RUMORS
RACE
and
RIOTS

I find the people strangely fantasied;
Possess'd with rumours, full of idle dreams,
Not knowing what they fear, but full of fear. . . .

—William Shakespeare (King John)

RUMORS
RACE
and
RIOTS

Terry Ann Knopf

ta

Transaction Books
New Brunswick, New Jersey

Library of Congress Catalog Number: 73-85098
ISBN: 0-87855-063-1

Printed in the United States of America

CONTENTS

To John P. Spiegel

PREFACE

For six years I was on the staff of the Lemberg Center for the Study of Violence at Brandeis University and for much of this time I was associated with a research and service division known as the Civil Disorder Clearinghouse. The purpose of the CDC was to gather and analyze data on racial disorders. We collected material on thousands of disturbances and issued reports on trends (we had the dubious distinction of correctly predicting that schools would become major centers of unrest) and subjects such as citizen security patrols, sniping incidents and press coverage of racial disorders.

Our research operation was unique because we were able to utilize different kinds of resources: (1) two news clipping services which provided relevant news stories from most of the 1,750 newspapers in the country; (2) consultation with groups immediately involved in civil disorders—mayors, police chiefs, reporters, community leaders, human relations people and others; and (3) access to the research community—not simply the universities, but study groups such as the Southern Regional Council and the various commissions on violence.

My interest in the subject of rumors initially grew out of the phenomenon of rumor control centers which cropped up in scores of cities in the late 1960s and reflected a growing concern on the part of public officials, especially about racially divisive rumors. My intellectual appetite was further whetted by indications that relatively little research had been conducted in this area. Moreover, what had been done centered on rumors generally, with a notable lack of attention to the social settings in which rumors thrive. *The Psychology of Rumor* by Gordon W. Allport and Leo Postman, written more than 25 years ago, is considered the definitive work on the subject. However, my previous work in collective violence suggested that the authors' individualistic bias made the book largely irrelevant to the recent riots and other group confrontations. By focusing this new study in the specific context of racial disorders, I have approached the subject from a different perspective, hopefully one that provides fresh insights into how and why rumors emerge.

More than three years were spent gathering the material. Excluding the data used for historical and theoretical purposes, the material generally encompasses the 1967-1969 period and includes nearly 500 cases of rumors taken from local and national news stories, investigative accounts (including previously unpublished reports) and a survey questionnaire sent to police chiefs whose cities experienced racial disorders.

The standard practice of publicly acknowledging the guidance and support of those close to a project carries with it a certain sadness here because the Lemberg Center has now closed. Both from a professional as well as personal standpoint, these were important years for me—although not lacking in occasional irony. The one time Brandeis was hit by a nine-day student takeover of Ford Hall, I found myself at home in my kitchen drafting a report on sniping. I can remember the trepidation my colleagues and I felt the night we debated some local SDS leaders before a Brandeis student audience—the subject being whether or not the Lemberg Center should be shut down. And I am still just a little embarrassed that I didn't get my first taste of tear gas until 1972 at the Republican National Convention in Miami Beach—a war story for my future grandchildren.

I do hope that the research we carried on has contributed to public understanding in some small way and would like to take this opportunity to express my personal appreciation to a few individuals in particular:

—To John P. Spiegel, director of the Lemberg Center, who made so much possible and to whom this book is dedicated.

—To Ralph G. Lewis, associate director, for his valuable suggestions on methodology and for reminding me why I didn't major in math.

—To Ronald L. Breiger, Rose LeBlanc, May Jean Louie and Laurence T. May, Jr., for their superb research assistance. Their enthusiasm and dedication will always be remembered.

—To Lillian Oates who typed most of the manuscript.

—To Mary E. Curtis, my editor, and Irving Louis

Horowitz, president of Transaction Inc., both of whom treated me so well.

—To my friends, especially Martha and Matt, and Mrs. K—because they were there.

—And finally, to the Beach Boys, whose music could frequently be heard above the din of my typewriter—and because they make me smile.

October 1973   Terry Ann Knopf
Cambridge, Mass.

1. THE PERVASIVENESS OF RUMOR

DEFINING RUMOR

On March 8, 1970, a woman in Washington, D.C. queried *Parade,* the Sunday weekly magazine: "I have been told that Mrs. Dean Martin plans to name 240 'other women' in her divorce suit. Is this true?" The woman's question is a good example of rumor. A proposition is offered for belief (in fact, two propositions are involved here: first, that there were 240 "other women" in the singer's life; and second, that they were about to be named in Mrs. Martin's divorce suit), and passed along from one source or person to another ("I have been told that"), without secure standards of evidence. The only evidence was that someone, probably a friend or acquaintance with no direct knowledge of the situation, happened to mention it.[1]

Other elements of rumor may be seen in this story itself. First, rumors refer to a particular person, object, event or issue. In this case, the woman's account is quite specific in detail, referring as it does to Dean Martin, Mrs. Martin and 240 "other women." Second, the story is of a topical nature and of some interest to the public, since Dean Martin has been a popular television and motion picture personality. Furthermore, the circulation of this rumor coincided with a public announcement that the Martins would shortly be divorced.

Note that nothing has been said about the validity of the woman's story—in other words, whether or not the rumor was true. Contrary to the popular view, falsehood is not necessarily a feature of rumor. The key factor which sets a rumor apart from information is that the report, account, story or allegation is *unverified*—but such an inverified report may later turn out to be true or false.

One may ask what constitutes "secure standards of evidence." To begin with, the origin or source of the evidence should be easily identified and considered reliable. Statements which begin: "Did you hear the latest?" or "Someone told me" or "I have it on good authority," raise serious questions about the quality of what is being reported. Proximity to the source is another important feature. A report that is based on second- or third-hand evidence may be far less reliable than a report stemming from the original source.

Next, the source should be regarded as objective. The report of the Advisory Committee to the Surgeon General, linking cigarette smoking to lung cancer, is likely to be more impartial and credible than the press releases issued by the Tobacco Institute, a lobbyist group for the tobacco industry. Some people would protest that objectivity is a myth and that some sources are merely less biased than others. In that case, the argument can be put another way: know the bias of your source. In September 1973, Chile's democratically elected government headed by Marxist President Salvador Allende was toppled by a military coup—the first in 46 years. Immediately, many "underground" newspapers in this country charged the CIA and American business interests were involved, while discounting the President's reported suicide. Perhaps the charges were true. However, the leftist bias of such publications cannot be denied and suggests the need for additional investigation.

Finally, the source should be defined as authoritative. For example, the public has traditionally held the news media in high esteem as a valuable and trusted source of information. Many Americans refused to believe that President Franklin D. Roosevelt had died until the reports were confirmed by the media. As Shibutani points out:

> Whether communication occurs through personal contact, writing, print, or some electronic device, if the channel is defined as authoritative, it serves as the standard against which reports attributed to all other sources are checked.[2]

Of course, any evaluation of evidence requires some judgment on the part of the recipient, since some standards of evidence are more secure than others. Sometimes it is hard to tell whether secure standards are actually present and thus whether the report falls in the realm of information or is simply a rumor. Conflicting reports just before the Senate voted on the nomination of Judge G. Harrold Carswell to the Supreme Court illustrate this point.

Both the *New York Times* and CBS News are regarded as reasonably objective, reliable and authoritative sources. Both undertook senatorial nose-counts on the eve of the

Carswell vote. Yet each of the investigations turned up a different set of conclusions. On April 7, 1970, the *Times* reported that "confirmation is likely." Later in the day, on the CBS Evening News, Walter Cronkite more cautiously rated the vote "a toss-up." It turned out that both reports were off the mark. The Senate defeated the nomination of Judge Carswell by a vote of 51-45—a fairly decisive margin, considering the earlier reports.

It is not clear why the *Times* and CBS erred in their reporting. Perhaps the political situation was more fluid than they realized. Perhaps some Senators changed their minds at the last moment. Perhaps, under the pressures of deadline reporting, they were not so thorough in their investigations as they should have been. In any event, individuals reading the *New York Times* that day or watching Walter Cronkite that night would have found it extremely difficult to judge the quality of the reports—and to tell how secure were the standards of evidence.

Another difficulty arises in situations where the informant is the sole source of evidence. Some time ago, a tourist in South Africa insisted he had seen a pink elephant in Kruger National Park. The man was quite specific in his account: "The brush of the tip of its tail was snow white and its skin was pearly pink." As described by a newspaper account, the gentleman was "sober" and "firm" in his story. Albino characteristics have been discovered in many animals; elephants might similarly be affected, and an albino elephant could very well appear pink. Nevertheless, given the uniqueness of the situation—there are 7,700 elephants in Kruger Park and this was the first time a pink elephant was reportedly seen by an individual whose credibility had not already been established—additional verification would seem to have been in order.

RUMOR IN OUR LIVES

Few of us are completely objective and reliable in seeking, disseminating and verifying information. Nor are we experts on most subjects. To a greater extent than we realize, we are all prone to formulate and circulate rumors. Gossip, whether it be of the back-fence or petty-office variety, constitutes rumor in its simplest form. But rumor exists on other levels as well, permeating and affecting virtually every phase of human activity.

In 1969, for example, rumors swept the country that California would soon fall into the sea. Soothsayers, mystics, and visionaries all prophesied that a cataclysmic earthquake would occur on April 4th of that year. "Earthquake fever" was especially conspicuous in California itself. Popular songs, jokes, books, records and cartoons appeared there, all commenting on the impending disaster. Stores held pre-earthquake sales. Stories circulated that many people were taking April vacations. While these reports were never confirmed, it is a fact that Governor Ronald Reagan, who has long been interested in astrology, happened to be in Arizona on April 4.

Several months later, another rumor circulated on college campuses, that Paul McCartney of the Beatles was dead, prompting the following satirical news story in *Time* magazine on October 31, 1969:

> LONDON (AP)—Paul McCartney vigorously denied today the rumor that he is alive and well. At a resurrection ceremony held at London's Highgate Cemetery, the 24-year-old Beatle, who would have been 27 had he lived, emerged from his tomb to insist that he was decapitated in a car accident three years ago.

Rumors play an extremely important role in the business world. This is especially true in the stock market, which is based upon the willingness of businessmen to risk buying and selling stock in the expectation of profiting from future market fluctuations. On September 20, 1973, rumors of a possible devaluation of the French franc set off a wave of speculation on world money markets, dragging down the dollar and putting pressure on the French currency. Underscoring the sensitivity of the stock market to rumor, on more than one occasion the New York Stock Exchange has opened an inquiry into the possibility that widespread and erroneous rumors had been spread deliberately as part of a plan to manipulate the market.

Specific details, facts, information and candor are frequently at a premium in politics, making the political arena another fertile breeding-ground for rumor. In 1970, an unfounded rumor spread that the RAND Corporation had been asked by the White House to study what would happen if the presidential election of 1972 were called off. This "scare" rumor originated with the Newhouse News Service and was subsequently picked up by the *Village Voice,* a Chicago *Sun-Times* columnist and several underground newspapers.

Throughout the Vietnam War, there were rumors of every variety. Unconfirmed reports of a schism in Hanoi's leadership over whether or not to continue the war, expectations by U.S. commanders of sharp rises in infiltration by the other side, and allegations that Saigon planned an invasion of North Vietnam, all received widespread circulation at one time or another.

Now that direct U.S. involvement in this tragic war has ended, and with the release of the Pentagon Papers, more secret documents may become available to the public, thus paving the way for a more objective and accurate assessment of the real situation. It will be vitally important for us to see the extent to which the information flowing from a vast complex of sources—the State Department, the Pentagon, the South Vietnamese government, the American embassy in Saigon—was defective, and the extent to which crucial decisions were made in Washington on the basis of these faulty data. Even now, certain public statements made in the early stages of our commitment there, concerning Vietcong strength and support, projections of their growth rate, reports that our troops "had turned the corner" and were winning the war, suggest the existence of a serious information gap.

The precarious state of race relations—about which we shall have much to say later—is mirrored in many explosive rumors which have swept through communities across the United States. Ralph E. Featherstone, a prominent black activist, and an unidentified black man were killed on March 9, 1970, when an explosive device shattered the car in which they were driving. Immediately, rumors spread that the unidentified man was Featherstone's close friend, H. Rap Brown. (The explosion occurred two miles from the courthouse where pretrial hearings were being held for Brown, who had been charged with arson and incitement to riot in Cambridge, Maryland.) Additional rumors swarmed through the black community that the dead men had been victims of an assassination plot. Meanwhile, rumors in the white community suggested that the two men were bringing dynamite to the courthouse area for the purpose of a terrorist raid.

A series of police raids on the Black Panthers, notably in Chicago and Los Angeles in late 1969, precipitated charges of a national conspiracy directed from Washington. In particular, the Department of Justice, under the conservative leadership of John Mitchell, was said to be "out to destroy" the Panther organization. In a similar vein, stories still persist that the federal government plans to establish concentration camps for blacks.[3]

RUMOR THROUGHOUT HISTORY

Thus far, we have seen that rumors encompass an extremely broad range of human endeavor: personal relationships, business, race, politics, international affairs and the like. But the importance of rumor goes far beyond its pervasiveness in our lives. The point is not simply that we are all so susceptible to rumor—that we are willing to listen to, formulate and circulate unverified reports—but that we are frequently willing to *act* on the basis of rumor. Indeed, history abounds in examples where men and women have created, miscalculated, explored, exploited, even killed—at least partly in response to rumor.

In Athens, stories that Socrates was corrupting the youth and inciting them to violence helped send the philosopher to his death. During the Age of Expansion, explorers managed to voyage all around the world, motivated partly by sketchy reports of gold and other treasures, fountains of eternal youth and gigantic sea monsters. An episode in history known as La Grande Peur (The Great Fear) provides a clear-cut, if not classic, case of people responding to rumor.[4] Contrary to popular belief, the fall of the Bastille on July 14, 1789, did not trigger the French Revolution—for the provinces were already in flames before such news reached the peasantry. Earlier in July, a panic had seized large parts of the country, affecting even Paris itself. From village to village, word spread that the nobles were sending "brigands" into rural districts to massacre the peasants; that royalists were planning to starve them by raising the price of grain; and that city-dwellers were about to march upon the fields to cut down the harvest. Acting upon these rumors, landless farmhands, unemployed workers from neighboring towns, vagrants and desperate criminals banded together. Thus, even before the news of the Bastille arrived, several provinces were in full rebellion against their feudal masters. Rural police were unable to restore order, while the king could not count upon the troops of the regular army. The Great Fear really signalled the end of the old order in France.

The first World War provides another means of demonstrating the rumor-response phenomenon. Take, for example, the assassination of Archduke Francis Ferdinand which, as every schoolchild knows, was the immediate cause of the war. On July 28, 1914, the Archduke (heir to the throne of Austria-Hungary) and his wife were assassinated in the streets of Sarajevo, the capital of Bosnia, which Austria had annexed in 1908. The assassin, Princip, was a Serbian nationalist, and Bosnia had long been desired by the Serbs. Alarmed by the ambitions of the Serbian nationalists, the Austro-Hungarian government sent a strongly worded ultimatum to Serbia. Following Serbia's refusal to accept the ultimatum in its entirety, Austria declared war on Serbia. Within a week, all the great nations of Europe were at war.

Austria's actions were based on reports that the Serbian government had some previous knowledge of the assassination plot and therefore should have given her warning. In fact, these reports were true, but positive proof was lacking at the time.[5] Nevertheless, because of the reports, and also because she wished to check Serbian agitation, Austria prepared the ultimatum and later declared war.

Rumors continued to play a significant role as the war continued. Frightening stories of German atrocities based upon seemingly irrefutable evidence, as well as unconfirmed reports that the "Potsdam gang" had planned the war step by step, helped consolidate public opinion in neutral countries (such as the United States) in favor of the Allies. These reports were not only undocumented but also were largely untrue. Nevertheless, they did create a climate more favorable to the Allied cause—a climate which foreshadowed the eventual involvement of the United States on the Allies' side, beginning in 1917.

The history of our own country is replete with illustrations of a similar sort. For example, in Boston on March 5, 1770, a street fight broke out between a crowd of about 50 men and boys and a small band of British soldiers. Several civilians were killed and several more wounded. The citizens were at least as much to blame for this as the soldiers. During the fracas, seven soldiers under the command of a Captain Preston were surrounded by a large and hostile crowd which tossed insults at the soldiers and, according to some of the evidence, threw snowballs at them, attacking one soldier with a club.[6] Unfortunately, distorted accounts spread through the colonies claiming that peaceful citizens had been wantonly assaulted by bloodthirsty murderers and that the captain had ordered his men to fire on the crowd—an accusation that was never proved at the ensuing trial. Misrepresentation of the incident served to inflame passions and further polarize relations between the colonies and England. This episode stands as a small but significant prelude to the final break with the mother country.[7]

At times during our history, the state has legitimized the use of violence on the basis of rumor. When state troopers dispersed striking steel workers in Pennsylvania in 1919, officials justified the action by claiming that the strike leaders were "revolutionaries."

The preceding episodes are not meant to imply that history is just one big rumor-mill—that if it weren't for rumor, the New World would not have been discovered, the American Revolution would not have been fought, and World War I would still be waiting for an excuse to begin. Our central point is that rumor is an important factor, a contributing factor, in influencing the way people order their lives and ultimately shape the course of history.

RUMOR AND RESEARCH

Given the importance of rumor, we would expect the subject to have attracted investigators of every intellectual stripe: journalists, sociologists, historians, political scientists, psychologists. Surprisingly, this has not been the case. Relatively little research into rumor has been conducted, and it is difficult to explain why. Perhaps the elusive, fleeting quality of rumors, and the fact that most are not recorded, have led researchers to turn their attention elsewhere. In any event, our knowledge about rumor—its nature, cause and function—remains extremely limited.

The research that has been done in this area is deficient, or at least restrictive, in a number of respects. First, much of it is dated. Academic interest in the subject seems to have been greatest during World War II—a period when rumors were quite common. Some investigators were drawn specifically to "war rumors." Robert H. Knapp collected and classified a total of 1089 rumors during the month of September 1942. The rumors were collected by the Massachusetts Committee on Public Safety, with the aid of *Reader's Digest,* which had appealed to its readers to forward to the Massachusetts Committee any rumor they had heard.[8] While serving in the army, Theodore Caplow helped prepare a monthly intelligence report, which included a section on rumors. Valuable material was collected on the content, frequency and reliability of rumors within an army regiment. Unfortunately, an overzealous unit censor confiscated Caplow's materials during the period of demobilization. Nevertheless, a report based upon his experiences was published several years later.[9]

Other investigators working at that time focused their efforts on different aspects of rumor. Gordon Allport and Leo Postman's classic work, *The Psychology of Rumor,* published in 1947, goes well beyond the scope of the war. After the war, however, interest in the subject generally waned—at least until the 1960s.

A second problem is that much past research has centered on an aspect of rumor development known as "serial transmission"—the process by which rumors are successively reproduced and distorted in circulating from one person to another. This research attempts to isolate irregularities in faulty perception and inaccurate reporting. Using an experimental approach, the first subject in a series is either asked to describe a picture or given a predetermined message. The individual then repeats the account to the next subject, who then passes on what he or she has heard.

In addition to confirming the work of others,[10] Allport and Postman's book represents the most comprehensive study of its kind. The findings may be summarized in terms of three central principles:

1. *Leveling.* As the rumor is passed along, it tends to become shorter, more concise and more easily grasped. Fewer words are used and fewer details mentioned. In nearly all the experiments, names of places and persons were either dropped out or so distorted as to be unrecognizable.

2. *Sharpening.* Just as some details are dropped, certain details remain, becoming the dominant theme. The receiver tends toward selective perception, retention and reporting of a limited number of details from a larger context.

3. *Assimilation.* The rumor tends to become more consistent and coherent in accordance with the presup-

positions and interests of the receiver. Assimilation refers to the powerful attractive form exerted on the
rumor by the individual's intellectual and emotional
makeup. Expectations, self-interest, prejudice and the
individual's inclination to condense things are considered factors.[11]

In the years following Allport and Postman's work,
much research has been devoted to confirming, denying or
qualifying their findings and results. For example, T. M.
Higham conducted extensive follow-up experiments with
English subjects, and got essentially the same results.[12]
However, other researchers raised questions concerning
Allport and Postman's methodology. In particular, they
criticized the artificial confines of the laboratory, as opposed to the natural setting of the community; the arbitrary chain of listeners and tellers, in contrast to the spontaneous flow of actual rumors; the complicated and violent
nature of stimulus materials (such as battle or riot scenes);
and, finally, the psychological bias of the authors, which
caused them to treat rumor as an individualistic, rather
than a collective, phenomenon.[13]

Serial transmission is both an important and a fascinating aspect of rumor. However, it remains only one of
many possible avenues of inquiry. The origin, content,
frequency, distribution and reliability of rumors, in addition to their prevention and control, are equally important
aspects which have not received the attention they deserve.

Another problem is that rumors have not always been
studied systematically. For his book, *Improvised News,*
Tamotsu Shibutani examined 60 situations on which some
471 rumors developed. The material, however, was not
standardized in any particular way. Hopscotching his way
through history, the author selects one incident from 1789
and another from 1963. Physical settings include Hawaii,

Hiroshima and Harlem. Disparate events, such as a kidnap scare in Mexico, Cromwell's massacres in Ireland, an explosion in Canada, the execution of a Japanese general and the Chicago race riot in 1919, are casually lumped together.

In fairness to the author, Shibutani freely admits that his sources "are not of uniformly high quality," and that his sample is not representative.[14] Moreover, since his objective was merely "to construct hypotheses rather than to verify them,"[15] it can be argued his approach was justified. Nevertheless, this particular approach points up the need for a more systematic, more coherent research strategy.

Toward this end, a different research framework has been employed in this book, one that takes rumors out of the laboratory and into the real world, and one that attempts to study them more systematically, by isolating a particular type of rumor operating during a particular time, in a particular setting.

All of the rumors that were used in this study concern race. Directly or indirectly, the content of these rumors refers to events, issues, actions or activities of interest and concern to blacks or whites as members of a particular racial group. Moreover, these rumors are restricted to the context of civil disorders.

Our research strategy will be outlined shortly. But let us begin here, with an examination of the subject from a historical perspective, posing questions for further study.

2. RACE AND RUMOR: A HISTORICAL OVERVIEW

RACE-RELATED RUMORS

Rumors associated with race can be traced to the very beginnings of our country. Even before slavery was firmly entrenched in the colonies, rumors—some real, some fancied—circulated that the slaves were conspiring to rebel against their masters.[1] Alarmed by the growing number of blacks in the colony and by the widespread circulation of such rumors, Virginia enacted a series of laws in the middle of the eighteen century designed to check the importation of slaves. (Slave traders, however, continued to bring slaves into the colony, in larger and larger numbers.)

A little-known incident in colonial New York provides some insight into the early state of affairs between the races, while demonstrating the damaging effects of rumor. During the winter months of 1741, a Spanish vessel captured as a prize arrived in the colony. Part of the crew was comprised of blacks, who were to be sold at auction as slaves. According to J. T. Headley, a contemporary journalist, the slaves became "very intractable," and in spite of constant whippings, "uttered threats that they knew would reach their masters' ears."[2] In March, some mysterious fires broke out which damaged both the governor's house and the king's chapel. Immediately, rumors swept through the community that the captured blacks were responsible:

> The rumor now spread like wildfire through the town that it was work of incendiaries. ... Some thought the Spanish negroes [sic] had set the buildings on fire from revenge, especially as those of the Government were the first to suffer. Others declared it was a plot of the entire negro [sic] population to burn down the city.[3]

Panic now seized the community. Whole families were piled into every available cart and vehicle and spirited away to farms in neighboring towns. The lieutenant-governor issued a proclamation appointing a day of fasting and humiliation.[4] Blacks of all ages were arrested and hurried off to prison. A long, steady succession of executions of blacks followed, some by hanging, others by burning:

> The ashes of the wood that consumed one victim would hardly grow cold before a new fire was kindled upon them, and the charred and blackened posts stood month after month. ... The spectacle was made still more revolting by the gallows standing near the stake, on which many were hung in chains, and their bodies left to swing, blacken, and rot in the summer air, a ghastly, horrible sight.[5]

This episode is as intriguing as it is horrible, because it illustrates the journalist's own susceptibility to rumor. A good nineteenth-century liberal, Headley decries the trials of blacks that made a mockery of justice, and expresses revulsion at the brutal acts that followed. Nonetheless, he also concludes that slaves had planned and executed the fires. His evidence was a series of alleged threats made by the slaves against their masters, and certain plots reported in the past:

> That there had been cause for alarm, there can be no doubt. That threats should be uttered by the slaves, is natural; for this would be in keeping with their whole history in this country. Nor is it all all improbable that a conspiracy was formed; for this, too, would only be in harmony with the conduct of slaves from time immemorial. . . . There have been a good many servile insurrections plotted in this country, not one of which was a whit more sensible or easier of execution than this, which was said to look to the complete overthrow of the little city. That the fires which first started the panic were the work of negro [sic] incendiaries, there is but little doubt. . . .[6]

The fears of whites again were evident in rumors occurring at the time of the American Revolution. On November 7, 1775, Lord Dunmore, the royal governor of Virginia, issued a proclamation declaring all slaves free if they joined the British army. Stories then circulated throughout the colonies that Dunmore was holding secret meetings with blacks each night "for the glorious purpose of enticing them to cut their masters' throats while they are asleep."[7] It was also whispered that the king himself had promised every slave who murdered his master the plantation that had previously belonged to his owner.

Interestingly enough, colonial fears of the British proved greater than their fears of the slaves—at least in this instance. On December 31, 1775, George Washington announced a policy that permitted the enlistment of free Negroes into the ranks of the feeble Continental Army. As the war continued, most states, either by specific legislation or merely through a reversal of policy, began to enlist both slaves and free Negroes.

Rumors concerning the emotional issue of slavery had widespread currency during the antebellum period, particularly on the eve of the Civil War. These rumors reflected a growing polarization in the country—racial as well as sectional. In the South, the prospect of electing Abraham Lincoln as president was accompanied by dire predictions of more abolitionist agitation, more runaway slaves, more slave insurrections, more John Brown raids and more unfriendly federal legislation. The charges made in the Charleston *Mercury* are typical:

> When [the Republican] party is enthroned at Washington . . . the *under*-ground railroad will become an *over*-ground railroad. The tenure of slave property will be felt to be weakened; and the slaves will be sent down to the Cotton States for sale, and the Frontier States *enter on the policy of making themselves Free States.*

> With the control of the Government of the United States, and an organized and triumphant North to sustain them, the Abolitionists will renew their operations upon the South with increased courage. The thousands in every country, who look up to power, and make gain out of the future, will come out in support of the Abolition government. They will have an Abolition Party in the South, of Southern men. . . .

> If, in our present position of power and unitedness, we have the raid of John Brown . . . what will be the measures of insurrection and incendiarism, which must follow our notorious and abject prostration to Abolition rule at Washington?. . .[8]

That these rumors were so common is particularly ironic since Lincoln himself was no abolitionist, and had moderate views on the slavery question. On the other hand, these rumors were entirely consistent with the widely-held belief that the North was consciously seeking to annihilate the South.

Northerners at the time were also subject to rumors. Many individuals, especially abolitionists, charged the existence of a giant, monolithic Slave Power or "Slavocracy"—ascribing to its evil designs. This "conspiracy" was reportedly spearheaded by a secret and highly organized group whose aim was to systematically destroy personal and civil liberties. At least one northern paper inveighed against such a "thirty years' conspiracy":

> The present attempt at a forcible dissolution of the Union, is the result of a conspiracy which has been brooded upon and actively conducted by ambitious men for nearly thirty years past. . . . [S]ince 1832, [they have] steadily pushed on their plot, recruited their forces, and at last, confidant in their strength, they have openly announced their plans, and defied resistance to their execution. Their aim is to found a Southern Empire, which shall be composed of the Southern States, Mexico, Central America, and Cuba, of which the arch-conspirators are to be the rulers.[9]

These kinds of accusations helped unify the North, just as allegations made against the Abolitionists helped mold southern opinion. However, while the existence of slavery may well have posed a threat to the American tradition, and while an alliance of economic, political and social interests in the South undoubtedly did exist, there is no evidence of any actual plot. As Kenneth Stampp points out: "The South was never so completely unified as to reveal evidence of a definite conspiracy."[10]

The periodic episodes of lynching that occurred in this country are among the ugliest expressions of racial hostility. That rumors and lynching should be closely associated is logical since, by definition, lynching refers to punishment for *alleged* crimes or offenses in which the individual is put to death by a mob acting without legal sanction. Secure standards of evidence being absent, the individual's guilt is invariably presumed rather than proven.

Traditionally, lynching victims have been accused of

robbery, homicide, rape or attempted rape, mischievous deeds (such as insulting white persons) and numerous other "offenses." Between 1885 and 1914, there were more than 3,500 lynchings, most of which involved blacks.[11] The majority of these lynchings occurred in the South, although some northern states—notably those in the Midwest—made contributions of their own.

Thus far in this chapter, we have been tracing episodes in our history, some better known and more important than others, involving race-related rumors. While the emerging picture is sketchy and incomplete, we may draw several conclusions from it. First, these rumors have operated in a variety of settings and circumstances. They are not limited to any one period in our history; nor are they limited to any particular geographical region. (The rumors concerning Lord Dunmore's proclamation in Virginia are more than matched by those occurring in the colony of New York.) Second, the rumors have been generated without reference to the formal status of blacks. Some occurred when Negroes were slaves, while others occurred following the Civil War, when they were officially free. Third, the rumors have elicited, or have helped elicit, many different responses. In some instances, the response has been relatively mild. For example, following the rumors about Lord Dunmore's proclamation, certain so-called "troublemakers" were rounded up, while nightly patrols were instituted to enforce a strict curfew for blacks. At other times, the response has been more extreme—witness the panic in New York and the thousands of lynchings that occurred in the late nineteenth and early twentieth centuries.

A final point here is less a conclusion than an observation. Virtually all the rumors examined thus far have centered on a theme of plots or, more generally speaking, threats made against the people spreading the rumors—i.e., whites.[12] Reports that slaves planned to burn down the city of New York; alleged meetings to encourage slaves to cut their masters' throats; predictions of more runaway slaves, John Brown-type raids and slave insurrections; charges of a Slave Power conspiracy—all of these examples underscore the threatening quality of the rumors. However, whether or not this is a dominant theme in race-related rumors remains to be seen.

Equally unclear at this time is the cause (or causes) of the rumors. In this case, at least, the data supply a few clues. These rumors appear to be linked with *existing social conflict*—specific issues, events and grievances that were important at the time. The dire predictions of the South, coming at the height of the slavery crisis, provide the most obvious example of this; but others can be cited as well. The rumors circulating in colonial Virginia followed a significant increase in the number of slaves there; the panic in New York roughly coincided with the arrival of a foreign ship carrying slaves—an incident which had an unsettling effect on the local white population.

We should, however, mention a second possible factor. Many of the situations appear to be characterized by *ambiguity*. The fires leading to the panic in New York were mysterious in origin—it was never clear who set them. The rumors circulating in the South on the eve of the war coincided with a presidential election fraught with uncertainty, including the possibility of electing a "black Republican" (Abraham Lincoln) as president, a man thought to be an enemy of the South. Thus, at least two potential explanations concerning the source of rumors have emerged. These and other alternative explanations will be explored later in our inquiry.

RACE RIOTS IN THE TWENTIETH CENTURY

Violent clashes between the races are not new to this nation's history. The so-called "Draft Riots" occurring in New York and in other northern cities during the Civil War are probably the best-known illustrations of earlier violence. Even prior to these disturbances, riots took place in various cities, including Cincinnati (1829), Pittsburgh (1839) and Philadelphia (which experienced five "major" outbreaks of racial violence between 1832 and 1849).[13] Whites invariably initiated this violence, which took the form of mob action against defenseless blacks. Sometimes, the victims were simply stoned or beaten up; at other times their homes and churches were burned or destroyed. Occasionally, they were not only driven from their homes, but also forced to leave the city.

But while riots are not a new phenomenon, the twentieth century ushered in a new and in some ways more painful era of racial conflict. Allen D. Grimshaw has identified 33 "major interracial disturbances" that took place in this country between 1900 and 1949.[14] The two World Wars represent peaks in the number of such outbreaks. Eighteen disturbances are recorded between 1915 and 1919; five are recorded between 1940 and 1944. With the exception of the 1943 race riot in Detroit, however, none of the later outbreaks was as serious as those occurring at the time of World War I.[15]

Information is more readily available about some of these riots than about others. The largest-scale riots tend to inspire the greatest amount of descriptive and analytical material. Moreover, whatever information is available is of varying quality. While acknowledging these limiting factors, let us now examine the role of rumor in these riots. Specifically, we will concentrate on the following: 1) common themes or types of rumor; 2) emerging patterns concerning the occurrence of rumor, i.e., at what points in time the rumors were salient; and 3) unofficial and official group behavior—including that of the participants, the civil authorities, and the press—in originating and spreading rumor. Our purpose here is two-fold: first, to raise additional questions and thus establish the foundation for our formal inquiry into the racial disorders of the late 1960s; and second, to provide a frame of reference for later analysis.

East St. Louis (1917)

Many of the riots that occurred during World War I followed a mass exodus of blacks from the rural South to the urban North. In trying to escape the racial oppression of the South, the new arrivals were searching for better economic, political and educational opportunities. In East St. Louis, Illinois, the number of blacks jumped from nearly 6000 to perhaps as many as 13,000 between the years 1910 and 1917. The increase in the percentage of blacks relative to the total population was even more startling, rising from 10 percent to perhaps 18 percent during those years. Not surprisingly, the white population felt threatened by this influx of southern blacks. Its fears were greatest in the areas of housing, where the migrants came to "invade" white neighborhoods, and jobs, due to the increased competition. Further complicating this situation was a new determination on the part of blacks to claim their fundamental rights, particularly in the areas of decent housing, jobs, transportation and recreational facilities.

The situation was ripe for one of the largest race riots in our history. Actually, the East St. Louis riot consisted of two separate outbreaks, the first coming in late May; the second, and far more serious one, coming about a month later, in early July. By the end of the second outbreak, 9 whites and about 39 blacks had been killed, while approximately 300 buildings had been destroyed.

At the time of the first outbreak, tensions in the community had been running high due to a labor strike at an aluminum plant; these tensions were further increased when the company hired black workers. On May 28, a labor union delegation called on the mayor and the city council to request that curbs be placed on any further migration of blacks to the city. As the men were leaving City Hall, they heard that a black man had accidentally shot a white man during a holdup. Within a matter of minutes, a barrage of rumors spread through the white community: the shooting was intentional and the victim had died; a white woman had been insulted by a black man; two girls had been shot; a white woman had been shot.[16] As many as 3000 people congregated on the streets to talk about this occurrence. The shooting incident, accompanied by the series of rumors, precipitated several days of rioting.

Even before the shooting, however, anti-Negro rumors had been circulating in the white community. Widespread stories maintained that blacks were forcing whites from their neighborhoods, that they were planning to assault white women, and that employers were to blame for the influx of blacks. A witness testifying before a Congressional committee investigating the East St. Louis riot described white sentiments just prior to the outbreak:

Mr. Chairman. . . . Everyone felt that something terrible was going to happen. On the street corners, wherever you went, you heard expressions against the negro [sic]. You heard that the negro was driving the white man out of the locality . . . by moving into the white neighborhoods. That the whites were being forced out of their localities. Stories were afloat on the streets and on the streetcars of the worst kind that would inflame the feelings. For instance, I heard one story so persistently that I commenced to think later on there might be some truth to it. . . . I heard stories of this kind and I heard it no less than a dozen times on the streets of East St. Louis, that negroes had made the boast that they were invited to East St. Louis; that great numbers of white people were taken away for war purposes, and that there would be lots of white women for the negroes in East St. Louis. . . . The whole country became fearful. You could hear the same discussions away from East St. Louis. People were inflamed and their feelings were directed against big employers of East St. Louis, feeling that they were responsible for the great influx of negroes. . . . Everyone seemed to realize that something fearful was going to take place.[17]

That there was no evidence to support these stories is beside the point. What is relevant is that they received such widespread circulation, and were believed by a great many people.

Rumors continued to circulate among whites and blacks following each of these initial outbreaks. During the early morning hours of May 29, crowds of whites gathered at a railroad depot to "meet" a train supposedly arriving with 500 migrants. Only when the rioters realized that there was no truth to the report did they finally go home.[18] Later, other rumors among whites spread concerning an imaginary smallpox epidemic. In discussing and reporting the outcomes of these riots, both whites and blacks exaggerated the number of casualties. Whites asserted that between 250-400 blacks had died, while groups such as the NAACP and the Chicago *Defender* put the figure at approximately 100-200. Blacks were especially skeptical of the Congressional investigating committee's figure of 39 black deaths. The discovery of several mutilated bodies in a creek on July 4 and 5 seemed to provide the first bit of evidence that whites had indeed disposed of their victims in this way. Blacks believed that 25 such corpses could be recovered from the creek. However, no more bodies were forthcoming. Other people asserted that the corpses of the adult blacks were entirely consumed in flames, leaving no traces of their bodies. But once again, no evidence could be found to support these charges.

At times, both blacks and whites were susceptible to variations of the same rumor. For example, during the entire month of June, whites charged that blacks were secretly arming and planning a massacre on July 4, in retaliation for the May riots. (Thus, it was not surprising when, during the July riot, police officers relayed false reports of reprisal attacks by blacks on the outskirts of the city, thereby diverting valuable manpower away from the downtown areas.)[19] Blacks, for their part, were convinced that the whites were preparing for a bloodbath on the same date.[20] While there has never been any evidence to support the contentions of either side in this case, the tragic effect of such rumors was to help create a climate that encouraged the slaughter that actually did take place on July 2.

The role of the press during the riot deserves special mention for several reasons. First, all statements emanating from the press are distributed to an extremely wide audience—far greater than when individual citizens communicate with one another. Moreover, because the press has traditionally been considered an authoritative source of information, its statements are bound to carry more weight than those of average citizens. During crisis situations, therefore, the news media are invariably bombarded with calls from anxious citizens seeking information, clarification, verification of what they have heard elsewhere. For this reason, the press has a grave responsibility to check all facts and thus avoid the unnecessary spread of rumor.

Viewed in this light, certain glaring deficiencies in press reporting during the East St. Louis race riot become apparent. Unverified statements, unfounded stories and unsupported conclusions were frequently issued by the press as indisputable facts. Even more damaging was the character of press rumors, which reflected—and intensified—the deepest fears of whites.

Of course, a certain amount of misreporting is understandable, considering the chaos that prevailed at the time of the riot. This is the problem with most early statistical reports. For example, the East St. Louis *Daily Journal* exaggerated greatly when it reported that more than 6,000 blacks had left the city.[21] In fact, some blacks (though considerably less than 6,000) did go to St. Louis between May 29 and May 30, probably to avoid trouble. But several days later, when the riot had subsided, most returned to their homes. Newspapers also overstated the situation in reporting that the mobs were comprised of "10,000 blood-crazed whites."[22] While the active participants undoubtedly enjoyed the support of thousands of bystanders along the streets, the groups of assailants were actually quite small, usually comprised of 25 persons at most.

Far more reprehensible and dangerous were the journalistic lapses into rumor-mongering which exploited white fears. Misreporting of testimony allegedly given at the coroner's inquest after the East St. Louis riot provides an appropriate example, in which unconfirmed and unsupported rumors were reported as unassailable facts. The St. Louis *Republic* ran a banner headline: "25,000 Whites Were 'Doomed' in Negro Murder Plot." According to the account that followed, the riot on July 2 had actually forestalled a plot to massacre innocent women and children on July 4. Prominent citizens were reportedly marked for assassination, while blacks were supposedly making preparations to march through the city, killing and plundering along the way. Other newspapers added their own embellishments to the story. The East St. Louis *Daily Journal* asserted that this black "army" was to contain 1500 men in three divisions. According to its story, the invasion would have been carried out, were it not for an alert police officer who discovered the plot.[23]

Following publication of these stories, the St. Louis *Post-Dispatch* interviewed members of the coroner's jury and found no evidence whatsoever to support charges of a plot.[24] Unfortunately, the net effect of such inflammatory stories was to condone, rather than explain, the riot and to usher in another tense period bordering on hysteria. In the weeks following the riot, stories about a powerful black invasion force were told everywhere. Frightened families were unable to sleep; some whites in middle-class sections actually fled their homes; while other towns-people formed vigilante committees.

Without doubt, the most irresponsible act of "rumor-reporting" by the press in this case came on the eve of the second wave of violence—indeed, the press's handling of an incident helped precipitate the riot. On the evening of July 1, a Ford car (or perhaps two) driven by whites fired gunshots into the homes of some black residents. The second time around, the residents were better prepared and returned the fire. No action was taken by the police in regard to the white assailants. However, after receiving a report about armed blacks, a squad car—significantly, a Ford—was sent to the scene; it was also met by gunfire, and two detectives were killed. The next day, the St. Louis *Republic* asserted that the blacks had arranged these killings beforehand. Other newspapers followed suit, charging that the killings were both planned and unprovoked.[25]

Testifying later before a congressional committee, the reporter who covered the story for the *Republic* admitted that the killings could have been a case of mistaken identity. But this admission had come too late. An excited population, already on the verge of a major riot, had been given all the "proof" it needed to marshall its forces for a bloody massacre.

"The Red Summer" (1919)

The most serious interracial violence that our country had experienced until that time occurred during the summer of 1919, which James Weldon Johnson called "the Red Summer." During that period, an estimated 25 race riots[26] were recorded in American cities, large and small, northern and southern. Actually, the term "Red Summer" is misleading in several respects: the "summer" began in early May and ended in late September; moreover, only six or seven of the outbreaks were of major proportions. Still, there can be no doubt that this period was one of intense social conflict and upheaval.

The race riot that occurred in Washington, D.C. during the month of July was the first to receive national attention. At least 1,000 white citizens participated in the violence, and 2,000 federal troops were called in during the four days that the rioting lasted. But for our purposes, the chief significance of this riot is that it was precipitated by a series of rumors prominently featured in the local press. Prior to the riot, the daily newspapers, especially the *Washington Post,* needlessly and incorrectly played up alleged attacks on white women by blacks. These news stories included large front-page headlines, as well as predictions of lynchings following the capture of the assailants.

One story printed on July 19 was especially provocative, and directly triggered the riot. On the second page, the *Post* reported another case of an alleged with the headline:

NEGROES ATTACK GIRL . . .
White Men Vainly Pursue

The body of the story indicated that the "attack" consisted of an incident in which two blacks jostled a young woman on her way home from work and tried to take her umbrella. After their "insulting actions" were met by resistance, the two men fled. Significantly, the original story mentioned that the victim was the wife of a man who worked in the naval aviation department. In a matter of hours after the story appeared, some 200 sailors and marines lynched two black suspects who had been released by the police, and then began indiscriminately beating other blacks, both men and women. The riot had begun.

In its voluminous report, the Chicago Commission on Race Relations states that the total number of alleged assaults previously reported in Washington newspapers was seven.[27] In each case, it was claimed that a black man had assaulted a white woman. In fact, four of the seven assaults involved black women. Furthermore, three of the suspects arrested and held for assault were white men, and at least two of the white men were later prosecuted for attacks on black women.

To assert that there would not have been a riot had the press been more restrained and more accurate would be to oversimplify the situation considerably. Other underlying factors also played a part. A large influx of southern whites and blacks, competition for wartime jobs and the increased frustration and anger of blacks over discrimination, must be acknowledged as important contributing factors. Nevertheless, irresponsible reporting on the part of the press served to whip up passions and clearly helped set the stage for the riot. As Arthur Waskow observes: "The existing conflicts were brought to a boil by opportunistic journalism."[28]

Following an initial outbreak of violence in Knoxville, Tennessee, on August 30, 1919, rumors proliferated, influencing the behavior of white civilians and law enforcement officers as well. In the riot's early stages, rumors spread that blacks had fired upon some whites, and robbed others.[29] The next morning, in response to these reports, a group of 100 armed whites headed for the black section of town, but were met by gunfire from blacks who had set up barricades. Next, National Guard troops, which had been rushed to the scene, proceeded to "shoot it up" when a false rumor circulated that blacks had killed two white men.[30] The troops also responded with violence when it was reported that the blacks were firing again. However, the only individuals injured were two National Guardsmen who were shot when the troopers' own machine guns misfired.[31] Both men died.

A riot in Omaha, Nebraska, evolved from a highly disturbed social climate. Months before the outbreak, blacks were repeatedly denounced as criminals by the local press, the chief of police and members of organized labor. Coinciding with these public denunciations were "groundless stories" that blacks accused of rape were being allowed to go free.[32] Thus, it was not surprising that the riot began on September 28 with an especially vicious lynching of a black man accused of raping a white girl. After forcing the man's release from jail, a mob of whites dragged the helpless man through the streets, shooting more than a thousand bullets into him. The mob then proceeded to burn the mutilated body, leaving it to hang from a trolley pole in a busy downtown area. As the violence continued, a considerable amount of property damage was reported and several blacks were badly beaten. Federal troops had to be dispatched to restore order.

With the soldiers standing guard, tensions decreased the next day; but rumors continued to fly. At 6 P.M. the troop commander telegraphed his superior as follows: "Persistent rumors indicate outbreak tonight."[33] By October 2, when order had been fully restored, 59 of the rioters had been

rounded up and arrested. However, rumors were spread
(presumably within the black community) that some
policemen were failing to supply the names of certain
known participants in the violence.[34] The situation was
not helped by the disappearance of several known ring-
leaders from the city.

Rumors surrounding the riot in Elaine, Arkansas, in
early October are of special interest because of the
widespread attention they received outside the local
community. Several days after the riot in Omaha, rumors
of a black insurrection burst upon the nation. "Organized
negroes [sic] armed with high powered rifles" were
reportedly massing from all over the county,[35] as southern
sheriffs and politicians appealed for federal troops to quell
the presumed "uprising."

These rumors had their origin—at least in an immediate
sense—in a meeting of sharecroppers held in a country
church. Dissatisfied with the abusive practices of the
plantation owners, the blacks had organized a "Progressive
Farmers and Household Union of America." The group's
purpose in meeting was to formulate a strategy that would
force the landlords to make an equitable settlement.
Unfortunately, the meeting came to an abrupt end with a
violent clash between a group of deputy sheriffs and the
Progressive Union.

Two entirely different versions of what had happened
emerged later, with each version developed along racial
lines. According to the "white" explanation, prominently
cited by the press, the deputy sheriffs had been traveling in
the area for reasons that had nothing to do with the
Progressive Union, and were not even aware of the meeting
inside the church. Stopping in the vicinity of the church
because of a flat tire, the group was suddenly fired upon
by black guards who feared the discovery of the union's
plot to murder whites. Thus, members of the Progressive

Union had initiated a savage attack on the sheriffs' group and other whites.

Blacks said that no plan to murder whites existed; that the white deputies had panicked after somehow learning about the prospective demands on the plantation owners; that on September 30, a barrage of shots had been fired into the church; and that a large group of armed whites burned the church the next day in order to destroy any evidence of their unwarranted attack.

In a careful review of the evidence on both sides, Waskow concludes that:

> the weight of the evidence indicates that the original white version of events in Phillips County was false, and that the Negroes who joined the Progressive Union were not planning a massacre.[36]

At that time, however, rumor proved to be a more potent force than either reason or restraint. Word spread like wildfire that the blacks had launched a full-scale insurrection. In the ensuing reign of terror, a few whites and many blacks were killed (although the exact numbers involved are not known). After the riot, in trials lasting less than an hour, 12 black farmers were sentenced to death, and 67 others were given severe prison terms. The Supreme Court later nullified these decisions, declaring that the blacks had not received a fair trial.

The Chicago Race Riot (July 1919)

Of all the race riots that occurred during "The Red Summer," the one that took place in Chicago stands out. First, it was by far the most serious outbreak. The violence there raged for four days; 38 persons—23 blacks and 15 whites—were killed; of 537 injured, 178 were whites and

342 blacks—the racial identify of 17 persons was not recorded—and about 1,000 persons were left homeless. Beyond the pale of these statistics was the stark reality of extreme racial polarization. As John Hope Franklin points out:

> When the authorities counted the casualties the tally sheet gave the appearance of the results of a miniature war. . . . It was the nation's worst race war and shocked even the most indifferent persons into a realization that interracial conflicts in the United States had reached a serious stage.[37]

A second distinguishing feature of the 1919 Chicago race riot was that it became the basis for the most exhaustive study of its kind ever made. Following the appointment of the Chicago Commission on Race Relations by the Governor of Illinois, an investigation was launched into the conditions underlying the riot. The Commission examined more than 5,000 pages of testimony taken by the coroner's jury; it also studied records of the state's attorney, Police and Fire Departments, hospitals and other institutions; interviewed public officials and citizens; and held a series of conferences to which key individuals in government and law enforcement were invited. The result of all this was *The Negro in Chicago*—a massive document of more than 600 pages. Publication of the report in 1922 produced little significant change in programs and policies concerning blacks. Nevertheless, the study continues to be a major resource for scholars, particularly historians and sociologists. In addition, the study is dotted with references to rumor. While the source of rumor-related data is not always made clear, the report still represents the best historical treatment of the role played by rumors during a race riot.

According to the Commission's report, rumors operated at three separate junctures: prior to the riot, immediately following the precipitating incident and during the course of the violence. Before the riot, rumors were spread predicting violence on July 4. Signs were posted in Washington Park, warning that blacks would be driven from the park on that date. The effect of these rumors was to heighten tensions in the community and to help set the stage for the tragedy on July 27:

> All this expectation undoubtedly caused preparation for trouble. It is conceivable that this preparation at least accentuated the violence of the riot which began on July 27.[38]

On Sunday, July 27, late in the afternoon, Eugene Williams, a 17-year-old black, went swimming at a local beach. Although the beach was used by both races, there was an unofficial boundary line dividing it into two parts. Williams entered the water from the area used by blacks, but drifted into the "white" area. Stone-throwing broke out when more blacks arrived on the scene. Meanwhile, Williams, who had remained in the water during the melee, suddenly went down. Efforts by both blacks and whites to save the young man proved futile. No stone bruises were found on the body when it was later examined and, in the opinion of the coroner's jury, the youth had drowned because his fear of stone-throwing kept him from going ashore. Nevertheless, a rumor swept through the crowd that the boy had died after having been hit by one of the stones. A second rumor sprang up that a police officer had refused to arrest the murderer. The accused policeman further increased the tension of the situation by arresting a black on a white man's complaint. Blacks mobbed the policeman, and the riot was on.

The Commission was apparently unable to determine whether or not the second rumor was true. Its report merely points out that police officials denied that one of their men had refused to arrest the stone-thrower. There is little doubt, however, that the drowning, coupled with reports about the policemen's behavior, triggered the riot:

> The two facts, the drowning and the refusal to arrest, or widely circulated reports of such refusal, must be considered together as marking the inception of the riot. Testimony of a captain of police shows that first reports from the lake after the drowning indicated that the situation was calming down. White men had shown a not altogether hostile feeling for the Negroes by assisting in diving for the body of the boy. . . . There was every possibility that the clash, without the further stimulus of reports of the policeman's conduct, would have quieted down.[39]

As the violence raged unabated for several days, rumors were a common occurrence on both sides. At times, these rumors were "the first step" in forming crowds and transforming them into mobs;[40] at other times, they were the basis of retaliative actions by members of both races.

Both sides were susceptible to the same types of rumors. For example, each group exaggerated the number of casualties. The "Bubbly Creek" rumors were among the most persistent in this respect. Bubbly Creek was a small tributary of the Chicago River into which flowed waste material from the local slaughterhouses. Because of its murkiness, the stream would have made an ideal dumping ground for dead bodies and, according to rumors, it did. Stories were told that the bodies of many riot victims had been disposed of in this way. Despite the fact that several attempts to dredge up these bodies turned up nothing, the rumors continued to fly. A juror at the coroner's inquest said:

> A man told a friend of mine, I can furnish the name of that man; a man told him that he saw 56 bodies taken out of Bubbly Creek.[41]

Another juror stated:

> There is a story that was repeated on the floor of Congress that numerous colored people were caught down there [at the Stock Yards] and thrown in Bubbly Creek, and their bodies never recovered. A congressman from our district . . . told me that on the floor of Congress it was recently stated that a man with a dumb-bell in his hand stood there at the big rock entrance of Exchange Avenue and knocked a half-dozen of these colored men on the heads as they passed through that rock door there.[42]

In a similar vein, the number of police deaths was also greatly exaggerated. One report, later traced to the half-joking remark of a policeman, suggested that more than 75 officers had been killed in the Chicago riot.

Policemen seem to have been extremely likely to circulate rumors. Following the riot, a study was conducted with a class of students from the University of Chicago, to determine how they received information during the riot and the extent to which the information they received was distorted. Specific questions were asked concerning the number of deaths reported and the source of this information. Students getting their information from policemen and relatives placed the average number of persons killed at 209—by far, the highest average of the lot.[43] The lowest average figure—55—came from students who were out-of-town and received most of their information from newspapers published elsewhere. These findings suggest that those closest to the riot situation are more inclined to distort or exaggerate the facts.

In this context, two incidents involving police officers during the riot are worth mentioning. In one instance, police officers asserted that more than 2,000 blacks had been killed and another 8,000 wounded,[44] a gross exaggeration of the facts. Given the chaos that prevailed at the time, these outrageous figures probably seemed quite reasonable at the time. The other incident, involving a couple of deputy sheriffs, had more serious consequences. The deputies had heard stories that local blacks were planning to destroy factories in the area. While patrolling the streets, the two men saw a dark form in an alley. The deputies panicked and fired on an innocent black who lived in a nearby house.[45]

While both blacks and whites were susceptible to similar kinds of rumors, each group was frequently the object of vilification in the rumors circulating in the opposing group. Rumors of arms caches fall into this category. Throughout the riot (in fact, long after the violence had ended), whites were convinced that blacks were stockpiling arms and ammunition. False rumors spread that blacks had broken into an army regiment's quarters, looking for guns and ammunition. Following the riot, unconfirmed reports circulated that Pullman porters and white prostitutes were storing arms. Meanwhile, Mexicans were supposedly helping the blacks manufacture bombs and hand grenades. Detectives later drew up lists of addresses where ammunition was reportedly being stored, but these reports were never confirmed. On their part, blacks were convinced that local whites had large amounts of guns and ammunition hidden in the cellars of their homes; that white men were organizing gun clubs in preparation for another riot; that a department store sold guns to whites before the riot, while refusing to sell to blacks; and that pawn shops sold guns to white people without permits from the police.[46]

Hand in hand with rumors of an arms buildup went numerous reports of conspiracy. In the fall of 1919, the Chicago office of the United States Army Intelligence Bureau sent to Washington information linking the NAACP to the Industrial Workers of the World (IWW), a radical labor group. The intelligence report suggested that the civil rights organization was "planning to flood the colored districts with IWW literature."[47] However, the Commission could find no evidence of a connection between the two groups, and denied that the NAACP had ever planned to distribute IWW literature.

White people did not have a monopoly on conspiratorial notions. The migration of blacks from the South to Chicago and other northern cities coincided with stories that the Germans were on their way through Texas to capture the southern states, and that the federal government was planning to transport all blacks from the South, in order to break up the Black Belt. Another rumor, that the Indians were coming back after several hundred years to reclaim their land, appears to have been related to the encampment of some gypsies near Meridian, Mississippi.[48]

Knapp, and later Allport and Postman, termed such rumors "wedge-driving," because of their hostile intent and the divisiveness they engendered.[49] Regardless of the label, the effects of such rumors could be devastating, particularly where alleged atrocities were concerned. For example, following unconfirmed reports of killings by whites, a group of young blacks stabbed to death an old Italian peddler. A white laundryman met his death in the same way. An even more serious incident stemmed from rumors that a white occupant of the Angelus apartment house had shot a young black from a fourth-story window. A crowd of about 1500 blacks massed around the building as frightened white tenants called the police, crying out for the "culprit" to be apprehended. Tensions increased with the subsequent failure of the police to locate him after searching the building. Someone threw a brick at the police, who responded by firing into the crowd. Four blacks were killed and many others injured.[50]

Elsewhere, a racial clash was narrowly averted when a white man was caught crawling under a house where blacks lived, with a bottle of kerosene in his pocket. When asked to explain his behavior, the man recited the current rumor that blacks had set fire to houses in which whites lived, "back of the Yards."[51] In another incident in the Italian district, such rumors proved more costly when it was alleged that a black had shot a little Italian girl, either wounding or killing her. As these rumors intensified, an innocent black happened on the scene and was met by a crowd of highly agitated Italians. Following a chase, the victim was dragged from his hiding place in a basement and murdered by the crowd.[52] The coroner's report indicated the man had been repeatedly beaten, stabbed and shot. The frequency of similar atrocity stories during the Chicago riot, together with the brutal and violent reactions they provoked, suggest that such "wedge-driving" rumors were an extremely important spur to retaliative action on both sides.

Of all the groups in positions of responsibility and power, none received more extensive criticism than the press. Basically, the press was accused of contributing to the poor state of race relations by its handling of general news concerning blacks. Studies conducted by the Chicago Commission disclosed that local newspapers tended to overemphasize crimes involving blacks against whites, while underplaying crimes in which whites were the aggressors against blacks. The effect was to convey a stereotyped picture to the reading public, in which the entire black race was branded as criminal.

With reference to the riot, much of the criticism concerning the press centered on numerous instances of inaccuracy, distortion, exaggeration and sensationalism— much of which fell into the realm of rumor. For example, several weeks before the riot, the press added to the tensions in the community by misreporting an incident in which a white saloonkeeper died of a heart attack. Accounts appearing in the local papers indicated that the man had been killed by a black.[53] That evening, a raiding party of young whites riding in an automobile fired on a group of blacks.

During the riot itself, the press continually misreported the number of casualties. By comparing the figures given in the Chicago *Tribune* and the *Herald-Examiner* during the first four days of the violence with later figures obtained from the Police Department, the State's Attorney and various hospitals, the Commission found that the newspapers had understated the number of injuries. Interestingly enough, however, while under-reporting the total number of injuries, these newspapers asserted that 6 percent more whites than blacks were injured, when, in fact, there were 28 percent more black than white casualties.[54]

The low injury figures reported by the press were at variance with those asserted by the general public, which tended to inflate such figures. In many cases, however, the press merely echoed rumors already circulating in the community, thereby giving them additional credence. The following list of headlines from local newspapers should sound familiar to the reader:

Ald. Joseph McDonough Tells How He Was Shot at on South Side Visit—Says Enough Ammunition in Section to Last for Years of Guerrilla Warfare.
   —*Daily News*, July 30, 1919 Subheadline
Negroes Have Arms
   —*Herald-Examiner*, July 28, 1919 Subheadline
Four Bodies in Bubbly Creek
   —*Daily News*, July 29, 1919 Subheadline
RED PLOT NEGRO REVOLT
I.W.W. Bomb Plant Found on South Side
   —*Herald-Examiner*, January 4, 1920

In each case, the headline was either not explained, not

elaborated on or not documented in the body of the story.
And the local press was not alone in its preoccupation with
racially oriented plots and conspiracies—indeed, such sentiments were even more pronounced outside the Chicago
area. The *New York Times,* for example, was an early
advocate of the conspiracy idea. In a strongly worded
editorial one day after the riot broke out, the *Times*
charged that the outbreaks in Chicago and Washington
were not spontaneous, and that they involved "intelligent
direction and management." The editorial made reference
to another news story appearing the same day, in which an
unidentified federal official exhibited to the *Times* a
supposedly seditious black periodical. This magazine
(which was not named) reportedly contained articles
urging blacks to join the IWW and other left-wing socialist
organizations. Adding a more sinister cast to the story was
the unexplained revelation that the magazine "was illustrated and is printed on the finest of newsprint paper."[55]
The *Times'* case for conspiracy also rested on the
assumption that, because the riots in Chicago and Washington were closely linked in time, they must therefore be
part of some master plan. The following excerpt from the
editorial indicates just how flimsy the evidence was:

> The outbreak of race riots in Chicago, following so closely on
> those reported from Washington, shows clearly enough that the
> thing is not sporadic. . . .

> In the TIMES this morning is printed some evidence which goes
> far toward suggesting that the Bolshevist agitation has been
> extended among the negroes [*sic*], especially those in the South,
> and that it is bearing its natural and inevitable fruit. It is rather
> hard to believe that in such widely separated cities as Washington
> and Chicago there could be an outbreak of violent animosity
> within a certain number of days, and all without influence or
> suggestion from any outside source. There is no use in shutting
> our eyes to facts; and we know that in the early days of the war

there was a pro-German and pacifist propaganda among the negroes, which may well have turned into a Bolshevist or at least Socialist propaganda since.[56]

The inclination to explain the riots in Chicago and elsewhere in terms of conspiracy was by no means limited to the public or the press. In fact, this view permeated the highest levels of government. At about the time of the Chicago riot, the federal government was compiling reports to show that blacks were the victims of a "vicious and apparently well financed" propaganda effort. Predictably, federal agents attempted to link the IWW to blacks.[57] It is noteworthy that the Chicago Commission, which could find no connection between the IWW and blacks, maintained that such allegations showed "the absurd ignorance frequently manifested by members of the white group concerning the activities of Negroes."[58]

At the congressional level, Representative James F. Byrnes rose in the House to blame the recent riots on "incendiary utterances of negro [sic] leaders circulated through negro publications."[59] In his speech, the Congressman urged the government to proceed against such individuals under the Espionage Act.

Several strands in Byrnes's argument deserve mention here. First, he felt that the riots' proximity in time, coupled with the geographical distance between them showed their cause was "not local"—rather the cause was "these articles." In quoting from "these articles," Mr. Byrnes seemed to equate vigorous protest against oppressive conditions with sedition against the government. The following excerpt from *Crisis,* the official magazine of the NAACP was the basis for his request that the Justice Department institute proceedings against W.E.B. Dubois, the magazine's editor:

This country of ours, despite all its better souls have done and dreamed is yet a shameful land. It lynches***It disfranchises its own citizens***It encourages ignorance***It steals from us***It insults us.

Another point in Byrnes's speech was that the riots in Chicago and Washington coincided with publication of *The Messenger,* edited by A. Phillip Randolph and Chandler Owen. This connection in time between the two events was taken to show that black leaders "had deliberately planned a campaign of violence." The fact that the magazine was printed on a fine quality paper was simply further proof that the publication was "supported by contributions from some source ... antagonistic to the United States."

The entire speech of Representative Byrnes is characterized by gigantic leaps in logic and an obvious lack of hard evidence. Nevertheless, the speech is significant, not simply because its message came from a prominent public servant, but also because it was so typical of official thinking at that time. It was not surprising that, one day after the speech was delivered, the Department of Justice issued a supporting statement which said the IWW and Soviet influence were at the bottom of the recent riots. No details were given.[60]

Between World Wars: Harlem (1935)

In the years following World War I, the amount of racial violence in this country declined sharply. During the thirties, only one major disturbance was recorded—the Harlem riot of 1935.

This riot began with a seemingly minor incident which was compounded by a series of rumors. On March 19 at about 2:30 P.M., Lino Rivera, a 16-year-old youth, was caught stealing a knife from a dime store in Harlem. A brief scuffle ensued between the store manager, his assistant and Rivera, during which time the boy hit the hands of his captors. After the fracas had ended and Rivera had been subdued, the store manager declined to press charges. In order to avoid anxious shoppers on the scene, a policeman took the youth to the rear entrance of the building, via the basement. Unfortunately, this precautionary measure only seemed to lend credence to the hysterical cries of a black woman that they had taken the boy away "to beat him up."[61] An odd set of circumstances now combined to strengthen this rumor. An ambulance which had been summoned to dress the wounds of the boy's captors appeared on the scene and seemed to confirm the woman's charges. Adding to the confusion was a hearse which happened to be parked in front of the store—which in turn led to a second and even more inflammatory rumor among the shoppers that the boy was dead.

A group of about 100 shoppers was now transformed into an angry crowd. The possibilities for disseminating the rumor to a large audience were further enhanced by the decision to close the store earlier than usual.

> The closing of the store did not stay the rumors that were current inside. With incredible swiftness the feelings and attitude of the outraged crowd of shoppers was communicated to those on 125th street and soon all of Harlem was repeating the rumor that the Negro boy had been murdered in the basement of Kress' store.[62]

Shortly afterwards came the sound of the first window being shattered.[63] So strong was the belief within the community that the youth had been killed that the police decided to circulate a photograph of the unharmed Rivera with a police officer who was black. This dramatic gesture not only failed, but also led to still another rumor that

Rivera was part of a police coverup and was being used as a substitute for the "real victim."

The violence was terminated by the end of the next day, amid charges that the riot was not spontaneous and was part of some conspiracy. For example, District Attorney William C. Dodge attributed the whole affair to a Communist plot and initiated a grand jury investigation.

At this point, the activities of two organizations during the riot should be mentioned. The Young Liberators were a militant group, comprised mostly of blacks, whose avowed purpose was to protect blacks. Although it was not a Communist organization, the Young Liberators did have some Communists in its ranks. On the day of the riot, late in the afternoon, the rumor that a black youth had been beaten and killed reached the group's headquarters. The president went immediately to Kress's store in order to verify the rumor, but was refused entrance to the store. He then went to the police station but was turned away once again. Accepting the rumor as true, the Young Liberators printed and circulated an angry handbill:

CHILD BRUTALLY BEATEN!
WOMAN ATTACKED BY BOSS AND COPS
CHILD NEAR DEATH

One hour ago a 12-year-old Negro boy was brutally beaten by the management of Kress' Five and Ten Cent Store.

The boy is near death, mercilessly beaten because they thought he had stolen a five-cent knife. A Negro woman, who sprang to the defense of the boy, had her arm broken by the thug and was then arrested.

WORKERS! NEGRO AND WHITE

Protest against this Lynch Attack of Innocent Negro People.

Demand Release of Boy and Woman.

Demand the immediate arrest of the management responsible
for this lynch attack.
Don't Buy at Kress.
Stop Police Brutality in Negro Harlem.

JOIN THE PICKET LINE.[64]

The Young Communist League issued a similar handbill at
about the same time.

According to the testimony presented to a Commission
officially appointed by Mayor Fiorello H. LaGuardia,
neither handbill appeared on the streets before 7:30 P.M.,
when the riot was "already in full swing." While both
groups bore some responsibility for fueling the rumors, the
Commission could find no evidence to implicate either the
Young Liberators or the Young Communist League in a
plot:

> the outbreak was a spontaneous and unpremeditated action on
> the part, first, of women shoppers in Kress' store and, later, of
> the crowds on 125th street that had been formed as a result of
> the rumor of a boy's death in the store.... At no time does it
> seem that these crowds were under the direction of any single
> individual or that they acted as a part of a conspiracy against law
> and order.[65]

Considering the climate of the time, the Commission's
praise of the Communists' constructive role during the riot
was quite bold:

> While one, in view of the available facts, would hesitate to give
> the Communists full credit for preventing the outbreak from
> becoming a race riot, they deserve more credit than any other
> element in Harlem for preventing a physical conflict between
> whites and blacks.[66]

The findings of the Commission indicate that the charges
of a conspiracy had no basis in fact and, like so many

rumors at the time, were rooted in the mind of an excited public.

WORLD WAR II

In examining the incidence of major racial disturbances during the first half of the twentieth century, Allen D. Grimshaw found that the total number of riots recorded during World War II (five) was significantly lower than those recorded in World War I (18). Nevertheless, the period of World War II ranked second in terms of riot peaks. We therefore turn our attention to a series of urban riots, all occurring in 1943, where rumors are known to have played a part: in Los Angeles, Detroit, Harlem and Beaumont, Texas.

Beaumont and Los Angeles

In all four cases, rumors helped trigger the riot; in two of these cases, the rumors involved sexual assault. In Beaumont, the riot was sparked by stories that blacks had raped white women. Similar reports were prevalent at the time of the so-called "zoot-suit race war" in Los Angeles, although the situation appears to have been more complicated. The riot began there on a Thursday evening, June 3, when a group of young men of Mexican descent assembled at a police station to discuss ways of preserving peace in the community. At the conclusion of their meeting, the youths were driven in a squad car to the area where most of them lived. Shortly thereafter, the boys were attacked in what proved to be the first of a series of vicious assaults made over the next few nights. The disturbance reached its height on Monday evening, June 7, when a crowd estimated at 1,000 persons, mostly soldiers and sailors, set out to unleash its fury on every "zoot-suiter"[67] it could find. Angry mobs of people invaded downtown movie houses, bars and streetcars, all in search of victims. Chicanos and a few blacks were dragged through the streets, kicked, beaten and, in some instances, stripped naked and left lying on the pavement. In keeping with historical precedent, the police were notably lax in apprehending the aggressors, on some occasions contenting themselves with accompanying the mob, watching the beatings and arresting the victims.

In their appraisals of the riot situation, most observers have found it difficult to isolate a single precipitating incident. However, in the aftermath of the violence, the most common charge levied from each side was that the other had molested its women. On the one hand, there were rumors that the so-called "zoot-suiters" had repeatedly attacked the wives and relatives of servicemen. Similar claims were issued by the Mexican community, to the effect that servicemen were guilty of insulting and molesting Mexican women. Although other rumors were present at the time, the sexual motif was dominant:

> While many other charges were reported in the newspapers, including unsubstantiated suggestions of sabotage of the war effort, the sex charges dominated the precipitating context.[68]

Turning to the causes of the riot, a number of investigators have assigned the major responsibility to the press. In an article for the *New Republic*, Carey McWilliams charged that for more than a year before the riot, the local press—especially the Hearst newspapers—had whipped up anti-Mexican sentiment.[69] The press was

accused of needlessly headlining every case in which a
Chicano was arrested, prominently displaying photographs
of Mexican-Americans in zoot suits and continually prod-
ding the police to make more arrests. In their more
scholarly inquiry published many years later, Ralph H.
Turner and Samuel J. Surace reached essentially the same
conclusions. For their study, these two researchers used a
content analysis of the Los Angeles *Times,* the largest of
the four area dailies, considered responsibly conservative,
and a newspaper with no connection to the Hearst chain.
The analysis spanned ten and one half years, from January
1933 until June 30, 1943, encompassing the riot period.
The findings showed a trend in the newspaper's terminology used to describe persons of Mexican descent. Where
earlier the newspapers had made reference to "Mexicans,"
a term which evokes ambivalent reactions, by the time of
the riot that term had been effectively displaced by the
term "zoot-suiter," a symbol with predominantly negative
connotations. Unlike the term "Mexican," which conjured
up visions of the distant and romantic past, the latter
phrase suggested only the sordid picture of a social
outcast, lacking in moral character and, as a deviant
individual, not entitled to the usual standards of justice
and fair play. The phrase was associated with sexual
offenses, gangster activities and other crimes, including
draft-dodging. It thus became the basis of the following
proposition: all Mexican-Americans were "zoot-suiters";
all "zoot-suiters" were criminals; therefore, all Mexican-
Americans were criminals.[70] The effect of this on the
mind of the public was to encourage a stereotyped picture
of Mexican-Americans, one with almost exclusively negative connotations.

There is enough evidence against the press to suggest
that the thrust of the arguments of both McWilliams and
Turner and Surace was correct. The press at the time was

irresponsible in its handling of news and did help create a climate of fear and reprisal in the community. However, the final judgments of these observers are open to some question. In their view, the case against the press was so strong as to suggest that no riot would have occurred had there been no press. Along with the police, McWilliams placed "immediate responsibility" for the outbreak on the shoulders of the Los Angeles press. For Turner and Surace, the "zoot-suiter" symbol, embedded in the mind of the public by an incautious press, resulted in community feelings which could accomodate and support aggressive crowd behavior:

> This new association of ideas relieved the community of ambivalence and moral obligations and gave sanction to making the Mexicans the victims of widespread hostile crowd behavior.[71]

The difficulty with this view is that, given the dynamic, complex nature of riots and the multiplicity of forces—historical, political, social, psychological, cultural, economic —at work, it is virtually impossible to establish a direct causal relationship between any one single factor, such as the press, and an outbreak of violence. In the case of the Los Angeles riot, this point holds in both an immediate as well as a fundamental sense. Furthermore, any such conclusions would lie outside the scope of this study.

What is clear and relevant here is that the stereotyped picture of Chicanos fostered by the press found expression in a series of rumors during the riot. These rumors were disseminated by the major newspapers of the city and constituted the "official version" of what had happened.

The "official version" was woven together with the following strands. First, press reports suggested that the Chicanos were the aggressors, while the servicemen had merely acted in self-defense. While some Mexican-Americans may have initiated attacks in a few cases, in reality, the servicemen were the main perpetrators of the violence. Nevertheless, as soon as the violence in the city had subsided, news stories appearing in late-afternoon editions of the Hearst newspapers (the Los Angeles *Examiner* and the *Herald & Express*), along with Harry Chandler's Los Angeles *Times,* warned of an armed attack by "zoot-suiters" that night: "We're meeting 500 strong tonight and we're going to kill every cop we see." The *Herald & Express* blazoned: "ZOOTERS THREATEN L.A. POLICE."[72] It is significant that these predictions were based upon nothing more than a purported anonymous call to police headquarters. It is also significant that the worst of the violence occurred that night, as soldiers, sailors and white civilians took to the streets, following publication of these reports.

Second, news stories conveyed the misleading impression that all the young Chicanos were criminals, gangsters and hoodlums. For example, the *Examiner* blared: "Police Must Clean Up L.A. Hoodlumism." The first paragraph of an editorial stated: "Riotous disturbances of the past week in Los Angeles by zootsuit hoodlums have inflicted a deep and humilitating wound on the reputation of the city."[73] In fact, while juvenile delinquency had been increasing in the city since the start of the war, it had risen less among Chicanos than any other ethnic group. Furthermore, there was no such thing as a "zoot-suit gang," in the criminal sense of the word. The so-called "gangs" in the area were actually loose conglomerations of neighborhood or geographical groups, with little or no organizational structure. Many of these groups were, in Carey McWilliams's words, "boys' clubs without a club house."

Even the term "zoot-suiter," with all its sinister overtones, was misapplied by the press to fit the rumor formula. The attacks on Mexican-Americans were indiscriminate; many of them were not wearing zoot-suits.

McWilliams estimated that "perhaps not more than half" the victims wore zoot suits. Nevertheless, contemporary press reports used the term repeatedly in situations where it did not apply. In one instance, a story appearing in the Los Angeles *Times* indicated that the police had rounded up 200 youths, and that "only a few" were wearing zoot suits.[74] Yet other related headlines, captions and stories—all in the same newspaper—made reference to "zoot clashes," "zoot-suit gangs" and "wearers of peg trousers." Even *Time* magazine, which took a constructive stand in criticizing the Los Angeles newspapers, chose to title its story "Zoot-Suit War."

For sheer inventiveness, however, the Los Angeles *Daily News* surpassed all other journalistic efforts at the time by condensing the largest number of rumors into the smallest space possible. A headline appearing over a story read simply: "Zoot-Suit Gangsters Plan War on Navy."[75]

Harlem

The riot that occurred in Harlem—the "Negro capital of the U.S.," as *Time* called it—was set against the backdrop of wartime conditions. Added to the usual indignities which black people had long been accustomed to were additional forms of mistreatment, ranging from discrimination against black workers in the defense industries, to segregated fighting units, to the outright murder of black soldiers by white civilians. The irony of their position was not lost upon the millions of black Americans living in this country, or upon the three-quarters of a million uniformed blacks who were fighting to defend "the arsenal of democracy." It is against this background that the riot—and the rumor which precipitated it—must be examined.

The immediate origin of the Harlem riot was an incident occurring in a hotel lobby on August 1, 1943, in which a white policeman sought to arrest a black woman for disorderly conduct. Private Robert Bandy, a military policeman who was also black, happened to be checking out at the time and intervened in the dispute on the woman's behalf. Following an exchange of words, Bandy was alleged to have struck the policeman across the face with his own nightstick. The policeman then drew his gun and fired; and Bandy was hit in the shoulder.

Although Bandy's wound was not serious, within a few minutes, word raced through Harlem that a black soldier had been killed by a white policeman. Angry crowds surrounded and attacked the policeman. Throughout the night, attempts were made by the community to terminate the rumor. Blacks who were well-known to the people of the area rode in sound trucks which blared the message that the rumor was false. But such efforts did little to ease the situation.

Another rumor was recorded during the early morning hours, when the police department received word that an ominous-looking crowd of whites was massing in the area. Mayor LaGuardia himself sped to the scene with a group of policemen. However, the report proved to be false. In fact, as in the Harlem riot of 1935, most of the violence was directed against property, not people, except for several clashes with the police.[76]

While Mayor LaGuardia was later praised by such distinguished black leaders as Walter White as a moderating influence during an explosive period, the mayor was not above contributing to the spread of rumor. In assessing the riot, LaGuardia charged that the criminal elements in the community were behind the riot: "What happened was the thoughtless, criminal acts of hoodlums, reckless, irresponsible people. Shame has come to our city, and sorrow. . . ."[77]

The implication of his remarks was that all the rioters were criminals and that this one particular group has initiated and sustained the violence in order to achieve certain private ends. Adding weight to this charge was the fact that it came from a high-ranking, respected public official. Nevertheless, no documentary evidence was offered and not even a simple explanation was forthcoming.

Detroit

A number of the conditions surrounding the race riot in Detroit were similar to those found in many cities at the time of the first World War. In the years prior to its 1943 riot, Detroit witnessed a spectacular increase in the number of blacks—the largest of any northern city. Coinciding with the growth of its black population was a large influx of lower-class whites from the South. Sharp divisions between the races surfaced in the areas of housing, jobs, transportation and other essential services. The resulting tensions were reflected in a number of disruptive or violent incidents. In 1941, blacks and whites confronted one another during a strike at the Ford River Rouge Plant. An interracial clash between students was reported at Northwestern High School during the same year. In 1942, a disturbance took place in the Sojourner Truth Housing Project. Several months before the riot, a series of strikes broke out over the issues of hiring and upgrading procedures for blacks. And five days before the outbreak, a group of young blacks was prevented from entering an amusement park by a group of stone-throwing white youths.

The immediate setting for the violence was Belle Isle, a large recreational area spanning nearly one thousand acres. Included in the island's facilities were baseball fields, tennis courts, picnic grounds and beaches. During the 1920s and 1930s many blacks from nearby Paradise Valley, a large black community on Detroit's East Side, frequented the island. As the number of blacks coming to the area increased over the years, many whites came to resent the presence of blacks and eventually sought other places of recreation. Still, thousands of whites continued to come to the island, even though some of them openly expressed their displeasure in having to share its facilities with blacks.

June 20, 1943, a Sunday, was hot. By mid-afternoon, the temperature had climbed above 90 degrees as nearly 100,000 persons, the majority of them black, swarmed over the island. A number of minor incidents were reported during the day. Two youths, a black and a white, scuffled at a pony stand; two black women charged that they had been assaulted by a white man and woman; five blacks and two whites clashed over the use of a picnic oven. As nightfall came, the police continued to receive such complaints. At 8:00 P.M., a fight was reported at the skating pavillion. Minutes later, a white youth was reportedly beaten by several blacks. Shortly after at 9:00, police were dispatched to the ferry dock to investigate a report of a pushing and shoving match.

By 10:00 P.M., the Belle Isle Bridge was crowded with cars and pedestrians. A fist fight between a black and a white man proved to be the last straw in the already fragile situation; it was followed by a free-for-all on the bridge. Before long, about 200 blacks and whites were battling one another, while others rushed to the scene. A full-fledged race riot had come to the city of Detroit.

A question might be raised as to why this particular fight, which appeared to be no different from similar incidents reported throughout the day, should have triggered a massive outburst of violence. According to the report of a special committee appointed by Michigan's governor, the violence would not have spread beyond the bridge were it not for a provocative rumor. This rumor was first recorded when a 17-year-old black, coming upon a crowd near the entrance of the bridge, said that a black woman and her baby had been drowned. Except for the arrival of police reinforcements on the scene, the crowd might have listened to the young man's suggestion that they go to Belle Isle. The rumor had far more serious consequences when it reached the Forest Club, a night spot located in the heart of Paradise Valley, about three miles from Belle Isle. In fact, the committee report cites this episode as "the principal cause" of the riot.[78] At about midnight, just as the band was finishing a number, a black man suddenly jumped on the stage, seized the microphone and identified himself as a police officer. The man urged the audience to get even with the whites for ostensibly killing a black woman and her baby by throwing them off the bridge. The rumor about this killing was false. In fact, it was later discovered that the individual was not a policeman, but an employee of the Club. Yet, upon hearing this man's alleged report, many of the 700 black patrons became extremely agitated, and began heading for the exits:

> Pandemonium broke loose! Some of the dancers dashed out of the building; others jumped out of the windows. Tamble Whitworth, a special officer working at the ballroom, attempted to dissuade the people from leaving, but to no avail.[79]

The crowd spilled out into the streets and began stoning white-operated automobiles and white-owned businesses. By 12:40 P.M., the riot was out of control.

Complicating the situation was a second rumor now circulating among whites, to the effect that blacks had raped and murdered a white woman on the bridge.

However, there is some disagreement among investigators in pinpointing the exact source of this report. Lee and Humphrey trace it to white workers leaving war plants before midnight,[80] while Shogan and Craig claim the story was spread by "white rioters chased from the bridge by police."[81] In any event, many whites were spurred to action because of this rumor.

Variations of both sets of rumors also sprang up: whites threw a black baby from the bridge; blacks threw a white baby from the bridge; blacks attacked two white women on the bridge; white girls were attacked by blacks while swimming; sailors insulted white girls and blacks intervened.

By 3:00 in the morning, the situation had deteriorated. Looting had become extensive and at daybreak crowds of blacks and whites attacked streetcars containing workers on their way to war plants. The violence raged for 30 hours, leaving 34 persons dead (25 black and 9 white), and property damage estimated at several hundred thousand dollars.

Rumors continued to be recorded throughout the violence; the police were bombarded with calls. On Monday afternoon, word was received that a mob of blacks was about to descend on the police station. This "mob" turned out to be a group of blacks on their way to police headquarters to volunteer their services as a security patrol. Lee and Humphrey state that the police received many "fake telephone calls."[82] However, it is not clear from their text whether these were merely crank calls or whether there were indications that they had been placed deliberately by some individuals or group for a specific purpose.

The news media were directly involved in a rumor at least once during the riot. On Monday afternoon, a newscaster named Harold True went on the air, and announced that the State Police had been alerted about carloads of armed blacks from the Chicago area who were headed for Detroit.[83] No source was mentioned and, as it turned out, Mr. True's report was false.

FINDINGS

Our review of rumors and race riots occurring in the first half of the twentieth century suggests the following conclusions:

Association of Rumors and Riots

Rumors were found to have occurred at all stages of riots, particularly at three distinct points in time. Some occurred during the pre-riot period. For example, in East St. Louis there were numerous rumors that blacks were forcing whites from their neighborhoods; that blacks were planning to assault white women; and that large-scale employers were directly responsible for the enormous influx of blacks. In Chicago, it was rumored that violence would occur on July 4. (The riot actually erupted three weeks later, on July 27.) In Omaha, the riot was preceded by "groundless stories" that blacks accused of rape had been allowed to go free.

The data revealed an even stronger coincidence between rumors and collective outbursts following the initial outbreak. In some cases, rumors were connected with the massing of crowds—witness the LaGuardia Commission's finding that "crowds formed here and there as the rumors spread";[84] or the finding of the Chicago Commission that rumors were "the first step" in transforming crowds into angry, hostile mobs. At other times, rumors were linked to panic situations, as when National Guard troops in Knoxville proceeded to "shoot it up" after hearing an erroneous report that blacks had killed two white women. The shooting of an innocent black by two deputy sheriffs in Chicago who had heard that blacks were going to blow up factories is another example of this sort. Rumors were also linked to retaliatory actions, as when young blacks killed an old Italian peddler and a white laundryman following reports of killings by whites.

The association between rumors and precipitating incidents was especially striking. Rumors were an apparent factor in triggering most of the riots—9 out of 11—under discussion. In a few instances, an inflammatory rumor appears to have been the precipitating incident itself, as in Beaumont and Los Angeles, where unconfirmed reports of sexual assaults were followed by violent outbursts. In most instances, however, a specific—and at times, trivial—incident, accompanied by one or more rumors which distorted or exaggerated the incident, was then followed by an eruption of violence. In Harlem, the 1943 riot was touched off by a fight between a black military policeman and a local white policeman, coupled with false reports of the black man's death. In East St. Louis, the riot was precipitated by the accidental shooting of a white man by a black man. At that point, no less than five inflammatory rumors—all of them false—sped through the white community, over-emphasizing and distorting the shooting incident.

It is usually very difficult to pinpoint the exact sequence of events—much less the approximate time of their occurrence—during a riot. Nevertheless, insofar as this information was available for the riots examined, an important connection was disclosed between the precipitating incident, the circulation of rumors surrounding the incident, and the massive outburst of violence. The time lapse between these events was frequently no more than several hours. In Detroit, an ordinary fist fight between a black and a white was reported at about 10:00 at night. The rumor about the black woman and her baby being thrown from the bridge made its way to the Forest Club at around midnight. By 12:40 A.M., the violence was raging and was officially termed "out of control" by the Dowling Commission. In East St. Louis, a union labor delegation received word of an accidental shooting just as the men were emerging from a meeting at City Hall. Within minutes, various rumors about the shooting swept through the local white community, as crowds began to gather. By the time the mayor had rushed outside his office to try to persuade the crowds to return to their homes, as many as 3,000 people may have taken to the streets. The extremely short time lapse between these events underlines the strong connection between the rumors and collective violence, and raises a question about causation which will be discussed shortly.

Themes

Certain similarities of content were found among the rumors, regardless of the racial group in which they circulated. Most were hostile, and directed against members of the opposite race. In addition, they bore varying relationships to reality.

Sometimes, there appeared to be no truth to the rumors. The "Bubbly Creek" rumors espoused by both blacks and whites fall into this category. Sometimes, there was a core of truth which was perverted or, at least, enlarged. The black military policeman in Harlem had, indeed, been shot by a white policeman. The wound, however, was not serious and the individual was very much alive at the time—rumors to the contrary. The large influx of blacks into East St. Louis did necessitate some changes in the established housing patterns of previously all-white neighborhoods. However, it did not mean that "hordes" of blacks were engaged in a concerted effort to "invade" these neighborhoods and "force" whites from their homes.

Almost all of the rumors uncovered by the data were either false or merely partial statements of fact. This finding does not mean that those rumors which were essentially true were necessarily absent from the riots. The difficulty is that accurate rumors were much less likely to have been remembered, recorded or thought of as rumors at the time.

Perhaps the most important finding was that the same kinds of rumors tended to occur again and again— independent of the time, setting and circumstances involved. Moreover, the rumors' themes were highly differentiated along racial lines. Three major themes were discerned among whites.

1. *Rape Rumors.* Sometimes rumors of sexual assault operated prior to the riot, as in East St. Louis, where it was reported that blacks were planning to attack white women. However, such rumors were even more prominent in the precipitating context. In approximately half the riots studied—five out of all 11 cases—reports of alleged rapes were the apparent triggering factor, suggesting that rape rumors were extremely inflammatory among whites.

2. *Black Brutality Rumors.* All sorts of violent, criminal acts were attributed to blacks in these rumors: beatings, bombings, stabbings, shootings and killings. Subsumed under the general heading of "black brutality" are several other themes, including predictions of violence, exaggerations of casuality figures, and so-called "atrocity stories"—

tales of outrageous, horrible deeds allegedly committed by blacks. In Detroit, blacks were supposed to have thrown a white baby from the bridge. In Chicago, it was said that blacks had murdered a little Italian girl. Atrocity stories were of a highly provocative nature and were often tied to acts of reprisal as extreme as the stories themselves.

Other brutality rumors took a more subtle form, involving alleged violations of the "proper place" relegated to blacks by whites. These rumors contained a strong sense of trespass or encroachment against the rights and privileges considered the exclusive domain of whites—hence the charges in East St. Louis that blacks were forcing whites from their neighborhoods and that a black man had insulted a white woman.

Interestingly enough, exaggerations of the number of casualties represent one of the few rumors which did not follow racial lines precisely. Whites were not above inflating such statistics pertaining to blacks, as shown in their contention that 250-400 blacks had died in the East St. Louis riot.

3. *Conspiracy Rumors.* Reports that blacks were plotting actions specifically directed against whites were among the less inflammatory rumors. They did not occur often in conjunction with precipitating events; nor were they strongly identified with specific acts of violence, as were atrocity stories and rape rumors. Nevertheless, "conspiracy rumors" were distinctive in that they displayed a persistence—a kind of "staying power"—much stronger than that of other rumors. In one riot after another, unconfirmed reports of massacres, armed shoot-outs, uprisings and insurrections flourished—prior to riots, during riots, even between riots. We might also point out that conspiracy rumors were a common occurrence in non-riot situations involving the two races—for example, during the slavery period. The durability of this kind of rumor was

truly remarkable, if not puzzling, in view of the impressive amount of evidence marshalled by official investigative bodies which invariably denied the existence of such plots.

Turning to rumors commonly circulated among blacks we find that another set of three themes stands out.

1. *White Brutality Rumors (Civilian).* Closely paralleling black brutality rumors were those which attributed violent, criminal acts to whites: stonings, beatings, burnings, stabbings, shootings and killings. At various times, "white brutality rumors" took the form of predictions of violence by whites, exaggerated casualty counts and atrocity stories. Among blacks, atrocity stories were reminiscent of those among whites; only the distribution of races was different. The script for these stories was also similar, in that they were often tied to a tragic chain of events: rumor-reaction-reprisal. The incident at the Forest Club in Detroit is perhaps the most graphic illustration of this phenomenon. The reader may recall the scene in which hundreds of patrons, in an agitated state, headed for the streets upon learning about the black woman and her baby on the Belle Isle Bridge.

2. *Police Brutality Rumors.* In these rumors, police actions were depicted as inhumane, arbitrary, discriminatory and abusive.

For example, in Omaha, blacks charged the police were withholding the names of white rioters. The riot in Harlem in 1943 was, in part, triggered by the rumor a black soldier had been killed by a white policeman.

Both white and police brutality rumors were closely related, in that the alleged offenses were frequently the same—beatings, shootings, and so on. Moreover, the identification of civilian whites and policemen with "brutality" was such that the two groups often merged into the same or, at least, related rumors. In Chicago, the drowning of a young black was immediately followed by two successive rumors: first, that the victim died from stones thrown by a white person; and second, that a police officer on the scene had refused to arrest the murderer. In Harlem, it was rumored that a youth caught stealing a pen knife had been beaten—by the store management officials *and* the police. Underscoring the combustible qualities of white and police brutality rumors is the fact that both sets of rumors in Chicago and Harlem touched off major riots.

3. *Conspiracy Rumors.* Rumors that whites were preparing for violence did, at times, wend their way through the black community. Prior to the second outbreak of violence in East St. Louis, blacks charged that whites had scheduled a massacre for July 4. Included in the rumors in Chicago were assertions that whites were stockpiling guns and ammunition in their homes, and organizing gun clubs, and that the federal government was planning to transport all blacks from the South in order to break up the Black Belt.

There was, to be sure, a certain amount of overlap in themes between the races. Brutality as well as conspiracy rumors circulated in both the black and white communities. But race-based differences were also noted. No police brutality rumors were recorded among whites; and, with one exception,[85] no rape rumors were recorded among blacks.

Rumor Transmission

1. Informal Groups. The data confirmed that these rumors were an essentially social phenomenon, in that most were disseminated among the members of a particular group. Each group—black and white—was, of course, comprised of individuals. However, these individuals neither related nor responded to the rumors as isolated or

independent units; rather, they did so as part of a larger aggregation which overshadowed the individual's needs and attitudes. The collective aspect of rumors went beyond the fact that more than one individual—or thousands of individuals, for that matter—was involved in the rumor. What was especially significant was that there was a *community* of interest and concern over issues regarded as important: civilian brutality, police brutality, rape, conspiracy and the like.

The data also affirmed the spontaneous quality of rumor. Detroit was the only case in which the possibility of planned or deliberate rumors was raised—and, even there, the "fake" calls to which Lee and Humphrey refer may well have resulted from a few cranks or overly emotional citizens. In every other instance, the rumors seemed to spring up by themselves, free of manipulation or prompting.

Specific questions about various rumor publics were left unanswered by the data—questions such as: how many members of the community heard the rumors; how many people believed the rumors; how many people repeated the rumors; and finally, how many people became active participants upon hearing the rumors? In the absence of studies conducted at the time, it is unlikely that these questions will ever be fully answered.

2. Formal Groups. Insofar as official agencies or groups were involved in the riots, the data suggested that they were not immune to the spread of rumor. Moreover, in keeping with the pattern discerned among citizens, the kinds of rumors transmitted by these groups were, in large measure, determined by race. Civil rights or activist organizations comprised of, or representing, blacks were inclined to reproduce the same rumors sweeping the black community. For example, at the time of the riot in East St. Louis, the NAACP grossly exaggerated the number of

casualties, asserting that 100-2000 blacks had died. When rumors that a youngster had been badly beaten traveled through the streets of Harlem, hand bills stating that the boy was "near death" were immediately drawn up by the Young Liberators and the Young Communist League.

Political groups representing a predominantly white constituency, and comprised mainly of whites, were likewise inclined to mirror the kinds of rumors prevalent among whites. Law enforcement agencies, for example, fell into this category. When National Guard troops in Knoxville sprayed the black community with bullets, they were responding to a rumor that blacks had shot at whites while robbing others.

The findings concerning public officials, governmental agencies and the press are especially significant. Each of these groups occupied an important leadership role in the community; each was charged with placing the public interest above narrow, petty or partisan considerations; each was regarded as an authoritative source of information; and each was responsible for providing accurate and objective news to the public, particularly during the crisis period.

Despite their pivotal position, the data suggest that, on occasion, these groups performed their functions with a notable lack of distinction. All too often they represented one segment of the community in blatant disregard of the other; all too often they conducted themselves in a short-sighted, irresponsible manner.

The problem was not simply that groups in an official capacity were susceptible to the spread of rumor during a time when reliable information was urgently needed—furthermore, they continually echoed the sentiments of the white community. Among public officials and governmental agencies, the theme of conspiracy on the part of blacks was especially strong. A New York District Attorney's attribution of the 1935 Harlem riot to a Communist plot, the denunciation of respected civil rights leaders by a United States Congressman for supposedly planning violence, the attempt by the Department of Justice to link the riots in 1919 to a radical labor group and the Soviet Union—all without any real evidence—indicates that these official agents of the government, whether consciously or not, were catering to their predominantly white audience.

The deficiencies in news reporting were even more glaring. Rumors disseminated by the press[86] ran the gamut of the rumors circulating in the white community. In unsubstantiated and sensationalized stories, headlines and editorials, blacks were frequently seen beating, raping, shooting, murdering and plotting against whites.

Such misreporting was found prior to, as well as during, the riot period. In two cases, inaccurate or distorted press reports actually constituted the precipitating incident: in Washington, D.C., where a distorted and inflammatory headline implied that blacks had sexually assaulted a white girl; and in East St. Louis, where unverified news stories charged that blacks had arranged to ambush the police. In one other riot (in Los Angeles), the worst of the violence followed upon rumored predictions of trouble by the so-called "zoot-suiters," which received major coverage in the local newspapers.

A key responsibility of the press during the riots involved sifting through various fragments of information in order to piece together a story—accurate, objective and balanced—about precisely what happened. In discharging this responsibility, however, numerous instances were uncovered where the "white version" of events was impulsively, if not automatically, adopted by the press—thereby becoming the only "official version" of those events. All too often, and on the basis of virtually no evidence, blacks were incorrectly faulted as the aggressors and main perpetrators of the violence. A news story appearing in the *Arkansas Gazette*[87] at the time of the clash between some deputy sheriffs and blacks in Elaine, Arkansas, is instructive. The body of the article made reference to "numerous stories and rumors and suspicions" circulating among whites:

> Returning possemen brought numerous stories and rumors and suspicions, through all of which ran the belief that the riot was due to propaganda distributed among the negroes [sic] by white men. It was clearly indicated, they said, there was an organization of negroes antagonistic to the white residents in the southern part of the county.

By the end of the article, the tenuous views of the white possemen had meshed with those of the white reporter filing his report, to the point where the two sets of views were indistinguishable. The last paragraph read:

> It is stated on good authority that negroes [sic] of the vicinity of Elaine have been holding secret meetings at night and that unidentified white men had been circulating literature among them.

(It was not clear who or what this "good authority" was.)

The tendency on the part of the press, as well as other groups in positions of authority, to echo rumors found in the white community—in the face of no evidence, insubstantial evidence, or even contradictory evidence—amounts to a clear and unmistakable bias. To be sure, not every rumor emanating from those in leadership positions was traceable to this bias. There were instances in which a given rumor simply stemmed from the general chaos of the time. This appears to have been a factor in the exaggerations of the size of crowds and the number of casualties. Nevertheless, the receptiveness of these powerful groups to so many rumors that were hostile in content, directed against blacks, and rooted in the white community, does indicate a serious bias.

3. THE FORMATION OF RUMOR: THEORETICAL PERSPECTIVES

In the last chapter, we examined rumors and riots from a historical perspective. In brief, we found that rumors and riots were strongly connected. We also found that a number of themes were salient; certain rumors tended to occur repeatedly—regardless of time, setting or circumstance. And, finally, we found that these themes were distributed among each race—not randomly among individuals. These findings, however, raise some important questions:

1. How should we interpret the relationship between rumors and collective violence? Did the rumors help cause the violence? Did the violence help cause the rumors? Or, were the rumors and the violence both caused by the same underlying process?

2. Why did certain themes occur over and over again? And why were the themes so strongly divided along racial lines? Was it a simple case of historical accident; or did the emergence of themes by race reveal something deeper and more significant about the way rumors circulate?

We also need to examine why the rumors arose, and what were the underlying factors that generated the rumors in riot situations.

With these questions before us, we move to a discussion and evaluation of three models of rumor formation. These models may be labelled: psychological, functional and conspiratorial. Within each school of thought, most investigators address themselves strictly to the general question of rumor formation, without reference to a particular situation or setting. Such a broad treatment of rumor formation by no means precludes its applicability to riots. Nevertheless, wherever possible the author will draw from materials previously applied to riot or, at least, crisis situations.

THE PSYCHOLOGICAL MODEL

Proponents of this model maintain that rumors stem from the needs, drives and interests of the individual. The formation and circulation of rumors is seen as an emotional outlet—a defense mechanism—against feelings which, if confronted directly, might be unacceptable to the individual or at least difficult for him to handle. The rumors may relieve feelings of guilt, anxiety, fear, anger, resentment and hostility.

For example, Robert H. Knapp emphasizes the importance of individual anxiety in wartime rumors.[1] He cites the situation in England during the days of World War I when morale was extremely low. Throughout this difficult time, the country was rife with rumors that large numbers of Russian troops had landed. These rumors, which were false, continued to circulate despite repeated denials from public officials. Knapp explains the tenaciousness of the rumors by hypothesizing that they helped reassure an insecure, frightened population. A similar explanation is offered for the many disparaging rumors about Hitler, Mussolini, Tojo and other dictators during the Second World War. Knapp suggests that the hostile, aggressive quality of the rumors served "to reassure the individual, to make him feel stronger, to protect him from his anxiety."[2] Allport and Postman have a similiar view of rumors as a rationalizing force in the individual's emotional life:

> Rumor is set in motion and continues to travel in a homogeneous social medium by virtue of the strong interests of the individuals involved in the transmission. The powerful influence of these interests requires the rumor to serve largely as a rationalizing agent: explaining, justifying, and providing meaning for the emotional interest at work.[3]

Given this emphasis on the individual, we should not be surprised to find that personality traits are regarded as an extremely important factor in rumor construction. Indeed, many rumors are thought to have a neurotic basis. Among the more commonly cited rumors are those which serve to enhance a poor self-image. Bernard Hart points to the need of some individuals to be the center of attention, to achieve a distinctive place among their peers as the possessor of the "latest news." He also observes a tendency for the person transmitting the rumor to relate it as closely as possible to himself. A case is cited in which one rumor

propagator assures his audience of listeners that a box full
of bombs has been discovered in a nearby town, or in the
next street, or even in his cousin's house.[4] A similar
parallel might be drawn from the Chicago riot, where a
local resident recited a rumor that blacks had set fire to
houses occupied by whites just "back of the Yards."

Other investigators share Hart's "center of the stage"
view. Schall, Levy and Tresselt suggest that most rumors
serve as an attention-getting device.[5] Similarly, Peterson
and Gist contend that "inside information" about some
issue of concern to the public momentarily enchances the
individual's prestige and position.[6] The more credible-
sounding the story, the more secure the individual's
prestige. Consequently, the person transmitting the rumor
may be motivated to "forget" certain details which cast
doubt on the rumor, and stress those details which increase
its plausibility. The individual may even add a few
embellishments of his or her own.

Rumor formation is frequently treated as a projection
of repressed feelings, in which the rumors provide a
fancied view of reality. The individual imputes his own
motives to others, thereby giving vent to his own inhibi-
tions or secret desires. In some of the earliest and most
original work done in this area, Jung analyzed the case of a
13-year-old girl who was expelled from school for spreading an ugly rumor about her teacher's sexual activities.[7]
The source of the rumor was a dream the girl had, which
was subsequently repeated to some of her classmates. Jung
interviewed the girl and obtained written statements from
the other classmates as to what they had heard. He
concluded that the dream, repeated in the form of a
rumor, fulfilled the girl's desire for sexual union with the
teacher. The erotic fantasies of the girl's companions also
contributed to the spread of the rumor.

This interpretation could easily be applied to the riot

situations previously studied. For example, we could say that many of the unproved and unfounded tales of rape against white women were rooted in the personalities of repressed white men. Believing in the superior sexual prowess of blacks, and convinced of their own sexual inadequacy, these insecure individuals invented and spread rumors to relieve their pent-up feelings of guilt and anxiety, while bolstering their egos as the defenders of white womanhood.

Some investigators have postulated rumors as a pathological phenomenon, rather than something to be expected of all normal persons under certain conditions. In this case, rumors are thought to be initiated by persons suffering from severe emotional disorders. Indeed, psychiatrists have long observed patients in a state of panic who hallucinate, turning ordinary events into imaginary, frightening threats. These individuals may interpret a couple of people walking along the street as coming to attack them, or hear the siren of a police car as a person's screams. Hallucinatory rumors harbored by these disturbed individuals may take the form of atrocity stories. Hart states:

> Rumors of atrocities . . . have probably at least one root in the sadistic and masochistic complexes which, at any rate in an undeveloped or repressed state, are more widespread than is generally thought.[8]

Allport and Postman take a less extreme view. While acknowledging that rumors may, at times, be a pathological phenomenon, they do not go so far as to suggest that mental illness is a precondition for hallucinatory rumors. Instead, they contend that otherwise normal individuals may be inclined to hallucinate under conditions of severe strain. As an example, they cite the situation during the Detroit riot, when the police department was deluged with calls reporting various alleged incidents. One woman telephoned to report she had seen—with her "own eyes"—a white man murdered by a group of blacks. When the police arrived on the scene, all they could find was some girls playing hopscotch. Allport and Postman conclude:

> The fact that the caller claimed to have been an eyewitness suggests that rumor may, under extreme conditions of stress and excitement, be an outright pathological phenomenon.[9]

Another incident occurring at the time of the Detroit riot might be used to support the Allport-Postman position. The reader may recall the episode at the Forest Club when a black man, in a highly agitated stated, leaped on the stage and seized the microphone. Identifying himself as Sergeant William Fuller, the man announced that some whites had thrown a black woman and her baby off the Belle Isle Bridge. The rumor, of course, had absolutely no basis in fact; no one had been killed at Belle Isle. Moreover, the man on the stage was not Sergeant Fuller. Whoever the distraught man was who seized the microphone that night, it is conceivable that—for him, at least—the Belle Isle rumor had become a pathological phenomenon.

Despite its emphasis on the individual's personality traits and emotions, the psychological approach to rumor formation does not preclude social factors altogether. Some investigators see rumors as a social, as well as a psychological, problem. These people point to the prevalence of rumors during crisis situations such as panics, epidemics, wars, disasters and riots. In the preface to their book, Allport and Postman state: "Wherever there is social strain, false report grows virulent."[10] Moreover, as described by these investigators, the relationship between rumors and riots is extraordinarily close. In a statement that has been quoted many times over the years, Allport and Postman advance it as a "law of social psychology" that no riot ever takes place in the absence of rumors: *"no riot ever occurs without rumors to incite, accompany, and intensify the violence."*[11]

The introduction of social, alongside psychological, factors, however, points up some deficiencies of the psychological approach. The model grants the role of rumor in social situations, but fails to account for the social situation in which rumors form. As it is, conditions in the community—the environment, setting, circumstance—are largely neglected. The model retains the individual as the supreme factor in rumor formation at all times:

> Their [the rumors'] functional signficance in social life can be gauged only by probing into the deeper layers of personality and into the economy of the individual mental life.[12]

Likewise, the needs, drives, interests and actions involved in group behavior are ignored. Even during riots which pit group against group, the question of rumor formation invariably comes down to the individual. In reality, rumors are considered a social phenomenon only insofar as more than one person is necessarily involved:

> Certain large publics are susceptible to particular classes of hearsay. These rumor chains depend upon the suggestibility of the individuals who compose them. Whenever the excitement is more intense, more and more people become involved in the chain.[13]

Writing many years before Allport and Postman, Hart was already aware of the narrowness of this approach. He recognized the inadequacy of treating rumors as a single chain of reports among individuals. Unfortunately, in attempting to reconcile social with psychological factors, he merely succeeded in making the contradictions more glaring. In offering a provisional definition of rumor, Hart begins with the following statement: "Rumor is a complex phenomenon consisting essentially in the transmission of a report through a succession of individuals."[14] Later, he tells us that rumor "is something which occurs in communities, and has particular properties owing to that very fact."[15] Finally, he comes full circle in telling us that "crowds are without doubt the soil in which rumours grow and thrive...."[16] Hart's attempt to clarify individual versus group factors merely clouds the issue further.

Another weakness of the psychological approach involves a rather implausible assumption which helps to undermine the model. Rumors are viewed as having an emotional, frequently neurotic, sometimes pathological basis. It is therefore assumed that the more stable, rational individuals are necessarily less likely to start and spread rumors. This assumption belies an obvious fact of life: that *all* of us think and act daily on the basis of unverified reports. Moreover, the theory also supports the outmoded view of riots as irrational, senseless and without meaning, with active participants more rumor-prone *because* they are considered more neurotic.

Indeed, the psychological approach is especially vulnerable when it is applied to riot situations. For one thing, it is at variance with key findings presented in the last chapter. As we have seen, despite the serious attempt to introduce social factors into rumor formation, the psychological model remains firmly wedded to the individual and personality traits. The individualistic bias of psychologists and psychiatrists necessarily sets their theory apart from our previous finding that rumor is *essentially* a social phenomenon. It is not simply the case that large numbers of people construct and circulate rumors during the riots. The rumors reflected community concerns and issues: civilian and police brutality, rape, conspiracy, matters which are far beyond the personal concerns of the individual's daily life. In no way does the psychological approach account for, explain or substantiate these findings.

The psychological model is inapplicable to another finding as well. In our survey of riots over a 25-year period, we uncovered a series of rumor themes which emerged time and time again. In contrast, psychologically oriented investigators tend to posit the ephemerality of rumor. They view rumors as short-lived and of temporary interest only. Thus rumor content is presumed incidental and inconsequential—since it is determined by the whims and interests of the individual which, after all, are in a constant state of flux. According to Allport and Postman, different rumors are apt to come and go, "simply because the panorama of human interest changes rapidly."[17] Certainly, this view does not accord with our finding that a particular rumor will come and go in one situation, only to arise in another.

One of our previous findings does accord with the psychological model—namely, the close association between rumors and riots. Allport and Postman's proposition bears repetition: "no riot ever occurs without rumors to incite, accompany, and intensify the violence." That statement is a rather sweeping one, in view of the lack of substantive evidence presented. Nevertheless, the essence of that proposition is supported by our finding which showed strong temporal relationship between rumors and riots.

Allport and Postman's efforts are less than satisfactory in their failure to probe beyond the rumor-riot relationship. We still must answer the questions posed earlier: Did the riots help cause the rumors? Did the rumors help cause the riots? Or, were the rumors and riots both caused by the same underlying process? The Allport-Postman proposition does not readily lend itself to interpretation of this sort. To assert that rumors "incite" violence suggests that rumors are a causal factor; to assert that rumors "accompany" violence simply establishes a correlation; to assert that rumors "intensify" violence suggests an interaction with rumors as a control factor. The difficulty is that these issues are neither explained, expanded or explored.

The amount of literature which treats the psychological basis of rumors, while somewhat dated, is fairly large. But, aside from the fact that much of the reading is interesting and provocative, the weaknesses inherent in this model—its narrowness, its individualistic bias, its faulty assumptions—means that little is added to our understanding of rumors in relation to riots. Let us turn, therefore, to another approach which views rumor from a quite different perspective.

THE FUNCTIONAL MODEL

The most thorough inspection of rumor formation from a functional standpoint is found in the book *Improvised News: A Sociological Study of Rumor,* by Tamotsu Shibutani.[18] Not every component of Shibutani's model is new or original. However, in terms of synthesizing, refining and building upon previous efforts in this area, his book is by all counts impressive—the best work of its kind.

The psychological approach treats social factors in a perfunctory manner and not as an integral part of any model. In contrast, the functional approach is based on the premise that rumor is essentially a social phenomenon.

Social factors are stessed on two fronts.

First, rumors are regarded as a collective enterprise—not simply as the creation of any one individual. Shibutani speaks of a "collective transaction," in which rumors arise and take shape from the collaboration of many persons. Of course, individuals are involved; but they are interdependent. The participants do not simply parrot what they have heard. Instead, people are brought together to discuss matters of concern—matters of common preoccupation. There is give and take; ideas are shunted back and forth; different viewpoints are heard. A division of labor exists, in which different participants make different contributions. Some individuals venture opinions as to what might have happened; others predict what is going to happen; others make comparisons with previous situations; others introduce new bits of information. Opinions are weighed; statements are challenged; explanations are sought. From this mutual exchange of thoughts, ideas and sentiments, certain items of information begin to take precedence over others. In this way, a collective interpretation—a rumor—develops.

Second, interest is centered on conditions and circumstances. Rumors are seen rooted in the immediate situation whereby an unusual event—irregular, unexpected and unfamiliar—brings people together. The event may be highly dramatic—an assassination, a kidnapping, a "skyjacking," a flash flood, an epidemic, a riot. Or the event may be considerably less spectacular, although still out of the ordinary—a job resignation, a car accident, a siren, a police arrest. All of these incidents serve to alter the daily routine of life, paving the way for rumor.

The real importance of the situation, however, extends beyond the unusual quality of the event. What is even more important according to this model is that the event is clouded by ambiguity. It is not immediately clear what has happened, or what is happening, at a time when people need to orient themselves, to understand, to resolve questions and make decisions. For example, people living in an area where a riot is in progress may become preoccupied with questions such as: What precipitated the riot? Who is to blame? Is it safe to go outside? Are the police on the scene? Have any shots been fired? Has anyone been hurt or killed?

The problematic nature of the situation lies at the heart of the functional approach. Information is urgently needed to understand and adjust to changed and uncertain circumstances. In such situations, the public becomes highly responsive to news. This demand for news is related to the importance placed upon the event—the more important the event, the greater the demand for news:

> Demand for news varies with the importance placed upon events. "Big news" affects a large public and is about matters that require immediate attention. . . .[19]

Where does this news come from? The answer is: from any communications channel that is defined as authoritative and therefore reliable. The mass media, falling into this category, are undoubtedly the largest suppliers of news. Indeed, modern societies have established a complex communications network stretching across the globe. This vast network is able to speed the flow of news to the public almost instantly.

The mass media are not considered the only authoritative source of news. For example, a certain measure of public esteem and respect is automatically accorded individuals holding public office. However, these and other authoritative sources are severely handicapped by the number of people that they can reach directly. As a general rule, they are heavily dependent upon the media for communicating with the public—a fact which accentuates the media's importance even further.

Individuals, caught up in a situation which they do not adequately comprehend, tend to turn to the mass media—particularly radio, television and the newspapers—for clarification and verification of what they have heard. In this way, news provided by the media becomes the standard by which reports obtained from other sources are validated or supplanted.

The system is based upon the law of supply and demand, and works to the extent that the supply of news accords with the public demand. But problems may arise. The demand for news may exceed the supply made available through formal channels. An event may be so sensational that the best efforts of the news media may be insufficient to cope with the inflated demand. Or, for a variety of reasons, the news may be blacked out. Wartime censorship and newspaper strikes are two entirely different matters; but the effect in each case is to cut off the supply of news. Finally, there may be times when the news channels themselves are impaired or destroyed—during power failures, for example. In such cases, once again, the effect is to impede the flow of news.

Thus, occasions may occur where the system malfunctions—where ordinary communications are either not working adequately or suspended entirely. Under these conditions, information which the public vitally needs may not be forthcoming. Collective tension arises, which must be relieved. At this point, rumors are constructed as a form of "improvised news." Rumors are therefore functional—they explain what is not clear, provide details, answer questions, aid in decision-making and, above all, relieve collective tension. As Shibutani sees it, rumor construction represents a kind of collective problem-solving:

a recurrent form of communication through which men caught together in an ambiguous situation attempt to construct a meaningful interpretation of it by pooling their intellectual resources.[20]

In developing his model, Shibutani cites many different historical events. Let us take a closer look at his model—the functional approach—by examining in some detail a single event taken from recent history: the Chappaquiddick tragedy involving Massachusetts Senator Edward M. Kennedy.

On the night of July 18, 1969, a black sedan plunged off a narrow bridge on Chappaquiddick Island, Martha's Vineyard. The car, containing the body of a young woman, later identified as Mary Jo Kopechne, was discovered early the next day. Shortly after this discovery, which took place many hours after the accident, Senator Kennedy walked into the Edgartown police station and declared that he had been the driver of the car. Filing a brief statement with the police chief, the senator immediately left by plane for Hyannis.

From the beginning, this incident contained two important elements of Shibutani's model. First, the event was highly unusual. It is not every day that a United States senator drives his car off a bridge; and it is not every day that a senator is involved in another person's death. In addition, the event was of importance to the public, involving as it did a member of America's best-known and most important political family. The hundreds of curiosity-seekers on the scene, returning home with slivers of the now-famous bridge, attested to the enormous interest of the public at the time, as did the presence of reporters from all over the country. But huge assemblages of reporters did not simply reflect the public's preoccupation with the event. It was also indicative of the enormous

demand for news. At this point a third—and essential—in-
gredient of Shibutani's model was added to the situation:
ambiguity.

There were two problems with the statement filed by
Senator Kennedy. First, it was not immediately released,
at a time when both the press and public were anxious for
details of the accident. The delay in releasing the document meant that precious time had been lost which could
have been used to supply the public with some sort of
explanation of what had happened. A second problem was
that the senator's statement seemed to raise more questions than it answered. Both the press and public cited
numerous discrepancies; many found the statement con-
fusing, if not contradictory.

Other questions began to crop up. Why did the senator
leave the accident? Why did the senator wait nine hours
before reporting the accident? Why was there no autopsy?
How fast was he senator driving? Was the senator sober?
Why was he in the company of the young woman? Where
was his wife at the time? What was a second young
woman's purse doing in the car? The questions seemed
endless. Full and adequate disclosure was the order of the
day. Unfortunately for Senator Kennedy, many people felt
his official statement was neither full nor adequate. All
that was clear was that nothing was really clear.[21]

For the next week, there were two new cross-currents at
work in an already tense situation: a rising demand for
news on the part of a restless public, versus a virtual
blackout of news from the Kennedy compound at
Hyannis Port. An angry, tired, frustrated press was caught
in the middle. For three days, Senator Kennedy remained
out of sight, seeing no one but his closest associates, and
refusing to talk to even his most intimate contacts in the
press.

Filling the information vacuum was a series of rumors.

There had been a wild party. Mary Jo was four months pregnant. The senator had persuaded the medical examiner not to perform the autopsy. The Attorney General had been paid off.

The news blackout lasted for an entire week, ending with a nationally televised speech in which Senator Kennedy sought to explain himself to the American public. In this speech, the senator denied the rumors of immoral conduct on his part and that he had driven under the influence of alcohol that night. At the same time, he admitted leaving the scene of the accident, describing his behavior as "indefensible."

Public reaction to the speech was mixed. A flood of telegrams and letters were received supporting the senator; but doubt and skepticism remained strong in other quarters.

Our purpose here is not to assess the senator's explanation of the accident, but to explore this incident in order to understand better the process by which rumors are formed. The Chappaquiddick case appears to fit Shibutani's theory very well. All of the ingredients are there: an unusual event, an interested public, an inflated demand for news accompanied by an inadequate supply, an ambiguous situation culminating in an avalanche of rumors on the part of an anxious and confused public, trying to fit the pieces of the puzzle together.

Riot Situations

In developing his model, Shibutani studied 60 different situations, accounting for a total of 471 rumors. But few of these situations involved episodes of collective violence. In fact, only two of the 60 cases involved race riots—the Chicago riot of 1919 and the Harlem riot of 1935. These

two riots account for four out of the 471 rumors—an
extremely small proportion. Moreover, the Chicago riot is
only listed in the appendix of Shibutani's book; it is not
discussed or even mentioned in the text. This fact raises an
obvious question: to what extent is his model—or, more
broadly speaking, the functional approach—applicable to
riot situations?

In terms of the riot situations presented in the previous
chapter, much of that material seems relevant to Shibutani's model. In many instances, the appearances of rumors
was preceded by an unusual, and at times dramatic, event:
an interracial fight, a massing of crowds, a police arrest, a
shooting and so on. Even more important, many of the
situations were marked by ambiguity. Information to
supply details to a concerned or aroused public was absent
at the time.

The Harlem riot of 1935 may well be the best
illustration of Shibutani's model. The riot grew out of an
incident—far from spectacular, but out of the ordinary
nonetheless—in which a teenage boy was caught stealing
a knife from a five and dime store. A brief pushing and
shoving match ensued between the store manager, his
assistant and the boy, attracting the interest and attention
of the shoppers. To avoid stirring up emotions any further,
the boy was whisked away to the rear entrance of the
building via the basement. The boy's "disappearance" was
now complicated by the arrival of an ambulance on the
scene. In fact, the ambulance had been summoned to tend
to the wounds of the boy's captors. But this was not
immediately known to the excited shoppers in the store.
Where had they taken the boy? Why had an ambulance
come? The explanation was as simple as it was logical: the
boy must have been beaten up. Lending an even more
ambiguous cast to the situation was the fact that, by some
strange coincidence, a hearse happened to be parked in

front of the store. How to explain the presence of a hearse? The boy must be dead. One woman was heard to shriek: "They've come for the child's body!" Again, rumors seemed to explain what was not at all clear. The explanation may not have been correct, but it was at least plausible, and it did serve to define the situation.

An examination of riot situations in terms of Shibutani's model seems to demonstrate the validity of the functional approach. Apparently this explanation of rumors is as applicable to the Chicago race riot of 1919 as to the Chappaquiddick tragedy of 1969. But is this really so? When the riot situations are more closely inspected, serious doubts arise as to whether the functional approach is really adequate. Reservations are centered in three areas: the role of ambiguity as the dominant factor in rumor formation; the applicability (or, at least, relevance) of parts of the model to certain of our previous findings; and finally, the ability to deal meaningfully with the specific questions posed at the beginning of this chapter.

In the riots previously studied, ambiguity was most certainly a factor in the emergence of rumors. But was it the only factor at work? And was it necessarily the most important? The difficulty with Shibutani's model is that it fails to take into account other factors of a social nature which were built into the situations. Certain deep and complex factors—issues, complaints and grievances, all of which can be lumped under the general heading of "community conflict"—appear to have been as much a part of the situation as ambiguity, perhaps more so.

Take, for example, the rumors which helped precipitate the Chicago race riot. These rumors grew out of an incident at a local beach, in which a young black swimmer accidentally crossed an unofficial boundary line into the "white" area. While whites and blacks threw stones at one another, the young man, who had remained in the water,

suddenly went down. Efforts were made to revive the boy, but to no avail. A rumor immediately raced through the crowd that the boy had died as a result of being hit by a stone. A second rumor then spread, that a policeman had refused to arrest the boy's "murderer."

Obviously, the circumstances under which the young man had died were not clear to the crowds on the beach. Only later were officials able to determine that there were no stone bruises on the body, and that the young man had apparently died from drowning. It is perfectly understandable, given the excitement and confusion of the time, that unconfirmed reports of police misconduct might circulate. Shibutani's view that rumors develop in the absence of news seems to apply here.

Nevertheless, it can also be maintained—just as convincingly—that community conflicts were rooted in the situation, and that the rumors were some kind of expression or extension of these conflicts. Prior to the riot, friction had developed in white neighborhoods that had been "invaded" by blacks. Between July 1, 1917 and July 27, 1919 (the day of the riot), 24 bombs had been thrown at the houses of blacks and real estate men who had sold or rented property to the newcomers. Police were notably unsuccesful in locating the guilty parties and were accused by blacks of making little effort to do so. Five weeks before the riot, on two separate occasions, a black man was murdered—each the victim of a brutal attack. Assaults by white hoodlums had become a common occurrence, especially in parks and on local beaches. Indeed, the imaginary boundary line at the beach where the riot occurred seemed a perfect symbol of the division of the two races. In this scheme of things, the alleged murder of the young black swimmer appeared in the eyes of other blacks as the newest in a never-ending series of unjust, brutal acts by whites; reports of the policeman's unfair behavior appeared in the same light.

Let us examine one other situation from these two different perspectives—the hotel lobby episode which triggered the Harlem riot of 1943. The reader will recall that a white policeman tried to arrest a black woman for disorderly conduct. A black soldier intervened in the dispute, taking the side of the woman. Following a struggle between the two men, the policeman fired his gun, slightly injuring the soldier. *Time*'s account following the riot said that a "much garbled" version of the incident quickly spread through the streets, suggesting that the soldier was dead.[22] Thus, it would appear that the rumor emerged from an ambiguous situation, when the details of the shooting were not yet clear.

But, looking at the situation from a different vantage point, an equally strong case can be made that the rumors stemmed from wartime tensions widespread throughout the Harlem community. It is a fact that black soldiers (particularly those stationed in the South) were subjected to all sorts of indignities—from frequent taunts of "nigger," to having to sit in the back of the bus, to instances of outright murder. Three months before the Harlem riot, Judge William H. Hastie and Thurgood Marshall submitted a report on civilian violence against black soldiers to the National Lawyers' Guild. The report, later forwarded to the War and Justice Departments, noted that civilian violence directed against black members of the armed forces was increasing, and that the government had taken no action on the problem. In his article assessing the Harlem riot, Walter White indicates that the residents of Harlem were well-acquainted with cases of mistreatment:

> Naturally these soldiers [stationed in the South] wrote to their relatives and friends in New York. Harlem newspapers published the stories. They became another segment of many other tales from Southern camps such as the killing by a Louisiana state policeman of Raymond Carr, a Negro MP, when Carr refused to leave his post of duty at the order of a white civil policeman.[23]

Viewed in this light, the rumor that a white policeman had killed a black soldier was apparently linked to social tensions rooted in the community. The rumored death of the soldier became another example of the victimization of black people—even those employed in the service of their country.

Shibutani's model, like most explanations of rumor formation, rests upon an assumption of its universal applicability. Based upon the evidence accumulated so far, it appears that this assumption is false and that the model is more relevant to some situations than others. On the positive side, the theory seems finely attuned to situations such as Chappaquiddick, where the sequence of events is relatively straightforward and where a strong social context is lacking. The ease with which the model was applied to the Chappaquiddick tragedy is evidence of Shibutani's fine grasp of this type of situation.

But the applicability of this model to riot situations is quite a different matter. Here we are dealing with an infinitely more complex phenomenon, where innumerable forces and dynamics—political, social, economic, historical, cultural, psychological—are at work. Because of his heavy emphasis on the problematic aspects of the situation, Shibutani fails to appreciate the existence of other equally, if not more, important factors. Therefore, in the context of riots, his approach to rumor formation is both simplistic and incomplete. At best, it provides a partial explanation of why rumors are formed.

Indeed, there is some evidence to suggest that Shibutani overestimates the ambiguity factor altogether. In East St. Louis, for example, the riot grew out of an accidental shooting, the severity of which was distorted by rumor. In Rudwick's authoritative account[24] of the incident, there is nothing to indicate that ambiguity was an important part of the situation. The same point holds true for the race riot in Detroit which began with a fist fight, pure and simple, followed by the series of "bridge" rumors.

But while there is no evidence that either of these situations was problematic, it is noteworthy that community conflicts were much in evidence. In East St. Louis, the rumors immediately followed a highly emotional meeting at City Hall, during which a union delegation of whites had called on city officials to curb further migration of blacks to the city. An hour before the meeting was scheduled to begin, the street outside City Hall was packed with hundreds of people, including many union members. News of a holdup of a white man by a black was received just as the meeting was ending. The rumors about the holdup circulated among the crowds which had previously gathered, anxious to learn whether an agreement had been reached. Insofar as collective tension existed, it was apparently tied to the outcome of the meeting, rather than the details of the holdup. In Detroit, the fist fight which preceded the rumors was actually the last of a long series of interracial fights and incidents that had been reported in the area that day. Thus, while recognizing that the evidence at this point is not conclusive, there are some indications that the importance of ambiguity needs to be qualified. It appears that, while ambiguity is frequently a factor in rumor formation, it is not necessarily a prerequisite, and that other factors such as community conflict may be far more significant.

The incompleteness of Shibutani's model is underscored by his prescription for terminating rumors. Shibutani states that the process of rumor construction may be terminated when the situation is no longer problematic— when the demand for news drops or the supply of it becomes adequate. In crisis situations where collective excitement is intense, he says that rumors will be terminated when an acceptable explanation is provided by established channels—the news media, public officials, community leaders, etc.:

> rumor construction may be terminated by verification or refutation from formal news channels. . . . Especially where intense collective excitement has developed over some unusual event, tension drops suddenly when an acceptable explanation is provided in institutional channels. Conventional perspectives are quickly restored.[25]

Shibutani's solution, then, is really rather simple: supply the public with needed information, clarify the situation, and the rumors will go away. Unfortunately, this solution may be *too* simple. On several occasions during the riots described in the preceding chapter, attempts were made to combat rumors along the lines that Shibutani proposes. For example, as the violence raged through the streets of Harlem in 1935, following the rumor that young Lino Rivera was dead, desperate police officials blitzed the community with pictures showing the boy alive and well. For good measure, Rivera was photographed next to a black police officer. This effort by the police not only failed to stop the rumor, but also led to still another rumor, that Rivera was only a substitute for the "real victim" and was being used to deceive the people. Granted, Shibutani might well argue that the experiment failed because the police did not qualify as a trusted source in the eyes of the black community. The point would be well taken in this case. However, another similar effort, made during the Harlem riot of 1943, was equally unsuccessful, even though the plan was executed under circumstances that would presumably meet Shibutani's objections. In this situation, black leaders in the community—individuals who were well-known and respected—rode around in sound trucks which blared the message loud and clear: the rumor was false; the black soldier had not been killed. But the violence continued anyway. The message was ignored—at least by those who continued to participate in the violence. We are left to conclude that a fresh supply of information may not suffice in some situations, either because ambiguity is not central to the formation of rumors or because of the presence of underlying factors.

Further evidence of the model's shortcomings lies in the inattention given to rumor content. Let us suppose, for a moment, that Shibutani was correct—that ambiguity is at the core of rumor formation. The difficulty with this view is that it would explain the cause of the rumors, but not their content. In other words, the model merely explains why the rumors emerge, but not why *certain* rumors emerge. To pose the problem in Shibutani's terms, it is not clear why one "collective interpretation" is arrived at, as opposed to some other one.

At times, Shibutani seems on the verge of grappling with this selection process. There are references to "the importance of an event" and "the sensitivities shared by the people." But these are casual comments, rather than themes which are fully developed. Moreover, while these ideas are presented, they remain subordinate to the notion of ambiguity. Thus, Shibutani briefly takes stock of the importance of the event, but immediately cautions:

> It is not so much the intrinsic importance of an event but the existence of a problematic situation that converts what is otherwise ordinary information into news. Where the situation is ambiguous, where there are alternatives, where a decision has to be made, any item that might affect the outcome becomes 'live matter.'[26]

The narrowness of this approach is reflected in its emphasis on the perishable, transient qualities of rumor. Like Allport and Postman, Shibutani views rumors as "an ephemeral transaction," stressing that "most rumors are soon forgotten."[27] As we have previously noted, this view appears to be true only in the immediate sense that a given rumor will span the length of a given riot. More important, however, our findings also showed that certain kinds of rumors had great resiliency, appearing again and again— regardless of time, place or setting. It would appear that, where riots are concerned, old rumors never die; nor do they fade away. They simply lay dormant for a while until the next appropriate time appears—contrary to the views of Shibutani, Allport and Postman, and numerous other investigators.

Shibutani's efforts are equally unsatisfactory in his discussion about the relationship between rumors and riots. Because his theoretical treatment is so broad, Shibutani does not address himself specifically to the causal relationship between rumors and riots. However, he does attempt to probe the relationship between rumors and what he calls "collective excitement." Unfortunately, even at this level, his analysis suffers from the sort of incompleteness mentioned earlier.

Like Allport and Postman, Shibutani recognizes that conditions of social unrest provide a perfect spawning ground for rumor:

> Rumors . . . flourish in situations characterized by social unrest. Those who undergo strain over a long period of time—victims of sustained bombings, survivors of a long epidemic, a conquered populace coping with an army of occupation, civilians grown weary of a long war, prisoners in a concentration camp, residents of neighborhoods marked by interethnic tension—become restless and dissatisfied.[28]

But all of the above-mentioned examples simply represent empirical findings. Where Shibutani—like Allport and Postman—falls short, is in his inability or, at least reluctance, to deal with the causal implications of these findings.

Shibutani does attempt an explanation. In his particular scheme of things, rumors are thought to be determined by the amount of collective excitement:

> With intensification of excitement more and more participants lose their sense of individuality, and self-discipline in terms of conventional norms is gradually relaxed. . . . They also become immediately and uncritically responsive to one another, and rumors develop instantaneously.[29]

The difficulty with this scheme is that Shibutani does not really explain why the volume of collective excitement should suddenly increase in the first place. Statements such as "once collective excitement gets under way . . ." or "with the intensification of excitement . . ." beg for some kind of elaboration which is not forthcoming. As in other areas, Shibutani's scheme here is incomplete—or, perhaps, ambiguous.

It is ironic that, by positing a relationship between social unrest and rumor which appears to be correct, the weakness of both the psychological and functional approaches should be exposed. In both cases, the failure to fully probe this relationship indicates that social conditions are not an integral part of either model. To be sure, each model is posited on a different base. The psychological approach, stressing the needs and drives of the individual, is essentially emotional; while the functional approach is essentially cognitive. With the latter, people are seen putting their heads together, trying to solve a problem, attempting to define or make sense out of a given situation. But, in both cases, the attempt to broaden the social dimensions of the model fails, because the ideas presented are never really developed. The functional approach looks at the situation only in the immediate sense that it is problematic. The psychological approach virtually ignores the situation altogether. Thus situational factors, such as social tension or unrest, are not central to either model.

Our general assessment of Shibutani's model indicates that the functional approach has very definite limitations when applied to riot situations. The emphasis on ambiguity at the expense of other situational factors is probably the model's most serious defect. Still, the criticisms of it which have been expressed need to be tempered somewhat, or at least placed in a proper perspective—for, however serious our misgivings, they are not meant to detract from the particular merits of the model. The stress on rumor as a social phenomenon, the isolation of ambiguity as one important factor, the recognition of the special responsibilities of the news media, public officials and other official sources of information, all represent significant contributions to our understanding of the rumor process. As we have seen, the model is not adequate when it comes to riots. What Shibutani has done is to provide us with several small, but important, pieces in the rumor-riot puzzle. What remains is for us to try and find the other pieces.

THE CONSPIRATORIAL MODEL

Several years ago, an ugly rumor sept through the peaceful and prosperous region of France called Orléans. The rumor suggested that local Jewish merchants were drugging and kidnapping their women customers for the purpose of selling them into white slavery.[30] Certain aspects of this episode were highly unusual. Reportedly, Orléans had not had a history of racism or similar excesses. Yet the story, recalling the Middle Ages when Jews were accused of stealing gentile children to make matzoh, was apparently believed by large numbers of people. As the rumor fever reached a peak, women customers refused to go alone to the stores were the alleged atrocities took place. Instead, they came in threes or accompanied by their husbands or, according to the storekeepers, not at all. Perhaps the most significant aspect of the whole affair was the strong consensus—from high-ranking police officials to leading citizens within the community—that the rumors had been instigated by an anti-Semitic group as part of a slander campaign against Jews.

This last point serves to introduce us to a third and final model of rumor formation—the conspiratorial approach. Unlike the psychological and functional approaches, which treat rumors as spontaneous transactions, the conspiratorial model views rumors as manipulated or controlled artificially, as part of an organized effort.

Most investigators of rumor—including Knapp, Allport and Postman, and Shibutani—[31] grant that rumors are deliberately planted in some situations, particularly where there is a strong divergence of interests. Such rumors are generally used to advance or consolidate an individual's position. More specific objectives may involve winning new converts, finding out information or defeating the opposition by discrediting, demoralizing or dividing it. A variety of techniques can be employed, including the deliberate misrepresentation of facts, the exploitation of existing beliefs and values and the manipulation of the media. What is important is not that the uses of such rumors are so varied, but that their uses can be so deadly.

Anonymity is a major advantage of planted rumors; it is usually quite difficult to trace their source. Moreover, even if the source can be identified, it is often impossible to establish actual complicity. Another advantage is that once these rumors are launched, if they are credible or strike

some responsive chord, they tend to be self-propelling—
that is, once planted, they spread under their own power.

Because of the competing interests at work and the high
stakes involved, the financial world is especially conducive
to rumors spread deliberately. Recently, in a highly
unusual action, the American Stock Exchange disciplined
two of its floor members for rumor-mongering about the
financial condition of F.I. DuPont, Glore Forgan & Co.,
one of the security industry's biggest but most troubled
firms. Stories had previously circulated that certain wealthy
members of the DuPont family intended to withdraw substantial amounts of capital from the firm, and that DuPont
was about to announce its liquidation and withdrawal
from the securities business. The stories, which were false,
were traced to two men who were subsequently fined
$1000 each for circulating them. That the rumors warrant-
ed disciplinary action indicates how serious the situation
was considered. Dupont is one of the largest firms in the
country, so its collapse would inevitably have had a major
impact on Wall Street. Underscoring the market's sensitivity to manipulation of this sort is exchange Rule 3c,
which provides that "no member organization shall circulate in any manner rumors of a sensational character which
might affect market conditions on the exchange" and requires that "any such rumors shall be promptly reported
to the exchange."

The volatile world of politics provides still another
setting for contrived rumors. Political campaigns seem an
especially good spawning-ground. In 1972, for example,
charges of a "whispering campaign" reverberated during a
heated congressional primary contest in New York between Bella S. Abzug and William F. Ryan. Supporters of
Representative Ryan claimed that his opponent was
responsible for circulating "despicable and untrue" rumors
about Ryan's health. While the charges against Representa-

tive Abzug were never proved, Ryan died of cancer several months later.

The "dirty tricks" operation of President Richard M. Nixon's re-election campaign organization in 1972—which became an important aspect of the ugly Watergate scandal —provides us with an almost unbelievable case study in the manufacture of rumors. Donald H. Segretti, a young California lawyer and friend of White House aide Dwight L. Chapin, headed an elaborate program of political spying and sabotage designed to confuse and harass the Democrats. The secret projects, including the spread of false and malicious rumors, were carried on by a cross-country network. In February 1972, New Hampshire voters received phone calls late at night from representatives of the "Harlem for Muskie Committee" who, in obviously "black" accents, promised Muskie would deliver "full justice to black people." On February 24,—two weeks before the New Hampshire primary, the Manchester *Union-Leader* published a letter from a "Paul Morrison" of Deerfield, Florida, which linked Muskie (who was campaigning in Florida) to an ethnic slur against "Canucks." The newspaper then ran a front page editorial headlined "Sen. Muskie Insults Franco-Americans." Two days later an emotionally upset Muskie wept while speaking in front of the *Union-Leader* office. (To date, "Paul Morrison" has not been found.)

But Sen. Muskie was by no means the only political target. One "trickster" was dispatched to New Hampshire to make a contribution to the presidential campaign of Republican Congressman Paul N. McCloskey in the name of the Young Socialist Alliance. (The young man was originally supposed to represent a homosexual organization, but balked at the last minute.)

On March 11, three days before the Florida primary, phony letters on "Citizens for Muskie" stationery were mailed out to a list of Senator Henry M. Jackson's supporters. It was asserted that Sen. Jackson, while a high school senior in Everett, Washington, in 1929, had become involved with a 17-year-old girl and fathered an illegitimate child. The letter also claimed that he had been arrested on two different occasions on homosexual charges. But lest the other Democratic candidates feel slighted, Senator Hubert H. Humphrey was cited in the same letter for having been arrested for drunk driving in Washington, D.C. in 1967, after hitting two cars and a mailbox. For good measure, it was reported that in the car was a "well-known call-girl" who had been paid by a lumber lobbyist to entertain the senator. (Senators Jackson and Humphrey later denied the allegations and there was nothing in the police files to substantiate the charges.)

In late March, Segretti and his cohorts went to Milwaukee where the Wisconsin primary was scheduled for April 4. There they printed up a fake Humphrey press release announcing free food and drink, "balloons for the kiddies," and speeches by Mrs. Martin Luther King and actor Lorne Greene. The release was then passed out in the black neighborhoods of Milwaukee. In retrospect, the whole slew of "dirty tricks" was a part of the dirtiest political campaign in our entire history.

All of the foregoing episodes indicate that planted rumors can and do occur at times; that such rumors tend to flourish in situations where conflicting interests are at work; and that they are distinguished from other rumors by their malicious intent. The question before us now is whether such rumors were used in the context of the riots studied and, if so, to what extent.

Given the perpetual conflict between blacks and whites, some investigators have raised this possibility in the area of race relations generally; a few have gone so far as to posit that planted rumors have acted as an active agent during times of stress. Malcontents—both black and white—are pictured as deliberate rumor-mongers, planting their wares in appropriate places, sowing seeds of doubt, fear, hostility and suspicion.

In a small tract by Raymond M. Momboisse, entitled *Rumors,* the author tells about one case where rumors were deliberately and successfully used to force a retail store to capitulate to certain demands.[32] The rumors included charges of unfair employment practices and price gouging, as well as stories about contaminated goods. Even though the dispute was settled, Momboisse reports that the store suffered a permanent loss of business. Another instance is cited concerning the "shove and push day" rumor. Here deliberate rumors were supposedly spread that on a given day, members of minority groups were planning to physically harass whites whenever they came into contact with them. Momboisse says that no such plan for harassment actually existed; the rumor campaign was simply a ploy to increase general tensions and hostility.

In their book, *Race Riot,*[33] which is primarily an account of what happened in Detroit, Lee and Humphrey specifically raise the issue of planted rumors with respect to riots. These investigators assert that often on the eve of riots, more rapid dissemination of rumors occurs, along with a change in their type and tone. According to Lee and Humphrey, the rumors, which become increasingly vicious, go through three stages: reports of alleged insults and discriminations; stories of imminent violence, of arming by the other race, and invasion plans from another city; and inflammatory accounts of beatings, rapes and murders. The increased speed and changing character of the rumors are frequently the product of "artificial creation" and directly traceable to "the rumor-mills of demogogic groups":

> These rumor symptoms circulate with increasing rapidity in barber shops, beauty parlors, bars, church socials, in lobbies,

business gatherings, union meetings, and family conclaves, in
face-to-face talks, telephone conversations, and even in rare
instances over the radio and in the newspapers. Their origins are
difficult to locate until one considers *the significant fact that on
the eve of race riots, rumors frequently bear the earmarks of
artificial creation and abnormally rapid dissemination. This brings
us to the rumor-mills of demagogic groups. . . .*[34]

The "demagogic groups" to which Lee and Humphrey
refer include both the far Right and the far Left. In
Detroit, the anti-black groups listed as "demagogic"
included the Christian Frontiers (led by Father Charles E.
Coughlin of Royal Oak, Michigan), the Ku Klux Klan, the
Black Legionnaires, the Dixie Voters' League and the
United Sons of America. The anti-white organizations
named were the ("Japanese-inspired") Eastern Pacific
League, the Moorish Science Temple of Am, the Improvement of Our Own, and the Universal Negro Improvement
Association. These groups were seen as fostering stereotypes, thereby creating a climate of intolerance and serving
as "rumor-mills and propaganda-mills." The implication of
this last designated function was clear: these groups
provided the machinery for grinding out—manufact-
uring—rumors and all sorts of other propaganda deliberately designed to feed people's fears and prejudices. The
authors warn that as riot draws near, organized hate groups
are likely to operate more openly and more aggressively;
they also tend to play an active role "to demonstrate their
power" once the violence gets underway.

Lee and Humphrey's arguments favoring the conspiratorial approach to rumor formation are extremely weak in
several respects. First, although the authors are long on
generalizations, they are very short on evidence. Statements concerning a change in rumor content and more
rapid dissemination just prior to riots, along with assertions about the "artificial creation" of rumors, are
apparently based on only one riot—the Detroit riot of

1943. Obviously, one case is hardly a sufficient basis for sweeping generalizations. What is equally disturbing is that nowhere do the authors offer any *specific* evidence from the Detroit riot to support their claims. Instead, they content themselves with piling up one presumption on top of another, to arrive at their generalizations. For example, a presumed increase in the speed of rumor transmission is one basis for their conclusion that the rumors were planted. "Abnormally rapid dissemination" of rumors shows "artificial dissemination," or so the authors contend. But even if they *had* documented their point concerning the speed of rumor, such a finding would not necessarily lead to the conclusion that some form of manipulation was at work. It is just as conceivable that other factors—an increase in community conflicts, for example—might have been responsible.

A second weakness is that Lee and Humphrey fail to distinguish between rumors and beliefs. They note that hate groups tend "to propagandize against the Negroes and whites," but it is not really clear whether the authors are referring to generalized beliefs or rumors. Generalized beliefs would involve purported weaknesses, failings and evils attributed to one race, whereas rumors would refer to more *specific* accusations. For example, the notion that blacks are inherently licentious is a generalized statement of belief. The charge that blacks raped a woman on the Belle Isle Bridge is simply a rumor. While propaganda might include both rumors and beliefs, it is important that the two not be confused. Moreover, it is not clear whether the propaganda—whatever form it took in relation to these riots—sprang naturally from the views of each group toward the other, or whether it was part of a concerted effort to stir up trouble deliberately. Once again, our understanding is hampered by the investigators' failure to draw a distinction between intent and effect.

A third and final weakness involves a basic contradiction

in their line of argument. Lee and Humphrey assert that, just prior to riots, rumors are frequently the result of "artificial creation"—a claim which by definition must involve some sort of contrivance or planning. With respect to Detroit, the authors link their claim to the activities of certain "demagogic groups." Nevertheless, they immediately proceed to exonerate all such organizations from any direct role in precipitating the Detroit riot:

> we must know as much about such anti-democratic organizations as we can, even though it is generally agreed that none of those mentioned actually organized the Bloody Week Riots.[35]

With reference to this last issue, we should point out that—numerous rumors to the contrary—our historical survey failed to turn up any hard evidence implicating any particular group in plotting the riots. As we have seen, official commissions, independent investigators and later historians generally found the riots to be spontaneous affairs, without any real leadership or organization.

The same point applies to the racial disorders of the 1960s. Most investigative groups were in agreement with the National Advisory Commission on Civil Disorders that the disturbances "were not caused by, nor were they the consequence of, any organized plan or 'conspiracy.' " True, there were some instances where rumors appear to have been spread deliberately. But the number of such cases was very small, and they were mostly viewed as isolated events, rather than as part of any pattern. For example, in their study of the Watts riot in 1965, Cohen and Murphy state:

> Rioters monitored police calls on transistor radios. Some even went so far as to 'test' police capability to respond. They telephoned a report of a fire or a shooting at a certain distant address in the trouble zone, then determined by listening to their

radios how long it took officers to reach the scene of the phony
alarm.[36]

Nevertheless, when queried by this writer about whether
there was a great deal of deliberate rumor-mongering,
co-author Cohen replied as follows:

> Yes, I would say so, but only if you mean by a very, very small
> number of activists seeking to take advantage of the situation,
> make trouble, for whatever benefit they might have hoped to
> derive from doing so. But if you mean that large numbers of
> persons dealt deliberately in rumor—definitely not. Probably a
> great number of rumors were innocently circulated because of
> worry, concern and the tenseness of the time—just as in any
> crisis.[37]

We are therefore led to the conclusion that the conspiratorial approach does not provide us with a really valid
explanation of why rumors are formed.

Each of the three dominant models of rumor formation
has intrinsic merits. Each seems especially geared to certain
kinds of circumstances or situations, and each seems to
have at least some relevance when applied to riot situations. Although we have expressed reservations and criticisms, we have not dismissed outright any of these approaches.

If a central point emerges from our evaluation, it is that
none of these models goes far enough toward providing a
truly complete or satisfactory explanation with respect to
riot situations. For example, none of the theories really
comes to grips with the questions posed at the beginning
of the chapter—although by focusing on rumors as a social
phenomenon and drawing our attention to the situation
(at least in an immediate sense), the functional approach
probably comes closest.

All this suggests the need for an alternative approach,

which examines rumors from a different perspective. Let us therefore turn our attention to a new model of rumor formation.

4. RUMORS AND RACIAL DISORDERS: THE PROCESS MODEL

Since our historical review of riots, coupled with the inapplicability of traditional models of rumor formation, points to the need for a new approach, this chapter will be devoted to outlining and developing such a model. In successive chapters we shall attempt to test, apply and refine this model, exploring its practical implications.

Our new approach—called the process model—rests upon several premises. First, we must recognize that no single theory is valid in every instance of rumor formation. As we have seen, rumors are so varied in terms of number and nature that different explanations probably account for their emergence, depending on the particular circumstances or setting involved. Where collective violence—or, more specifically, racial disorders—is concerned, we are dealing with a unique and complicated phenomenon, where the social context is extremely important, and where a general or "single cause" model seems to have limited value. Consequently, a special model is required: the process model is offered specifically as an explanation of rumors with respect to racial disorders. Second, racial disorders are neither mysterious nor random occurrences; they arise out of the structural arrangements within society. This is not to say that protest, ideology and grievances are part of every disturbance involving blacks and/or whites. However, without denying the existence of "issueless riots," as Gary T. Marx calls them, or what Edward C. Banfield labels riots "for fun and profit," our concern is those disturbances—of which there have been thousands in this country—which have a protest character and are inspired by indignation and ideology. Third, rumors and racial disorders are part of the same process. It is not that rumors cause violence, or that violence causes rumors. Rather, rumors should be seen as one of a series of factors underlying the violence—one determinant out of many which increases the likelihood of violence.

We should stress that the purpose of this section is to present a model of rumor formation, not a complete approach to collective violence. But, given the third of our premises, some overlap between these two goals is bound to occur. Therefore, we shall draw upon various determinants of violence—but only insofar as they are a direct part of the process by which rumors are formed. The model itself has been developed from our earlier historical findings concerning rumors and riots, along with the writings of some prominent students of violence, principally Smelser, Grimshaw and Spiegel.[1] This approach represents a convergence of disciplines, drawing upon sociology, social psychology and history. It is sociological to the extent that structural features of society will be examined. Social psychological factors involving group attitudes and beliefs will be looked at as well, along with historical episodes taken from what is now generally recognized as "our violent past."

The process by which disorders occur is composed of a series of factors or determinants of violence. These factors must be present and, as a general rule, are sequentially dependent. No determinant by itself "causes" a racial outburst. Instead, each one in succession adds to the tendency toward violence. These determinants include: a rigid social structure, supported by a racist ideology; a hostile belief system; conditions of stress and rumors.

THE SOCIAL STRUCTURE

When outbreaks of racial violence have occurred in this country, the public's attention has generally focused on the violence itself—the culprits, the casualties, the amount of destruction, the duration of the disorder, the force necessary to stop it and so on. More serious observers have turned their attention to the "underlying factors" of the disorders—industrialization, migration, poverty and other conditions. While recognizing that these and other factors are involved in the violence, we must also examine what underlies the underlying factors. There may be something fundamentally wrong with our social environment, and these periodic episodes of violence may ultimately be the result of a specific malfunctioning of our social system. This basic defect, which Smelser labels "structural strain," involves the impairment of relations between blacks and whites—the inequality between the races which still exists, as it has always existed, in this country. There is a great deal of truth in Richard E. Rubenstein's observation, made after examining mass poli-

tical violence, that the "violence itself seemed a good deal
less important than the group relationships which produced it."[2]

Some form of structural strain must be present if an
episode of collective violence occurs. Where race relations
are concerned, strain in the form of inequality has been
built into our social structure—that is, institutionalized—
helping to ensure eruptions of violence at fairly regular
intervals. Behind all of the riots, lynchings, slave rebellions
—even the Civil War itself—the broad issue has been, and
remains, the relationship of the black and white races.

There are four basic aspects to the strain embedded in
our social fabric, all of them interrelated. The first is the
conflict between our democratic and elitist values. Americans are accustomed to thinking of themselves as unique
and democratic people. The United States was born out of
an anti-colonial revolution. It does not have a feudal past,
like the European countries. It is a land of immigrants,
enriched by the diversity of various groups. Moreover, the
United States has the most clearly-defined, best-advertised
set of democratic ideals in the world. The dignity of the
individual, the equality of all men, the rights to liberty,
justice and equal opportunity are the basic principles
which comprise the American Creed. These principles have
been written into our most important political documents:
the Declaration of Independence, the Preamble to the
Constitution, the Bill of Rights and the various state
constitutions. Every schoolchild pledges himself or herself
to a unified nation, "with liberty and justice for all" and
sings about "the land of the free and the home of the
brave," while committing to memory the tenet that every
individual is entitled to "life, liberty and the pursuit of
happiness." And Lord help the person who would dese-
crate the American flag by failing to fly or fold it correctly. (Indicative of our flag fetish is an incident that oc-

curred when Yippie leader Abbie Hoffman appeared on a national television show wearing a shirt in the form of a flag. The viewers at home were treated to a most unusual shot of Hoffman from the neck up—the rest of him was blacked out.)

Unfortunately, our democratic ideals have tended to mask our elitist values—which have not received as much attention but which are equally, if not more, important. By elitism we mean here a social-ranking process, a lineal arrangement whereby each member of society is assigned a definite place. Contradicting—or, more accurately, triumphing over—our egalitarian principles, our elitist values have been translated into a rigid, caste-like social structure which has excluded numerous groups from "the democratic process."

It is true that we are a nation of immigrants, but one in which the original dominant group, the so-called Anglo-Saxons, took early and effective control of the economic and political power in government, commerce and the professions. This elite group has been highly resistant to the upward strivings of other social, economic, religious, ethnic and racial groups, using its access to the levers of power to maintain its dominance to the present. Spiegel has suggested that, at the time when our country was founded, the American system of government was limited by six principles of inclusion/exclusion.[3] In order to be admitted to the system, one had to be white, Anglo-Saxon (or of some closely related national background), Protestant, middle or upper class, male and an adult. Naturally, these principles excluded far more than they included—indeed, our country at that time could hardly be called democratic. At one time or another in our history the following groups have been excluded from positions of power: non-whites, whether red, yellow or black; non-Protestants, be they Catholic, Buddhist or Jewish; working-class and poor people in general; ethnic groups, such as the Irish, Italians and Greeks; women; and youth, as well as young adults not considered sufficiently wise or experienced to engage in decision-making or significant kinds of participation. Historically, our has been a nation of dominants versus subordinates, the "ins" versus the "outs," the haves versus the have-nots, the powerful versus the powerless.

This conflict in values has been largely suppressed. However, the disparity between our democratic ideals and authoritarian practices, constituting another source of strain, has been more difficult to ignore. And in no other instance has the disparity been so great as it has been for blacks. The exclusion of blacks has been the most systematic and complete. No other group has been kept out of the mainstream of American life to the extent that blacks have; no other group has been given quite so low a position in the hierarchy; no other group has had to struggle with such a low rate of social mobility. The Kerner Commission's warning that "our nation is moving toward two societies, one black, one white—separate and unequal" is off the target historically. For we are not in the process of approaching something new; from the earliest beginnings of this country, we have maintained a dual system—what John Hope Franklin has called "two worlds of race."[4]

Less than 50 years after the first Negroes landed at Jamestown in 1619, they were set apart from the rest of the population and denied rights by custom as well as law. The Declaration of Independence may have asserted that all men were created equal, but it remained silent on the issues of slave trade and slavery itself. When the colonies were actually fighting for their freedom and independence, General Washington issued an order to recruiting officers that they were not to enlist suspected traitors, strollers, vagabonds—or Negroes.

The inferior status of blacks was most readily apparent in the whole master/slave relationship. The slave was totally removed from the protection of organized society, with his master retaining absolute control over him. The slave's marriage was not recognized, his wife could be violated, his children and his wife could be sold, and he could be subjected to unbelievable cruelty on the whim of his master. By law, the slave could not be taught to read or write, could not worship freely and could not even meet with friends, except in the presence of a white person.

The contradictions inherent in such a situation were a constant source of embarrassment. At the time the colonies were trying to secure their independence, when slavery was firmly entrenched, a troubled Mrs. John Adams wrote to her husband: "It always appeared a most iniquitous scheme to me to fight ourselves for what we are daily robbing and plundering from those who have just as good a right to freedom as we have."[5]

To this day the dilemma continues. Despite a steady stream of constitutional amendments, court decisions, executive orders and congressional legislation, this conflict between ideology and practice has yet to be reconciled. Some 22 million black Americans live under the vestiges of slavery, still struggling to emerge from their second-class citizenship. The dismal reality is that we have scarcely lifted a finger to eliminate the barriers which divide the races. Our black masses remain locked in ghettos from which there is virtually no escape; in overwhelming numbers our schools are still racially imbalanced. In fact, the class lines between the races are hardening; our cities are becoming racial islands, black ones in the inner city and white ones further out; our civil rights laws are frequently not enforced; and, with few exceptions, our elected officials continue to show themselves devoid of moral leadership.

Anti-democratic practices are now couched in new

rhetoric declaring the sanctity of "the neighborhood school," as well as opposition to "high density" developments, "low-income" housing and "forced integration" of the suburbs. The new terminology and techniques still mean "keep out"; know thy place in white society. It is clear that we are nowhere near the open, competitive, diverse society we profess to have. The institutions of the dominant majority have largely remained intact, while truly significant steps toward the elimination of racial barriers have yet to be taken. Tragically, the "two worlds of race" are still very much with us. If anything has changed, it is simply that the contradictions straining our social fabric have become more difficult to conceal. John Hope Franklin was painfully eloquent in his assessment of this situation.

> The reading of American history over the past two centuries impresses one with the fact that ambivalence on the crucial question of equality has persisted almost from the beginning. If the term 'equal rights for all' has not always meant what it appeared to mean, the inconsistencies and the paradoxes have become increasingly apparent.[6]

How has it been possible to justify a system which claims to be democratic but which has featured at various times forced labor, segregation and discrimination? The way out of the dilemma has been through the creation and maintenance of a racist ideology—a doctrine stressing racial differences and assuming the biological inferiority of Negroes. Where black/white relationships are concerned, color and other fixed biological traits have been the most important ingredients in the system of dominance and subordination, features which have distinguished the position of blacks from that of other minority groups.

During the pre-Civil War period, when the institution of slavery became firmly entrenched, a large body of unscientific literature came into existence to "prove" that the Negro was an imperfectly developed creature in mind and body. It was said that the Negro was an inferior variety of the human species, not capable of the same sorts of self-improvement as whites. Typical of the thinking of that time was the assertion by Dr. S.C. Cartwright of the University of Louisiana that the Negro adult's potential for learning was roughly equivalent to that of a white infant. This meant that freedom was not only unsuited to the Negro's temperament, but downright detrimental to his well-being and happiness. Racial stereotypes were an important part of the doctrine. Negroes were said to be lacking in intelligence, lazy, immoral, immature, happy-go-lucky, criminal, aggressive and close to their anthropoid ancestors. The idea of Negro inferiority was widely accepted among Southerners of all classes and among many Northerners as well. More than one anti-slavery society was divided on the question of whether or not to let free Negroes join. Long after slavery was ended, the stereotyped picture of blacks was perpetuated by our mass media—in newspapers, novels, short stories, the stage and later by movies, radio and television.

While the doctrine of racial inequality may not be quite so strong as it once was, it remains a potent force in American life. Public opinion surveys continue to document huge pockets of racism within our society. One out of every three white persons polled by *Newsweek* magazine in 1963 freely admitted to thinking that blacks were inferior to whites. Half felt that blacks had less native intelligence; 75 percent thought that they tended to have less ambition; 85 percent believed that they laughed a lot; while almost 70 percent were convinced that they had looser morals.[7] Three years later, a similar poll taken by the same magazine indicated that white attitudes toward blacks had remained substantially the same.[8]

It is ironic that the very doctrine used to justify the postion of blacks in society has proved to be an added source of strain on the social system. From the beginning, this doctrine was more a simplistic rationalization than a reasonable explanation of things. Parts of it were even contradictory. For example, blacks were thought to be lazy and inert, but also pushy and aggressive; they were happy with their position—there was no race problem at all—yet force was needed to keep them in their place. Equally important is the fact that black people themselves —especially young blacks—have begun to reject the racial stereotypes which white society has traditionally foisted upon them. The current preference for words like "black" and "Afro-American" over the word "Negro" (a term strongly associated with the racist doctrine); the predisposition to wear "Afro" hairstyles and clothes; the recent proliferation of black studies programs in schools across the country; the whole notion that "black is beautiful"— all of these things are the outward manifestations of the new racial pride. It is no accident that the latest cycle of interracial violence has coincided with a healthier, more positive black self-image, along with a repudiation of what has been called the "culture of subordination."[9]

A fourth and final source of strain can be found in the inequities themselves. The system of dominant-subordinate relationships between whites and blacks has left both groups perpetually insecure, hostile and suspicious toward one another. As the privileged group wishing to maintain its favored position, whites have felt threatened by the demand that they share their power, and have tended to resist efforts made in this direction. On the other hand, blacks have sought to adance their own position and to establish parity. The result has been an unstable accommodation, alternating with periods of open conflict. When violence has occurred, whites have tended to strike in the name of order, blacks in the name of justice.

This pattern has not been restricted to whites and blacks. In fact, we have had large-scale civil disorders whenever groups in an excluded category have made historically appropriate bids for admission to the seats of power. Historically, the poor began their struggle with a series of revolts known by such names as the Wars of the Regulators, the Shays Rebellion, and the Whiskey Rebellion. The anti-Catholic riots of the 1830s and 1840s, initiated by an intensely Protestant population, were meant to discourage the Irish from their bid for power. Following the Civil War, workingmen trying to organize themselves collectively engaged in more than a half century of violent warfare against the industrialists. As Jerome Skolnick has noted, the demand for participation has been an important motif throughout our history:

> A common theme, from the ghetto to the university, is the rejection of dependency and external control, a staking of new boundaries, and a demand for significant control over events within those boundaries.[10]

The situation between blacks and whites has differed only in that the struggle has been more prolonged and intense.

HOSTILE BELIEF SYSTEM

Another condition that is necessary for an outbreak of violence—and, as we shall see later, probably the most crucial variable for rumor formation—is the presence of a hostile belief system. By this term we mean a negative set of generalized views, perceptions and convictions held by one race with respect to another. These beliefs, which have varying relationships to reality, distinguish disorders having a protest character from merely deviant cases—as, for example, the victory celebration in Pittsburgh at the conclusion of the 1971 World Series.[11] More importantly, the beliefs reflect, not only the deep-seated antagonism between blacks and whites, but also the enormous amount of ignorance of each race regarding the other. Tragically, the gap—which in some cases is more of a gulf—in perceptions on so many issues, is the price we have had to pay for our racial isolation.

Before outlining these beliefs in detail, a few words about their general character would seem to be in order. The number of beliefs held by each race is almost endless. Fortunately, in this case we are only concerned with those beliefs which add to the tendency toward violence. In addition, we must acknowledge that racial beliefs, like other attitudes, are by no means static. A Gallup survey taken in 1958 found that fewer than 40 percent of the whites interviewed would vote for a qualified black person for president. In 1967, the figure had jumped to 54 percent—a majority. At the same time, however, there are many areas, particularly those which have a direct bearing on the relationship between blacks and whites, where attitudes and beliefs have not been modified to any great extent, and in some instances have actually worsened. Even if we allow for differences in age, sex, socioeconomic status, educational level and geography, the historical record demonstrates that hostile beliefs remain a powerful factor in our society, while contributing to the poor state of race relations.

Given the inequities inherent in the situation, the set of beliefs held by each race are quite functional. As we have seen, whites must live with the insecurity of trying to retain their favored position, while blacks must face the dilemma of a deprived minority trying to alter their status within a fundamentally hostile environment. Clearly, this

is an undesirable state of affairs for all concerned. Both parties live under constant strain; neither group has ever really been content with its lot.

Hostile beliefs among each group, therefore, serve to identify the source of strain and assign responsibility. For whites, blacks are the cause of trouble; while for blacks, the reverse is true. The argument can then be made that things will improve if the forces of evil are confronted, attacked, removed or destroyed. Symbols are convenient for pinpointing these forces. The Turner and Surace study demonstrated how the term "zoot-suiter" elicited a series of negative beliefs about Chicanos. For many blacks, the police are the personification of white authority and thus are similarly associated with a series of hostile views. What these beliefs do is remove the agent or object perceived as a generalized threat or obstacle. The way is then prepared for violence, since the next step involves the desire to move or mobilize against the forces of evil.[12]

The two assumptions that underlie this hostile belief system should be made explicit. Although the central purpose here is to explain, rather than assess the merits of these beliefs, we assume that each belief is part of a complex phenomenon in which fact and fiction are intricately meshed. We also assume that, while the hostile beliefs are found in varying degrees of intensity within each race, they are more highly pronounced among active or potentially active riot participants.[13]

In outlining these beliefs, the author has relied heavily on survey data accumulated by social scientists and professional pollsters. These public opinion surveys reveal surprising unanimity in their findings and provide important documentation for our contention that many hostile beliefs have remained strong, if not fairly constant, within our society.

Hostile Beliefs Among Whites: General Beliefs

1. *The status quo must be maintained.* Contrary to popular opinion, white people are not unaware of the existing inequality in our society; furthermore, they have shown some willingness to do something about it—at least in certain areas. The average white person knows that discrimination exists and does not approve of this. He thinks that blacks should have the right to vote, have decent housing, be served at the same lunch counters as whites, go to the movies of their choice and be able to shop at their favorite clothing stores. In recent years, large numbers of whites have favored spending millions of dollars to improve the ghettos, pass new legislation to eliminate rats in the slums, and create summer camps and large-scale government work projects to give jobs to the unemployed. So it would neither be fair nor accurate to accuse whites of being opposed to all change, per se. The "stop sign" is posted in those areas which involve more fundamental changes in the social system, and which would affect the lives of whites directly. It is one thing to support decent housing for blacks; it is quite another matter to let blacks into an all-white neighborhood. It is one thing to let blacks vote; it is something else when it comes to sharing political power on the local city council. It is one thing to favor quality education for all, but another matter when the issue of busing is raised. Clearly, in getting down to basics, white people are thoroughly committed to preserving the established order.

The reaction of whites to the latest cycle of violence, largely initiated by blacks, is significant. Thus far, most of the violence has been expressive rather than instrumental in nature—indicative of the rage, anger and frustration of a people who are not out to destroy the system, but who simply want "in." If we think of such violence as a revolu-

tion of sorts, it is, as Thomas Pettigrew has pointed out, a very special revolution:

> this is a revolution with a basic difference. It aims to modify, not to overturn, the society it confronts; it seeks to amend, not to ravage. Negro Americans are so firmly rooted in and shaped by their land that their revolution is attempting merely to guarantee full participation in the society as it otherwise exists. In short, they do not wish to depreciate or destroy that which they wish to join. It is, then, a peculiarly conservative revolution, a fact that in many ways gives it a special force.[14]

Nevertheless, whites have tended to perceive this violence as a direct threat to the system and all its institutions. As of 1967, 27 million white Americans, representing 54 percent of the nation's homes, owned guns. A nationwide survey by Louis Harris taken in the same year indicated that a majority of gun-owners were prepared to use their weapons "to shoot other people in case of a riot."

The message of the riots is really a plea for meaningful social change expressed in acute, dramatic and painful form; but by misreading the message, whites have merely increased their own determination to maintain the status quo.

2. *Blacks have a definite place.* Given the system of dominant-subordinate relationships, whites have created boundaries within the social setting which define acceptable modes or standards of behavior for blacks, principally with respect to social distance and respect for white authority. Many of these boundaries are actually physical. The Chicago race riot of 1919 began when a young black man was found swimming in the part of the beach reserved for whites. Similarly, the Detroit race riot of 1943 started at a hotly contested recreational area where racial tensions had long been simmering. Notwithstanding the public accommodations section of the Civil Rights Act of 1964,

there are still places in this country which will not cater to blacks, or where blacks dare not go.

There always seems to be some point at which whites draw the line, especially when it comes to social contact. Integrated housing remains a perilous collision point. A *Newsweek* poll conducted in 1966 found roughly half the whites opposed to integrated housing, even though a majority of those in the North and South supported federal legislation to help blacks improve their homes. At the same time, the location of low-income housing in the suburbs remains a volatile issue. And, predictably, the area in which whites come closest to unanimous agreement is the issue of interracial marriage. A Gallup poll released in November, 1972 found that 71 percent of the whites did not approve of marriages between whites and blacks.

The system does, of course, allow for some upward mobility. But the number of blacks who actually "make it" remains very small indeed. What is more, such success almost always comes on the white man's terms. Edward W. Brooke—the only black man to serve in the United States Senate during this century—has been quoted as saying he never even considered running for governor of his home state of Massachusetts, because he did not feel the voters would entrust a black man with executive responsibility. The reader may also recall the senator's obvious discomfort during the 1968 Presidential campaign when he was whisked around the country as the Republican Administration's showcase Negro. White America exacts a heavy price even from its successful black people.

But what of those blacks who are unwilling to pay the price and who openly defy the white Establishment? The list of notable casualties is long: Eldridge Cleaver, forced into exile in Algeria; Muhammad Ali, barred from the boxing ring during his prime; Fred Hampton, murdered by Chicago police; George Jackson, shot to death at San

Quentin prison under mysterious circumstances; the Reverend Dr. Martin Luther King, dead from a white assassin's bullet; not to mention the endless number of trials for civil rights activists, most of which have resulted in acquittal— but only after long and difficult trial periods. In a strange bit of irony, a sampling of white Americans by *Newsweek* at the close of 1969 found that 85 percent of them felt "black militants have been treated too leniently."

3. *Blacks wish to usurp the position of whites.* A natural consequence of the fact that whites occupy the top rung of the ladder is a constant fear of falling and losing their preferred position. White people have traditionally felt menaced by blacks, forever alarmed that blacks are encroaching upon their rights and prerogatives. A political tract called *White Americans,* circulating in Chicago some 50 years ago, is an extremely useful document, showing as it does the pervasive fear among white Americans that blacks had all but taken over the country. In descriptions that would surely amuse black power advocates today, Negroes were depicted as controlling national elections, manipulating public officials, and even taking over a major American city:

> In the United States Negroes not only vote and hold office, but the Negro vote is the deciding factor in the national elections, and also in many of the northern cities. . . . The Negroes control the great city of Philadelphia, and the press said the Negro delegates at the Republican Convention in Chicago openly offered to sell their support to the presidential candidate who would pay the most money. Just think this thing over, you sovereign United States citizens: the Negroes control the elections, and thus your law-makers, judges, and officials.[15]

And the belief lingers on. Many white people still feel that "If you give them you finger, they'll take your hand."

The wave of violence in 1967 solidified white beliefs

along these lines. For, as the pressure of the riots on our society has increased, so has the level of white resistance to black tactics and objectives. Witness, for example, the following excerpt from a Louis Harris poll released in June, 1967:

Changes in White Resistance

	1966 %	1967 %
Oppose open housing law	51	63
Feel Negroes asking for more than they're ready for	64	72
Oppose Negro demonstrations	63	82

These findings suggest that, the more pressure exerted by blacks for social change, the stronger the belief among whites that their favored position is in imminent danger.

Hostile Beliefs Among Whites: Specific Beliefs

Accompanying these general beliefs, and in large measure derived from them, are a series of specific beliefs. These beliefs attribute more concrete characteristics to blacks—characteristics which, in turn, are fraught with imminent danger where whites are concerned.

1. *Blacks are naturally violent.* In the public opinion section of its report, the Chicago Commission on Race Relations notes that there is "no section of the country in which is it not generally believed by whites that Negroes are instinctively criminal in inclination."[16] This statement was made in 1922. Some 50 years later (in 1963), a *Newsweek* poll determined that 44 percent of whites believed that "Negroes breed crime." This perception of

blacks as fundamentally different from whites, in that they are inherently criminal and unable to control their violent impulses, has been a dominant theme throughout our history. Moreover, there are indications that the periodic attempts at vigorous political protest by blacks have only intensified this belief. "People who weren't prejudiced before are now," a Seattle mechanic was quoted as saying in 1966. "When I see these demonstrations on TV, it makes me think of them as savages."

At first glance, the statistics on crimes involving blacks seem to support white views in this area. In fact, crime *is* prevalent among blacks. Even if other considerations are taken into account—discrimination in our laws, courts, arrests, sentencing and parole practices, in addition to crude and unreliable reporting procedures—the true rate of crime committed by blacks appears to be considerably higher than that for whites. Moreover, the disparity in rates for violent offenses is much greater than the differences between the races for offenses against property. For example, the rate for arrest for murder among blacks is 24.1 per 100,000 Negroes, 25 compared to 2.5 for whites—almost 10 times as high. In contrast, black arrests for burglary are only about three and one half times the rate for whites (378 to 107).[17]

Nevertheless, the high incidence of crime committed by blacks—particularly violent crime—needs to be placed in perspective. For the same social scientists who compile such statistics are almost invariably the first to stress social and cultural factors—as opposed to biological ones—in order to explain the differences between the races. Today, there is overwhelming evidence that criminal offenders are likely to be from the lower class, poor, slum residents of the largest cities, victims of family disorganization and community instability, young, unemployed and objects of extensive discrimination. The conclusion is widespread that group differentials in crime are not a consequence of race, but of life situation.[18]

Related to the belief that blacks are innately criminal is a belief that blacks consciously wish to harm whites physically. For example, it is commonly assumed that most violent crimes committed by blacks are directed against whites. This assumption, however, flies in the face of numerous studies which document the intra, rather than interracial nature of most crimes. For instance, President Johnson's Commission on Crime, with the cooperation of the Chicago Police Department, studied 13,713 cases of assaultive crimes against persons (exclusive of homicide) for the period of September 1965, to March 1966. The Commission found that blacks were more likely to assault other blacks, while whites were more likely to be victimized by whites. Thus, while black males accounted for two-thirds of all assaults, the offender who victimized a white person was most likely to be white. It was also found that a black man in Chicago was nearly six times more likely to be a victim than was a white man; a black woman's chances of being victimized were nearly eight times that of a white woman.

The District of Columbia Crime Commission uncovered similar relationships in its 1966 survey of serious crimes. For example, only 12 out of 172 murders were found to be interracial. Robbery was the only crime found to be predominantly interracial; and in 56 percent of the robberies committed in the District of Columbia, the victims were white.

Notwithstanding the results of these and other studies, whites persist in believing that blacks are naturally violent and represent a direct physical threat to the white community.

2. *Blacks are unusually promiscuous.* The race problem is and always has been inextricably tied to sex, with special

ramifications for the members of each sex.[19] Where whites
are concerned, it has long been feared and assumed that
blacks are not capable of exercising the social restraints
common to civilized persons. Indeed, a whole mythology
has grown up around this notion: the period of puberty
for black boys and girls is marked by special wildness;
blacks exude primitive qualities of physical dexterity and
bodily finesse; while the black man, dark and mysterious,
is pictured as a walking phallus.

A special component of the belief that blacks are
unusually promiscuous is the feeling that rape is always
uppermost in their minds, and that sexual assaults by black
men against white women are a common occurrence. Rape
statistics are therefore highly significant. Unfortunately,
attempted or forcible rapes are among the most difficult
crimes to classify. To begin with, these crimes often go
unreported to the police because of fear and embarrassment. Moreover, there are many instances in which the
offense results from prior association, making it difficult
to ascertain whether a crime was actually committed. But,
while recognizing these limitations, statistics compiled by
the Federal Bureau of Investigation and other organizations can still provide us with useful insights into the
nature and pattern of this type of crime.

According to the FBI's Uniform Crime Reports for
1972, there were approximately 46,000 forcible rapes in
this country, accounting for nearly 6 percent of the total
amount of violent crime committed in that year. Over 49
percent of the persons arrested for rape were black, 49
percent were white, and members of other races comprised
the remainder. In its 1966 survey, the President's Commission on Crime in the District of Columbia found that 88
percent of the reported rapes involved persons of the same
race. Among 121 cases of aggravated assault in which the
assailant's race was known, only 9 percent were interracial.

Finally, the Kerner Commission estimates that the probability of a black woman being raped is 3.7 times that of
her white counterpart.

On the basis of these figures, we can summarize as
follows: first, without attempting to minimize the seriousness of this type of offense, from a statistical point of
view, rape is one of the crimes least frequently committed
in our society; second, although blacks are dispropor-
tionately represented, equal numbers of whites and blacks
tend to be arrested for the crime; third, most rapes are
committed against persons of the same race; and, fourth,
white women are much less likely to be victimized than
black women.

The question therefore arises as to why whites display
such intense concern—it might almost be termed an
obsession—about the violation of "their" women. Without
denying certain relevant psychological factors—puritanical
attitudes about sex, the white man's self-esteem, guilt
about the inequities within the system—probably the best
explanation of this has to do with the "rape complex"
rooted in the Southern culture and brilliantly described by
W. J. Cash, in *The Mind of the South*.[20] Cash acknowl-
edges that, historically, the danger of interracial rape has
been relatively small. White women have had more of a
chance of being struck by lightening, as he put it.
Nevertheless, while conceding that black men did on
occasion sexually assault white women, and allowing for a
certain amount of realistic fear in this regard, Cash also
perceived the larger significance of the Southern "rape
complex." He suggested that any assault—real or imagined,
sexual or otherwise—represented an attack on the Southern system itself.

This point is brought home even more forcefully when
we consider that the Southern woman had long been
identified with the very notion of the South itself—she was

the mystic symbol of romanticism, the perpetrator of white supremacy, a creature completely inaccessible to the males of any inferior group. Therefore, the word "rape" applied not only to sexual assaults on white women by blacks, but also to any attempt at changing what Southerners called "our way of life."

The ideas which Cash grasped intellectually were later understood—and experienced—by Eldridge Cleaver, in more personal terms. In his book, *Soul on Ice*, Cleaver reveals how and why he consciously and willfully became a rapist of white women:

> Rape was an insurrectionary act. It delighted me that I was defying and trampling upon the white man's law, upon his system of values, and that I was defiling his women—and this point, I believe, was the most satisfying to me because I was very resentful over the historical fact of how the white man has used the black woman. I felt I was getting revenge.[21]

Defying the system, not to mention the statistics, was for Cleaver a kind of personal catharsis. Without attempting to pass judgment on his behavior (Cleaver himself later regretted these actions), we should note that Cleaver demonstrated an enormous amount of insight into the white psyche. He knew precisely where the white man was vulnerable.

According to the statistics, there is some evidence that white beliefs in this area have recently been modified somewhat and may even be changing. In the nationwide *Newsweek* poll of 1963, 69 percent of the whites believed that "Negroes have looser morals." Three years later, in response to the same question by the same magazine, this figure had dropped almost 20 points, to 50 percent.

If this dramatic change in figures truly reflects a change in white attitudes, and if we may be permitted to speculate a bit, the reasons appear to have little to do with diminishing white resistance (which has not occurred in key areas), and more to do with factors lying outside the area of race relations. It is interesting to note that the change in statistics coincides with certain other changes in our society, including what many people are calling a sexual revolution. Certainly, the 1960s were a time of enormous social ferment. The rise of the youth culture, changing attitudes about sex, a redefinition of sexual roles, the emergence of female liberation, gay liberation—and, more broadly speaking, heterosexual liberation—all of these things are evidence of significant changes in our society.

And it is possible that these changes in sexual attitudes and mores have sneaked in through the back door of our system of race relations. For, if the forces at work are, in fact, part of a genuine sexual revolution in which Americans—especially white Americans—are becoming less inhibited about sex and are recovering from an affliction which Malcolm Muggeridge originally ascribed to Englishmen as "sex on the brain," then it is entirely possible that white people are becoming less sexually intimidated by blacks.

Thus, concerning the hostile belief about blacks being unusually promiscuous, the following conclusion seems reasonable: the belief itself is still strong, but in view of the important social changes that have recently taken place in our society, the extent of its strength is now unclear.

3. *Blacks constantly conspire to undermine the system.* Historically, the notion of plots and conspiracies by blacks, aided and abetted by fanatical whites, has always had great currency in this country. Prior to the Civil War, Southerners frequently viewed Abolitionists as "outside agitators," trying to stir up the happy slaves. Violent interracial clashes during the First World War were said to be instigated by black activists and Bolsheviks, while the outbreak in Detroit in 1943 was similarly

attributed to an "Axis plot." The current wave of disorders has been blamed on individuals such as Stokely Carmichael and H. Rap Brown, and groups ranging from the Black Panthers to the Chinese Communists. In a survey of six northern cities issued by the Lemberg Center for the Study of Violence at Brandeis University in 1967, 77 percent of all whites interviewed believed that "outside agitators" were a major or contributing cause of such disorders. (This finding came in the wake of a statement by J. Edgar Hoover himself, who said that the FBI could find no discernible pattern of conspiracy in the riots.) When Los Angeles Mayor Sam Yorty subsequently blamed a rash of school disorders on a conspiracy of the Black Student Union, the Students for a Democratic Society, Communist sympathizers and the National Council of Churches—without so much as a shred of hard evidence— he was following a long, if not very honorable, tradition.

Here and there throughout our history, plots of a racial nature have, in fact, been executed. However, the number, frequency and scope of such schemes has been so limited as to render them a historical rarity. The susceptibility of whites to conspiratorial theories—amounting to a kind of knee-jerk reaction—is therefore both curious and fascinating, and begs for explanation. To some extent, conjuring up conspiracies helps to explain events which are surprising and unbelievable—an explosion, a blackout, an assassination or a riot. People also have a tendency to dwell upon plots when they cannot understand a situation; like memorizing baseball averages, it requires attention and interest, but no real intellectual effort.

While these factors are undoubtedly related to riots, the functional aspects of conspiratorial thinking are even more important. By focusing on the machinations of individuals or groups of "outside agitators" as a main cause of the violence, attention is shifted away from institutions and conditions largely created and maintained by whites. In this way, whites absolve themselves of the sense of guilt and responsibility they might otherwise have to face.

But the resort to conspiratorial thinking is far more than a guilt-reducing mechanism. It is, in addition, a useful, if not necessary, means of rationalizing and protecting the system—keeping things just as they are. In this sense, the "rape complex" of which we spoke previously, is paralleled here by a special kind of persecution complex among whites—what Richard Hofstadter called the "paranoid style" and saw as an important factor in group antagonism.[22] Hofstadter did not use the term in the usual psychological sense, to refer to necessarily disturbed human beings, but rather to definable feelings of persecution experienced by more or less normal people. The central preoccupation of the paranoid style is the existence of a gigantic, insidious, effective conspiratorial network designed to perpetrate acts of the most heinous nature. These acts are considered a dangerous threat to our traditional values and well-established way of life. At the core of these feelings is the fear that opportunities for whites are being reduced, that the old American virtues are being eroded, and that American security and independence are about to be destroyed by treasonous plots.

This conspiracy theme is painted in the grandest of strokes. For the spokesman of the paranoid style does not see his fate alone as being affected, but that of millions of people, a whole nation, an entire civilization. Rich and vivid details are given to support his charges, notwithstanding a notable lack of concrete evidence and giant leaps in logic and imagination. Again, we are not denying the existence of occasional plots in history, but rather attempting to draw attention to a tendency among whites in racial matters to see a vast conspiracy as the central motivational force in historical events. As perceived by the paranoid spokesman, the conspirator:

wills, indeed he manufactures the mechanism of history itself, or deflects the normal course of history in an evil way. He makes crises, starts runs on the banks, causes depressions, manufactures disasters and then enjoys and profits from the misery he has produced.[23]

He also organizes riots. The typical conspirator is seen as the devil incarnate: powerful, ubiquitous, cruel, cunning, amoral, sinister, depraved. He is the agent of an elaborate apparatus—well-organized, well-financed—whose activities are carried on in a clandestine manner. In short, he is *the enemy,* someone to be feared and hated.

Thus, the only way to deal with this terrible menace is to fight fire with fire, by waging an all-out crusade. The paranoid's tendency is to portray that which is imminent, but which may be avoided. Unfortunately, this absolutist approach leaves virtually no room for bargaining or compromise. What is seen as important is the will to resist, to stand strong, to defend the system at all costs from those who would destroy it.

Hostile Beliefs Among Blacks: Introduction

In general, black beliefs are a secondary reaction to the white system, while the hostile beliefs common among whites—since they outnumber blacks and largely run our society—are primary and superordinate. In several respects, however, the hostile beliefs held by most blacks are similar to those common among whites. First, they reflect parallel concerns: perceptions about the existing order, the relationship of the races to one another, and various behavioral traits attributed to the other group. In addition, these beliefs are functional, serving to identify the source of strain, ultimately spurring the group to action. Finally, the beliefs have remained extremely potent over time.

Because the cycle of racial violence beginning in 1964 was largely initiated by blacks—contradicting the historical pattern of white-instigated disorders—it is tempting to infer that hostile beliefs among blacks have somehow changed significantly. However, this has not been the case. The historical record suggests that these hostile beliefs have always been present, but they have recently become far more conscious and widespread.

Following a long tradition of largely peaceful protest and an alliance with white liberals, both of which have brought only minimal gains, we now find a tendency among blacks to band together, to confront whites more directly and to respond to their situation in harsher, more aggressive terms. The late Malcolm X both reflected and understood this new black consciousness. In his autobiography, he states: "Today, in many ways the black man sees the collective white man in America better than that white man can see himself. And the 22 million blacks realize increasingly that physically, politically, economically, and even to some degree socially, the aroused black man can create a turmoil in white America's vitals. . . ."[24]

At times, the confrontation has merely taken the form of verbal rhetoric: "Whitey, you are a racist!" On other occasions the confrontation has been violent. Between the years 1967-72 alone, the Lemberg Center's Civil Disorder Clearinghouse recorded hundreds of such disturbances. Nevertheless, it is important that we not lose sight of the beliefs at work amidst changing tactics and strategy. For, as we shall see, some are as old as the system itself.

General Beliefs

1. *The status quo must be changed.* While white Americans have become increasingly aware of "our violent

past," they are less cognizant of the long history of black protest in this country, aimed at resisting the system and altering its conditions. Suffering from historical amnesia, whites are inclined to think of protest activity as an exclusively twentieth-century phenomenon. Granted, the names of certain blacks who have led the struggle can be rattled off with ease—Booker T. Washington, W.E.B. DuBois, Walter White, Marcus Garvey, A. Phillip Randolph, Martin Luther King, Roy Wilkins, Whitney Young, Stokely Carmichael—while a number of alphabet organizations come readily to mind—the NAACP, SCLC, CORE, SNCC and so on.

But what is not generally realized, is the fact that this voice of protest and resistance dates from the earliest days of our history—perhaps from the sound of the first slave laying down his hoe out of disgust, despair or anger. Indeed, evidence of strong dissatisfaction on the part of slaves can be found throughout the entire slavery period.[25] While the majority of slaves adapted to the system, in the sense that a massive upheaval never occurred, many played a dual role: adjusting to the system and undermining it at the same time. Slaves frequently registered their feelings of discontent in subtle ways—for example, through work stoppages, loafing, feigning illness in the field or on the auction block, filching food, or seeking to learn how to read and write. Others engaged in more elaborate forms of sabotage: damaging tools, driving farm animals with a cruelty suggesting vengeance and ruthlessly destroying crops.

Spirituals were a means of escape to a different and better world—and another form of implicit protest. "Look Away in de Heaven, Lord," "Dere's a Great Camp Meetin' in de Promised Land" and "Heaven, Heaven, Everybody Talkin' 'Bout Heaven Ain't Goin' There" are not simply the happy chants of slaves going about their business in the fields, as many whites have assumed; rather, they suggest the slaves' deep dissatisfaction.

Occasionally the slaves' discontent took a more violent turn. Forests were burned, as were the houses and barns of the slave-owners. Some hated masters and overseers were actually poisoned or otherwise murdered. The number of conspiracies to revolt were, as has been pointed out, extremely rare. Nevertheless, the few that are on record—the most famous being the Gabriel revolt of 1800, the Denmark Vesey plot in 1822 and the Nat Turner insurrection of 1831—reveal a high degree of unrest common to many slaves.

The widespread practice of running away was especially irritating to the South. Some slaves disguised or armed themselves with free passes; others simply walked off the plantation. At times, runaways organized themselves into groups called "Maroons," and lived in their own communities. Federal and state legislation was passed to aid in their recovery, but many slaves managed to escape forever.

Our purpose here has not been so much to examine the slaves' reaction to oppression nor to destroy the myth of the contented slave, but to draw attention to the long and continuous struggle waged by black people in response to the existing order. Seen in this light, the collective outbursts of the 1960s and 70s—although more massive and more violent than anything that had previously occurred—must be seen as part of a historical progression. Public sentiment has tended to regard the riots as meaningless, purposeless, senseless and irrational.[26] Nevertheless, the extent of these disorders across the country and the high rates of participation, in addition to the tacit support given the rioters by large numbers of non-participants within the black community, suggest that the riots are an extension of more conventional forms of protest. In that case, the conclusions reached by Fogelson and Hill would seem to be warranted:

the 1960 riots were a manifestation of race and racism in the United States, a reflection of the social problems of modern black ghettos, a protest against the essential conditions of life there, and an indicator of the necessity for fundamental changes in American society.[27]

Partial proof that blacks will continue to push for change is the finding in *Newsweek's* 1966 poll, that fully half the blacks surveyed stood ready to march, picket or sit-in for their rights.

But the black man's rejection of the status quo, along with his determination to press his struggle, is seen even more clearly by a bookstore owner from Detroit:

White America is stupid. The white view is, 'We maintain the status quo, and don't you give us any lip. If you do, we'll exterminate you.' Armageddon is a possibility in America, and we know it, and we know the dangers of pressing our demands. But there is no use in living if you cannot be free.[28]

2. *White institutions are used to oppress blacks.* During a conversation with a white American ambassador in Africa, Malcolm X observed that "it isn't the American white *man* who is a racist, but it's the American political, economic, and social *atmosphere* that automatically nourishes a racist psychology in the white man."[29] In making these remarks, Malcolm X put his finger on two important concepts: the important interplay between institutions and people, and the extent to which institutions help shape individual attitudes and beliefs.

Today, the various levels of government, the political parties, the courts, the corporations, the schools, the prisons, the social agencies, the mass media—what blacks call the "white power structure"—have all come under increasing attack. The list of grievances against these and other institutions is long: blatant patterns of discrimination, a failure to distribute power along more equitable lines, an unwillingness to heed calls for change, excessive control over the lives of blacks, locking them into ghettos, denying them access to an open, free society. In a word, the feeling is that white institutions tainted by race have been and are being used to keep blacks "in their place."

Indications are that the chorus of angry voices is growing. A Louis Harris poll published in *Time* in 1970 found that, while most blacks were willing to work within the system, 9 percent—representing more than two million Americans—counted themselves as revolutionaries.

3. *White people wish to deny blacks their rightful place.* When Malcolm X was in grade school, he once had a discussion with a favorite teacher about his choice of careers. A bright student with excellent grades, he indicated he was thinking of becoming a lawyer. The teacher suggested that carpentry might be a more appropriate goal. Needless to say, Malcolm X would up in neither field.

What was for Malcolm X an extremely painful incident (he later called it "the first major turning point" of his life), reflects the widespread belief among blacks that white people—consciously or not—are opposed to blacks improving their position, and wish to deny them their rightful place in society.

In recent years the strong sense of injury and injustice which blacks feel toward whites has surfaced more and more. There is a pervasive feeling that what little gains have occurred are due to pressure exerted by blacks, rather than white identification with existing black problems. The results of a poll taken by the Columbia Broadcasting System in 1968 showed that six out of every ten blacks felt that whites were not sympathetic to their cause. A Louis Harris poll conducted in the same year revealed that alienation among blacks—the extent to which they felt that society did not care about them—had soared from 34 percent to 54 percent since 1966.

Mistrust of whites continues to be strong. And not surprisingly, black rioters have generally been found to display even more pessimism, hostility, mistrust and anti-white feelings than non-rioters.[30]

Specific Beliefs

1. *Whites are inherently violent.* Along with the recognition of "our violent past" has come the realization that much of that violence has been instigated by whites, against blacks. In the earliest days of our history, millions of Africans were forcibly removed from their homeland. No matter how many kindly slave masters past historians were able to dredge up, few today would deny that a system featuring whips and chains, beatings and rapes, not to mention the wholesale destruction of families, was at once brutal and violent.

Long after slavery was ended, the violent tradition continued—in the form of wanton lynchings, shootings and murders, along with white-initiated race riots. And today this tradition endures. From the attacks on the "Freedom Riders" testing segregation laws and practices, to the massive and sometimes violent resistance to school desegregation, the use of dogs and high-pressure water hoses on marchers in Birmingham, Alabama, the mob action against a black couple who "dared" to purchase a house in Cicero, Illinois, the burning of school buses by parents in Pontiac, Michigan, in opposition to busing—all of these incidents are tragic reminders that white-directed violence against blacks remains an important part of our history.

This historical reality has led may blacks to the conclusion that whites are *inherently* violent—paralleling a similar belief among whites about blacks. But, while this belief is understandable given past events, its validity is quite another matter.

In recent years, the amount of literature available about the nature of human violence has increased greatly. If we think of violence as being at one extreme of the pendulum of human aggression, many complex issues are raised: whether aggression is an inborn, instinctive trait which seeks spontaneous expression, as opposed to merely a response to adverse external circumstances; whether it is a primary or a secondary drive; whether it has positive as well as negative function; and whether group or individual differences are more significant.[31]

Concentrating on violence as an inherent trait within a particular group, we offer a number of propositions which provide the theoretical basis of the studies conducted at the Lemberg Center, in hopes of placing the issue in a reasonable perspective. (These propositions are similarly applicable to the corresponding beliefs among whites.)

First, as a form of human aggression, violence is an innate behavior which man shares with most species. Ordinarily, the internal, biological factors necessary for arousal are kept under control. The resort to physical force therefore represents an inherent potential—a capacity for human beings to behave in a certain way—i.e., to injure, subdue or destroy apparent obstacles in their path. Second, when violence does occur, it is elicited or brought about by external conditions—frequently, although not always, in an antagonistic situation where conflicting interests, goals, attitudes and beliefs are at work. Finally, individuals have different inherent capacities for violence; in other words, the destructive impulses vary from individual to individual. However, there is no evidence available at the present time which suggests that such variations are more salient among certain groups.

These propositions suggest, therefore, that while whites have frequently behaved violently toward blacks, as a group they are no more or less *inherently* violent than blacks, or any other group.

2. *The police and other symbols of white authority*

frequently abuse their power. The point has been made earlier in this chapter that symbols are a convenient way of pinpointing blame. Given their perceptions that white institutions are racist and that white people are fundamentally hostile, inherently violent and wish to prolong their favored status, blacks have singled out certain elements in our society—government officials, judges, merchants, school administrators and prison wardens, to name a few—who they hold responsible for their own exclusion from positions of power within white-dominated society.

But despite the wide range of establishment symbols, by far the greatest resentment has been lodged against the police. Since they are the most visible representatives of the society from which blacks (and other minorities) are demanding fair treatment and equal opportunity, the police are therefore seen as the arm of the white power structure, defenders of the status quo, instruments of the policy-makers, armed guardians of the social order.

Moreover, corresponding to white belief that blacks cannot control their sexual impulses, is the belief among blacks that the police are unable to control their aggressive impulses. Numerous studies,[32] as well as in-depth interviews conducted by specially trained teams from the Lemberg Center, have documented that blacks are more likely than whites to report that the police treat them disrespectfully, carry out searches without good reason and frequently use physical brutality. A Louis Harris poll in 1968 found that 52 percent of the blacks surveyed considered police provocation a major cause of disorder (compared with only 13 percent among whites). Attacks on police officers, interference with arrests, racial disturbances and riots beginning with police incidents, and verbal epithets—such as "pigs"—provide abundant testimony to the extreme hostility of blacks toward the police.

In one of the angriest passages from his book, Eldridge Cleaver describes the police as a chief symbol of terror and oppression. They are, he says:

> the muscles of control and enforcement. They have deadly weapons with which to inflict pain on the human body. They know how to bring about horrible deaths. They have clubs with which to beat the body and the head. They have bullets and guns with which to tear holes in the flesh, to smash bones, to disable and kill. They use force, to make you do what the deciders have decided you must do. . . .
>
> The policeman and the soldier will violate your person, smoke you out with various gases. Each will shoot you, beat your head and body with sticks and clubs, with rifle butts, run you through with bayonets, shoot holes in your flesh, kill you. They each have unlimited firepower. They will use all that is necessary to bring you to your knees.[33]

Even if we sympathize with the problems facing the police—inadequate manpower, dangerous working conditions, outdated equipment, unattractive salaries, and so on—it must be admitted that, on all too many occasions, they *have* behaved in an abusive, hostile and discriminatory manner toward the black community.

At the same time, however, we must not lose sight of a fundamental reality. The police did not start and cannot stop the convulsive changes at work in our society. Cleaver himself points out that, "behind police brutality there is social brutality, economic brutality, and political brutality."[34]

3. *The system is forever conspiring against blacks.* The belief among whites that they are constantly being subjected to plots is matched by a similar belief among blacks that various forces in society—government agencies, the police, the military, the news media—are out to

destroy their community. Indeed, many incidents from recent history substantiate this view.

In 1969, a series of police raids against Black Panther headquarters in cities such as Chicago, Los Angeles and San Francisco are believed to have been directed from Washington, chiefly by John Mitchell and J. Edgar Hoover, as part of a concerted effort to destroy the Party. Similarly, trials held for Bobby Seale and Ericka Huggins, Huey P. Newton, H. Rap Brown and Angela Davis are regarded in many quarters as a government plot designed to silence all black dissenters.

Drafting blacks into the armed forces and shipping them over to Vietnam was seen as a way of killing off the cream of black youth. Many blacks have opposed birth control measures on the grounds that they are a form of white-directed genocide—the deliberate destruction of future generations of blacks. The failure of the federal government to provide adequate funds for research into sickle cell anemia, a deadly disease peculiar to black people, is similarly viewed by many people.

While the conspiracy theme is found among whites and blacks alike, there are different dynamics at work within each group—dynamics which are largely determined by its vantage point. Whites, looking down from the top, see a menacing group of challengers threatening the status quo. Therefore the resort to conspiratorial thinking on their part is a guilt-reducing and rationalizing mechanism which shifts responsibility and helps to insulate the system. Blacks, looking up from the bottom, see an oppressive system designed to victimize them. The conspiracy belief among blacks is almost taken for granted, tied as it is to many perceptions about their daily lives.

During a riot in Boston in June 1967, for example, local black self-help organizations distributed mimeographed "survival kits" throughout the community. The kits came complete with instructions for preserving water and keeping rations, all in the belief that the police were determined to "exterminate" the black community. For the white observer on the scene, it was a rude awakening into the sensitivities of black people. Several years later in the same city, following some attacks by whites against black students, *The Black Panther* headlined a story on October 10, 1970: "PIGS PLOT GENOCIDE OF BLACK CHILDREN AT CURLEY SCHOOL." And, when a civil rights worker in Arkansas was shot to death in March 1971, a member of the local NAACP immediately assumed a "conspiracy by the whole city of Junction City." These examples indicate that many members of the black community regard such incidents as part of an ongoing conspiracy directed against them by the white-dominated system.

The purpose of this section has been to describe the hostile beliefs held by each race, while placing them in some sort of reasonable perspective. As we have seen, these beliefs are in fundamental conflict with one another, and therefore add to the conduciveness to violence. Nevertheless, this may be an appropriate place to caution the reader that descriptions of this sort are necessarily colored by the author's own biases. For whatever individuals say, is always said through cultural screens. But, insofar as we can take a value-free position, it seems that there is more validity to the hostile beliefs held among blacks, in that the broad sweep of history is on their side. Inequality is, after all, a central fact of their life; black people are still treated as second-class citizens; white institutions have been a source of oppression; and, while whites as a group may not consciously wish to harm blacks, many of their actions have had that effect. We are therefore led to the conclusion, however painful for both sides, that the sense of injury and injustice so keenly felt by blacks is in large measure justified.

With these thoughts in mind, we close this section with a summary in chart form of the hostile beliefs that are common among each race:

HOSTILE BELIEF SYSTEM

Among Whites	Among Blacks
General Beliefs	*General Beliefs*
1. The status quo must be maintained.	1. The status quo must be changed.
2. Blacks have a definite place.	2. White institutions are used to oppress blacks.
3. Blacks wish to usurp the position of whites.	3. White people wish to deny blacks their rightful place.
Specific Beliefs	*Specific Beliefs*
1. Blacks are inherently violent.	1. Whites are inherently violent.
2. Blacks are unusually promiscuous.	2. The police and other symbols of white authority frequently abuse their power.
3. Blacks constantly conspire to undermine the system.	3. The system is forever conspiring against blacks.

CONDITIONS OF STRESS

Many hostile beliefs permeate the environment without ever contributing directly to a collective outburst. These beliefs become significant only when conditions of stress are also present. Having already discussed the structural aspects of strain which have become established features of our social life, we turn now to situational features—cross-pressures at work in society—many of which have reappeared at periodic intervals.

General Conditions

Changes in an area's demographic composition, changes in broad ideologies (such as the rise of the black power concept in the sixties), urbanization, industrialization—factors usually referred to as the underlying or root causes of riots—must all be considered potential sources of conflict. These and other changes in society are likely to result in increased competition between the races for wealth, power, housing, jobs, recreational facilities and so forth. Under such conditions, existing tensions may reach new and dangerous heights. As Smelser states: "Such competition often brings diffuse hatreds between the races into the open; together these conflicts of interest, norms, and values may bring tensions to the boiling point."[35]

For example, each of the three riot cycles in this century has coincided with or immediately followed a wave of migration. At the time of the first World War, a serious labor depression gripped the South and sent wages there plummeting to a rate of about 75 cents a day. The damage done by the boll weevil to cotton crops in 1915 and 1916 meant the loss of jobs for many blacks who depended on cotton for their subsistence. Floods in the summer of 1915 left thousands of blacks homeless. The economic situation, therefore, sent many blacks to the urban North in search of more secure surroundings and better employment opportunities. Social factors also played a part in this process. Segregation, disfranchisement, lynching, the injustice of the southern judicial system, served as further encouragements for blacks to leave their homes for "the promised land" to the north.

Chicago—site of the worst riot during "The Red Summer"—was one of the northern cities most affected by this migration. Between 1910 and 1920, its black population jumped from 44,103 to 109,594, an increase of 148 percent. Most of this increase occurred in the years 1916-19. Similarly, many blacks emigrated to the North and West in search of employment during World War II. Approximately 50,000 blacks flocked to the city of Detroit at that time, along with 450,000 other persons in the three years preceding 1943.

The latest cycle of violence, which began in the mid-sixties, has come on the heels of another stream of blacks from the old Confederacy. Between 1940 and 1960, the black population outside the South more than doubled, from nearly four million to more than nine million, representing 48 percent of the nation's total black population. Most of this growth occurred in the central cities of our 12 largest metropolitan areas: New York, Los Angeles, Chicago, Philadelphia, Detroit, San Francisco-Oakland, Boston, Pittsburgh, St. Louis, Washington, Cleveland and Baltimore.

It is noteworthy that, with the exception of St. Louis, every one of these cities experienced one or more serious racial outbreaks during the most recent cycle of violence. However, the chief significance of this migration does not derive from the large influx of blacks per se, but rather from their disruptive effects on the old order. New arrivals mean new problems and adjustments; the additional factor of race makes for an even more delicate situation. The lack of housing, the relationship of blacks to organized labor, the presence of race-baiting demogogues, the reluctance of government to step in, all help to create an ideal atmosphere for a riot to develop.

War is another factor which has shaken the fabric of American life at various times—especially where race relations are concerned. In fact, each riot cycle in this century has occurred against the backdrop of an American military involvement abroad. A key element in the dissension found at home has been the black man's heightened awareness of his inferior position there. For example, each of the wars in which our nation has been involved has been fought for the goal of extending democracy abroad. During World War I we were going to "make the world safe for democracy"; in World War II, we were the "arsenal of democracy" fighting against Fascist dictators; and our engagement in Vietnam stemmed from a commitment to the South Vietnamese people to help ensure their right to "self-determination." The irony of the fact that our lofty rhetoric reserved for fighting wars abroad has frequently been at variance with the reality at home has not been lost on blacks. Indeed, the many contradictions within our society, which have periodically been heightened by war, have only increased the determination of black people to fight for their rights. During World War I, after a young black in Vicksburg, Mississippi, had been burned alive, *Challenge Magazine* of Chicago declared:

> The 'German Hun' is beaten but the world is made no safer for Democracy. Humanity has been defended but lifted no higher. Democracy never will be safe in America until these occurrences are made impossible either by the execution of the law or with double barrel guns. . . . I hate every Hun, and the worst I know are the ones that thrive under the free institutions of America.[36]

The increased urbanization of blacks is still another disruptive factor, for it has brought new expectations concerning wealth, status and power. Discrimination in a new urban setting is bound to be more psychologically disruptive than it was in the traditional South. In turn, the self-respect and cohesiveness generated among blacks in their new environment has had much to do with resistance efforts aimed at their would-be oppressors.

During the "Red Summer" of 1919, for example, blacks held numerous conventions and conferences. Following the lead of the NAACP, the National Equal Rights League, the National Race Congress and the National Baptist Convention all met on different occasions for the purpose of attacking specific practices—such as lynching, along with the general bigotry and injustice in our society. This rising tide of protest was met, in turn, with increased opposition on the part of whites. The Ku Klux Klan, which had been dormant for years, was flourishing again by 1919. At the close of the war, the organization had some 100,000 white-hooded knights in its ranks.

Each of the three cycles of racial disorders in this century has been characterized by increased political activity by blacks in the face of increased white resistance. Grimshaw feels that *every* period of racial violence in our history—from the earliest slave rebellions to the more recent race riots—has been determined "more by reaction of the dominant white community to attacks on the accomodative pattern by Negroes than by any conscious determination of policy by the white group."[37] Indeed, the whole black protest/white resistance syndrome has been an important aspect of the racial tensions within our society.

Immediate Circumstances

As grievances mount among one or both racial groups, tensions tend to focus on a specific issue or group of issues in the local community. Given the disturbed social climate, a chain of events—what the Kerner Commission calls "tension-heightening incidents"—is likely to occur a day, a week, a month or sometimes several months before the riot. These incidents are both a reflection and an extension of existing grievances, and add to the general unrest of the community.

Months before the Omaha riot, for example, blacks were repeatedly denounced as criminals by the local press, police and organized labor. In Chicago, where the housing controversy was extremely volatile, bombs were thrown at the houses of blacks who had moved into white neighborhoods. The police were completely unsuccessful in apprehending the guilty parties in this case, raising suspicions among many blacks. And, five weeks before the violence erupted, two blacks were murdered—both the victims of unprovoked, brutal attacks. In Detroit, a series of strikes over the upgrading procedures for blacks beset the city several months before the outbreak. Five days before the riot, a group of blacks were prevented from entering an amusement park by stone-throwing youths. And on the very day of the riot which began at Belle Isle, minor incidents—in the form of interracial fist fights and beatings—were reported in the area.

Each incident adds to community tensions until a point is reached where a final incident, commonly known as the precipitating event, occurs. Because of its apparently close association with rumors, the precipitating event merits attention.

By the precipitating event, we mean a specific incident —the proverbial "last straw"—which triggers an outbreak of disorder. As a generalization we can state that the vast majority of serious disorders begin with an identifiable precipitating event. In its examination of 24 racial disorders in 1967, the Kerner Commission was able to locate a precipitant in "virtually every case."[38] Similarly, in their

D.C., following an appearance of soul singer James Brown. Following what has become the classic script for modern-day disorders, young blacks clashed with the police, smashed windows and looted several stores. Nearly 100 persons were arrested. According to the police, this disturbance was caused by a rumor that Brown had been shot to death by a white man. The Washington *Star* headlined a story on October 15, 1968: "Police Quell Strife in NE, Blame Rumor."

The idea that a rumor can "cause" violence recalls another incident—little-known but quote extraordinary—which occurred the previous year at the same time that the Detroit uprising flared in the nation's headlines. Cedar Rapids, Iowa, has long been considered one of the most progressive and liveliest small cities in the Midwest. On July 28, 1967, word spread from mouth to mouth in this community that busloads of armed blacks were descending on the city. Late in the day the figure grew to 8,000 blacks who were ready to attack, as near-hysteria gripped the normally busy and preoccupied local people. The switchboard of the Cedar Rapids *Gazette* was jammed with inquiries asking about the course of the "race war." As the rumors ricocheted across the county, the police chief received numerous phone calls from armed volunteers who wanted to come at once to fight the blacks. Inside the city itself, lines of white customers waiting to buy guns and ammunition grew longer outside sporting goods stores. The governor was requested to call out the National Guard. But gradually the frenzy subsided. There was no holocaust, no violence, not even a broken window pane.

The foregoing episodes, each of which involved rumor, suggest two very different perspectives concerning its role in interracial incidents. In one case, a rumor was apparently a prime causal factor in the violence. In the other, a study of 76 race riots that occurred between the y 1913 and 1963, Lieberson and Silverman uncov precipitating events in all but four cases.[39] (It is n difficult to determine the precipitating event for sma scale disorders—mostly because such information is readily available.) Usually, the initial outbreak erupts quickly—frequently within a few hours—after the prec tating event, and in the same general vicinity.[40]

The precipitating event is usually characterized a trivial but inflammatory incident. This view, however somewhat contradictory, suggesting as it does that event is both unimportant and important at the same ti True enough, on a superficial level, the precipitating ev may not be of any great consequence—a routine arres simple fight, and so on. But, coming at a time of ris community conflict, the precipitating event derives significance as a concrete expression of the hostile beli held by the participant group(s). Such an event confirm even sharpens the definition of these beliefs. Thus, as actual incident, the precipitant becomes both a justifial target and an immediate mobilizer for aroused levels aggression.

The precipitating event represents a further refineme of these beliefs as applied to a specific situation. Seen this light, a more accurate term for the precipitant mig be the "crystallizing event"—the final incident whic crystallizes one or more hostile beliefs or, more broad speaking, the issue of public order versus social justice.

THE ROLE OF RUMORS

During the fall of 1968, sporadic violence lasting sever days erupted in the northeastern section of Washingtor series—in fact, a veritable avalanche—of rumors created confusion and near-panic, but did not lead to a collective outburst of any kind. Were we to judge from the Cedar Rapids experience alone, we would arrive at a different conclusion—i.e., that rumors do *not* have the capacity to bring about collective violence.

Precisely what, then, is the role of rumor with respect to racial disorders? To answer this question, we must return to the premise stated at the beginning of the chapter: rumors are part of the whole disorder-producing process— one of a number of determinants which enhance the prospects for a collective outburst. As we have emphasized before, rumors are part of an integral process involving successive steps, each of which must be taken if a disorder is to occur. By itself, a rumor cannot "cause" a disorder; it merely helps prepare the way for violence, operating along with all the other factors previously discussed.

In the case of Cedar Rapids, some, but not all, of the necessary ingredients appear to have been available. While the community's fears may have been stirred up by the fires raging in Detroit, in all probability the immediate situation at home was not sufficiently volatile to warrant an outbreak of disorder.

The situation in Washington, D.C., however, was quite another story. One week before the violence, a disturbance was triggered by a rally to protest the fatal shooting of a black pedestrian by a white police officer. The city's entire 3,100-man police force was mobilized to put the lid on the violence—temporarily. Thus, a tension-heightening incident, some violence, along with a massive show of force set the stage for a second round of disorder the following week. Even if blaming the latter spate of violence on a rumor was an oversimplification of reality, in so doing the city's officials did manage to divert the public's attention away from other issues smoldering in the community.

Of all the determinants, none is more important for rumor development than the hostile belief system. Rumors are functionally tied to this sytem in a number of ways: crystallizing, confirming, intensifying hostile beliefs, while linking them to actual events. At least in terms of disorders, the hostile belief system is what gives rumors their special character and force.

Crystallizing Function.[41] As noted earlier, hostile beliefs embody parallel concerns among each race: perceptions about the established order, the nature of behavioral traits ascribed to the other group. Furthermore, these beliefs serve to identify the various agents and forces of evil in society: the Negro race, the white man, the black militants, the police, the white power structure and so on. By holding these beliefs, each race is automatically predisposed to accept certain rumors—unverified reports, exaggerated stories and other distortions of reality—about the other race. The content of these rumors is largely determined or programmed by the hostile beliefs. In fact, the only difference between rumors and hostile beliefs is in terms of specificity and topicality; rumors are more explicit in substance, more definite in form and more relevant to the current scene. Exhibits 4.1 and 4.2 suggest that rumors are simply concrete representations—crystallizations—of the hostile beliefs already held by each race.

Two points should be made here. First, as the exhibits indicate, frequently more than one belief is involved in a particular rumor. Even more important, looming in the background and implicit in most rumors among each race, is the belief about the status quo, with whites seeking to maintain and blacks attempting to alter the existing order. We could easily tack this belief onto almost every rumor listed in our exhibits. Second, while the distinction between rumors and beliefs is a necessary one, it need not be absolute. There are times when the line between the

Exhibit 4.1
RUMORS AMONG WHITES

Disorder Place (Year)	Rumor(s)	Hostile Belief(s)
1. East St. Louis, Illinois (1917)	Migrants "invading" white neighborhoods and forcing whites out.	(1) Blacks have a definite place (2) Blacks work to usurp the position of whites
2. Elaine, Arkansas (1919)	Town almost completely surrounded by heavily armed blacks.	(1) Blacks constantly conspire to undermine the system. (2) Blacks are inherently violent
3. Chicago, Illinois (1919)	Predictions of violence on July 4.	(1) Blacks are inherently violent
4. Detroit, Michigan (1943)	"Bridge rumors": Blacks had raped and murdered a white woman on the bridge; blacks had attacked two white women on the bridge; blacks threw a white baby from the bridge; sailors insulted white girls and blacks intervened.	(1) Blacks are unusually promiscuous (2) Blacks are unusually violent (3) Blacks have a definite place

Exhibit 4.2
RUMORS AMONG BLACKS

Disorder Place (Year)	Rumor(s)	Hostile Belief(s)
1. East St. Louis, Illinois (1917)	Congressional committee figures of 39 deaths cannot be trusted; predictions that 25 more bodies would be found.	(1) System is forever conspiring against blacks (2) Congressional committee, symbolizing white authority, abuses its power (3) Whites are inherently violent
2. Chicago, Illinois (1919)	Department store sold guns to whites before the riot, while refusing to sell to blacks.	(1) Whites are inherently violent (2) White people wish to deny blacks their rightful place (3) Department store, symbolizing white authority, abuses its power (4) System is forever conspiring against blacks
3. Harlem, New York (1935)	Young black beaten by dime store management; black woman attempting to aid the youth gets broken arm and is then arrested by the police.	(1) Whites are inherently violent (2) Police, symbolizing white authority, abuse their power
4. Detroit, Michigan (1943)	"Bridge rumors": Whites drown black woman and her baby; black woman and her baby killed when whites throw them off the bridge; whites threw black baby from the bridge.	(1) Whites are inherently violent

two is extremely fine, or even quite blurred. For example, several years after the 1969 police raids on some Black Panther headquarters, reports of a government plot continued to circulate among many blacks. While this conspiracy charge is not really a public—or topical—issue any more, its continuance in segments of the black community over a relatively long period of time suggests that what was once simply a rumor has now assumed the status of a belief.

Earlier we saw that symbols have the capacity to isolate, identify and illuminate hostile beliefs, condensing and projecting them onto a single person, object or event. In the same way, symbols are an important feature of rumors, and part of their crystallizing function. During the Chicago race riot, for example, one rumor among whites maintained that blacks had broken into an armory (a white authority symbol) looking for guns and ammunition. Just before the Harlem riot in 1935, a rumor that a black youth had been beaten by a store's white management was at least partially inspired by not one, but two death symbols on the scene: an ambulance and a hearse. An identical rumor which swept both the white and black communities in between the two outbreaks in East St. Louis might be called variations on a symbol. The essence of the rumor was that the other side was planning a bloodbath for July 4. For whites, this day conjured up a frightening picture of violent upheaval and revolution; for blacks, it was day of promise—the victory of freedom over oppression. For both groups, the rumor summoned up differing beliefs about the existing order, and the other's race.

The term "zoot-suiter"—in this case, a wholly negative symbol—became the basis for many rumors during the riot in Los Angeles in 1943. "Zoot-suiters" were seen everywhere, doing all sorts of heinous things: raping the wives and relatives of servicemen, consorting with gangsters, threatening the police, plotting a war against the United

States Navy, with just enough spare time to start the riot. While these rumors had little to do with reality, they were completely consistent with contemporary views toward Mexican-Americans.

As the embodiment of white authority and its most conspicuous representative on the scene during civil disorders, the police remain the most enduring and most powerful symbol, where blacks are concerned. A major part of several hostile beliefs and numerous precipitating incidents, they are found in many rumors as well. Such rumors invariably involve some form of alleged police misconduct, ranging from unwarranted actions, such as increased patrols and reinforcements; to discrimination, such as making an unfair arrest; to outright brutality, such as manhandling, beating, shooting and killing black citizens without sufficient provocation. Without question, police brutality rumors are among the most pervasive and inflammatory within the black community.

The recent preference for the word "pigs" over police in some quarters simply represents the replacement of one symbol with another that is even more scornful. Its usage is a measure of the hatred with which many blacks regard the police.[42]

Confirming Function

If we could dissect and examine a hostile belief under a microscope, we would find that it had two parts. The first is the element of conviction; this is the emotional basis of the belief. In believing something, we hold our conviction about it partially as an article of faith, irrespective of the available evidence or proof. The second part is the cognitive element, the intellectual or factual basis of the belief; for we are convinced—or, so we like to think—that the belief is rooted in objective reality—i.e., that the belief is true.

When rumors flourish under conditions of stress, both of these elements are greatly intensified. Persons within a racial network (i.e., segments within the black or white communities) will hear an unverified statement or report over and over, thus strengthening their feelings of conviction. The cognitive aspects of the belief are similarly increased until a point is reached where the rumor is accepted as true—independent of verification. The following testimony from a citizen made before a Congressional committee investigating the East St. Louis riots provides a good illustration of rumors in action at this level:

> Mr. Towers: Mr. Chairman, yesterday I made the statement that the great influx of negroes [*sic*] was responsible for the riot. I want to try and show some of the feelings that developed after this great influx of negroes. It was a terrible feeling in the air. Everyone felt that something terrible was going to happen. On the street corners, wherever you went, you heard expressions against the negro. You heard that the negro was driving the white man out of the locality. ... Stories were afloat on the streets and on the street cars of *the worst kind of stories that would inflame the feelings.* For instance, *I heard one story so persistently that I commenced to think later on there might be some truth to it.* First I thought it was just originated by some who might want to inflame the feelings of the people. I heard stories of this kind and *I heard it no less than a dozen times on the streets of East St. Louis.*[43]

In other words, rumor closes the gap between a hostile belief and its embodiment as a "fact." Each confirms the other: the rumor ("You heard that the Negro was driving the white man out of the locality") proves the belief (blacks wish to usurp the position of whites), while the belief explains the rumor. Thus, rumors are not only a refinement and crystallization of hostile beliefs, but a realization of them as well—a confirmation by "reality"—reality as perceived by the group of people involved.

Because rumors connected with racial disorders operate within the framework of a pre-existing system of beliefs, there is a greater tendency, especially among riot participants, to accept them as facts. The dynamics at work can be reduced to a simple formula: "I have heard that . . . ." equals "I believe that . . . ." The veracity of the report is a secondary consideration. Of course, not every person accepts every rumor in every riot situation. The point is that people are made more susceptible to rumors in riot, as opposed to non-riot, situations. Indeed, given the perpetually strained state of black-white relations, there are indications that the degree to which people actually believe race-related rumors is unusually high even under normal circumstances. One year after the Detroit riot in 1967, the Detroit *Free Press* surveyed the blacks of that city and found that 17 percent ("a small but significant minority") had recently heard stories about groups of whites planning to attack black neighborhoods.[44] More important was the finding that almost half of the people who had heard these rumors believed they were true! Where the sensitive matter of race is concerned, hearing is often believing.

Intensification Function

Rumors also serve to intensify hostile beliefs. This intensification frequently occurs through gross exaggeration and distortion of reality: a crowd becomes a "mob," a shooting becomes a "murder," a brief scuffle becomes a "riot." What happens is that the behavior of the identified adversary (the object of the rumor) is magnified and seen as extraordinary, beyond the pale of expected norms.

Paranoid fantasies—on a group, not an individual level—are frequently incorporated into rumors. For example, feelings of persecution are found in "atrocity stories"—tales of outrageous, horrible deeds attributed to the other race. These tales involve brutal beatings, stabbings, rapes, murders, along with bloody massacres and insurrections. The details of these "atrocities" lend an air of greater authenticity, and can be quite impressive. In East St. Louis, 25,000 whites were "doomed" in a plot, set for July 4, to be executed by an invasion army containing 1,500 men, in three divisions—according to the widespread rumor.

Age and sex factors may add to the pervasive sense of horror. For example, crimes committed against women and children are considered more odious because these individuals are presumably less able to defend themselves than adult men. The shooting incident which triggered the first outbreak in East St. Louis involved two men. Nevertheless, the barrage of rumors which followed the shooting involved alleged offenses against women. Similarly, the two main protagonists in the "bridge rumors" in Detroit were a woman and baby, although neither was directly connected with any previous incident. Finally, the handbill circulated during the Harlem riot of 1935 asserted that a black woman had her arm broken before being arrested and a "child" had been badly beaten. Aside from the fact that no one had been hurt or mistreated, the "child" in question was actually 16 years old.

Other rumors center around the bizarre and have a wild, fantastic quality. Reports among blacks during World War I—that the Germans were on their way through Texas to capture the South, that the federal government had a scheme to transport all the blacks from the South, and that the Indians were coming to reclaim their land after several hundred years, had absolutely no basis in fact. But, ridiculous though they were, these rumors were accepted by some blacks and reinforced their belief that the system was constantly conspiring against them.

In keeping with their distortion effect, rumors are sometimes set in strange places—dark, eerie and mysterious. In both Chicago and East St. Louis, there were tales of dead bodies floating around in murky waters. The charge among white Chicagoans that blacks had stored large amounts of ammunition in their *cellars* was matched —in terms of setting—by a rumor connected with the first Harlem riot, that a black youth had been murdered in the *basement* of a store.

Linkage Function

In virtually every instance of rumor formation, the rumor is preceded by a tangible event. Most investigators would agree that the rumor is tied to this event in some way. For Shibutani, the chief significance of the event is that it is ambiguous—uncertain, unfamiliar and unknown. This ambiguity may have arisen because news about the event was lacking, or not clearly reported, or arrived in the form of several conflicting versions of the same story.

Certainly, many of the events discussed in the historical chapter of this volume could be characterized as ambiguous. In Chicago, a young man drowned, but it was not immediately clear why; in Elaine, Arkansas, a group of sharecroppers met in a church for reasons best known to themselves; in Harlem, a youth caught shoplifting was quickly whisked away, raising questions about his "disappearance"; and in Detroit, some individuals massed and headed for the police station, leading others to believe that "something was up."

But, while recognizing ambiguity as an important in-gredient in the event, we must also qualify Shibutani's arguments, on two fronts. The first concerns the origin of ambiguity. In many instances, ambiguity does stem solely from the absence of news. However, in connection with riots, the ambiguity is derived more from the fundamental strains between the races. Or, to put it another way, given the different experiences of the races, ambiguity is in the eye of the beholder. Take away the adversative aspects of an event and you take away much of its ambiguity. If, for example, a *white* youth caught stealing a knife had been removed from the scene, would the shoppers immediately have jumped to the conclusion that the *white* management had beaten him up? Or, if the sharecroppers meeting at the church had been *white,* would the deputy sheriffs and *white* citizens of the area have automatically assumed they were hatching a union plot to murder them? It is clear that, where riots are concerned, the element of race, more than news, is what makes the event ambiguous.

The second qualification of Shibutani's argument involves the importance of the event itself. Shibutani felt the ambiguity factor outweighed all others: "It is not so much the intrinsic importance of the event but the existence of a problematic situation that converts what is otherwise ordinary information into news."[45] With riots, however, the event itself *is* important, specifically as an outgrowth or expression of community conflict. The rumor may relate to the event either directly or indirectly. For example, efforts in the direction of integrated housing may result in a rumored "invasion" of white neighborhoods. On the other hand, the same event may produce stories of alleged rapes of white women.

The event comes in various forms: an incident, issue, grievance, complaint, or some sort of happening. But, whatever its shape, the real importance of the event, overshadowing its ambiguity, is that it induces or reflects conflict. Rumors serve to link hostile beliefs to this kind of event, making the event more inflammatory, more provocative and more ominous. Exhibit 4.3 demonstrates the linkage function as it pertains to rumors among whites around the time of the first riot in East St. Louis.

Hostile beliefs are a kind of alarm system—a warning device signaling danger. Tied as they are to incidents which highlight or heighten conflict, rumors help set off this alarm, mobilizing the public. As the public becomes disturbed, frightened and excited, it also becomes prepared for action.

In connection with racial disorders, rumors are part of the whole process by which violence occurs, one of a series of determinants, including: a rigid social structure backed by a racist ideology; a hostile belief system; conditions of stress; and rumors. In the absence of other contributing factors, rumors themselves are not really meaningful—a nuisance, perhaps, but not particularly effective or significant. Operating along with agents conducive to disorder, however, they can travel with the speed and impact of a bullet.

Like these other determinants, rumors are a measure of the extreme racial cleavage and isolation within our society. Ironically, they serve to increase polarization while, at the same time, strengthening solidarity within each group, in a negative sort of way. Like hostile beliefs, rumors create a "common culture" within which leadership, mobilization and concerted action can occur spontaneously. Crystallizing, confirming and intensifying hostile beliefs, while linking them to actual events, rumors often provide the "proof" necessary for mass mobilization.

The process model of rumor formation, therefore, denies the view of many social psychologists that rumors are based on the whims and interests of the individual, and affirms them as a social phenomenon arising out of group conflict.

Exhibit 4.3
EAST ST. LOUIS, ILLINOIS
May 1917

Hostile Belief(s)	Rumors (Among Whites)	Event
		Prior to Riot:
Blacks wish to usurp the position of whites	Blacks driving whites from their neighborhoods.	1. Some moves by blacks into white neighborhoods and increased job competition.
Blacks constantly conspire to undermine the system	Large companies conspiring with blacks to solicit migrants from the South.	
Blacks are unusually promiscuous	Blacks planning to assault white women.	
		Precipitant
Blacks are inherently violent	Shooting intentional and victim had died.	2. Black man accidentally shoots white man during holdup.
Blacks are inherently violent	Two whites girls had been shot.	
Blacks are inherently violent	White woman had been shot.	
Blacks have a definite place	White woman had been insulted by a black man.	
		During the Riot
Blacks wish to usurp the position of whites	Train of 500 migrants arriving from the South.	3. Outbreak.

This model suggests a number of propositions, which stem from two fundamental assumptions. First, rumors are functionally related to the basic and immediate conflicts which give rise to collective outbursts. Thus, both the rumors and disorders are part of the same process and have the same antecedents as causes. Second, rumors are a way of dealing with these conflicts through the medium of the hostile belief system. If these assumptions are correct, then the following propositions should follow logically:

1. Most racial disorders are characterized by rumor formation.

2. As a disorder becomes imminent, the number of race-related rumors in the community will tend to increase.

3. This increase in race-related rumors during the pre-disorder period tends to be associated with immediate conflicts in the community—more specifically, pending issues or events of a racial nature.

4. Since the event that triggers the racial disorder arises at a peak of community conflict, and since increasing numbers of rumors are tied to community conflict, rumors tend to be associated with precipitating events.

5. Since community conflict reaches a new peak during the course of the disorder, the volume of rumors increases at this time.

6. Due to the complementary aspect of hostile beliefs held by the white group and the black group, there will be some overlap in terms of thematic content for rumors circulating among both groups.

7. Because rumors are tied to the hostile belief system, the salience of themes common among each race does not differ markedly at different stages of the disorder.

8. Owing to the perseverance of the hostile belief system, within each race thematic content is similar for disorders —both past and present-day.

5. RACIAL DISORDER IN THE 1960s: THE PROCESS MODEL TESTED

The cycle of disorders spanning the early sixties and to a lesser extent the early seventies affected every section of the United States. These disorders occurred in cities large and small, and in diverse settings ranging from the streets to the schools, to the prisons, even to our military bases and carriers. While the data for earlier cycles of riots are not really comparable, indications are that this newest wave has been the longest, most extensive and most severe one in our entire history. Only a few of the "big-name" riots of the mid-sixties remain in the public mind—principally Watts (1965), Newark (1967) and Detroit (1967). Yet serious disturbances broke out as early as 1963 in places such as Cambridge, Maryland, Birmingham, Alabama, Savannah, Georgia and Philadelphia. In 1964, the arrest and conviction of civil rights demonstrators sparked some violence in Jacksonville, Florida; this was reportedly the first time Molotov cocktails were used. During the period of 1967-1969, the peak years of disorder, the Lemberg Center's Disorder Clearinghouse (CDC) recorded more than 1800 disturbances, involving nearly 600 different cities; over 200 deaths (mostly of civilians); at least 11,000 injuries; more than 70,000 arrests and countless millions of dollars in property damage.[1] Alongside these staggering figures were the higher costs exacted in terms of human loss and suffering which can never be measured. Far from being relics of a distant past, these most recent disorders were both tragic and disturbing reminders that our country had still not confronted the race issue directly.

In order to establish a context for the ensuing discussion of rumors, the reader is asked to accept the fundamental inequities in the system and a still-forceful set of hostile beliefs as given. Our attention can then be focused briefly on the underlying conditions of stress.

Increasing Urbanization

While the Depression may have slowed the migratory trend of blacks out of the South, World War II set the flow in motion again. More recently, the increased mechanization of agriculture and the expansion of industrial employment in northern and western cities has continued to stimulate the emigration of blacks, although at a less dramatic rate. From 1960 to 1963, the annual out-migration of blacks from the South dropped to 78,000; but it jumped to over 125,000 between 1963 and 1966. As of 1960, 48 percent of the U.S. black population lived outside the South. Equally important, this growth occurred in the central cities of the larger metropolitan areas. According to the Census Bureau, in 1966 almost 70 percent of all blacks in 1966 lived in metropolitan areas. Unfortunately, at that time most cities were ill-equipped, ill-prepared, and less than wholeheartedly committed to dealing with the conditions inherent in expanding ghettos. Poverty, discrimination, overcrowding, the failure to create new jobs, inferior education, poor housing, inadequate health facilities and other minimum services were miserable facts of life. The bitterness, rage and frustration so keenly felt by many blacks, especially young people, greatly increased the possibility that the cities would explode at some point. Indeed, the Lemberg Center's three-year report confirmed that the recent outbreak of disorders was essentially an urban phenomenon; they occurred most often in the largest cities, those with the highest proportion of black residents and low-income areas. The report concluded as follows: "The disorder phenomenon, then, is more likely to be related to the quality and character of urban life as experienced by poor youth rather than to summertime boredom or thrill-seeking."[2]

Relative Deprivation

It must seem ironic that the violence should have occurred at this particular time in history—a time of substantial racial progress. For example, a larger percentage of blacks now attend college than residents of the British Isles. Similarly, blacks in this country currently have a consumer buying power comparable to that of similarly populated Canada.

In point of fact, blacks *are* better off today than ever before. Indeed, the racial advances made during the last 25 years are unparalleled in our entire history. Impressive gains have been made in employment, as opportunities have been widened in professional, clerical and service fields. From 1950 to 1960, the median annual income for non-whites 14 years of age and older climbed 54 percent, and for non-white families, 73 percent. During the fifties the percentage of non-whites residing in census-defined "standard" housing doubled, while for the first time many blacks could afford to buy their housing without taking in boarders or other relatives. Important changes were also registered in the area of political power. Over one million more blacks voted in 1962 than in 1950. Significantly, during the 1960 presidential campaign, both major political parties tried to out-civil rights the other in their respective planks. The rise in black political power and pressure was also reflected in some significant changes at the national level. The landmark decision of the Supreme Court in 1954, striking down the "separate but equal" doctrine in education, would have profound effects on other areas of society as well. In 1957, Congress passed a civil rights law protecting the citizen's right to vote. It was a modest law, but it represented a remarkable reversal of the traditional hands-off policy of the federal government in matters of civil rights. Without question, however, the Civil Rights Act of 1964 was the most far-reaching law in support of racial equality ever passed by Congress. The attorney general was given additional powers to protect citizens against discrimination in voting, education and the use of public facilities; discrimination was outlawed in most places of public accommodation and in federally financed programs, while provision was made for withholding funds upon the failure to comply with this law.

Nevertheless, while recognizing the tremendous strides taken in recent years, many whites fail to take into account the other changes that have occurred, in the form of increased aspirations by blacks. For, in the face of the most rapid gains in our history, many blacks expected a swift and immediate elevation in their position. Unfortunately, however, their expectations far outweighed their advances. Therefore, while better off in absolute terms than ever before, many blacks feel relatively more deprived now than before the last 25 years of racial progress. Where blacks themselves are concerned, it does no good to compare their position to that of the Canadians or the British—only to that of white Americans. And what progress has been made is not sufficient to meet the hopes of a people beginning to view their inferior place in terms of the rest of our affluent society. This important social psychological principle, known as relative deprivation, helps to explain the tremendous dissatisfaction in blacks, born of racial progress. And, as Pettigrew points out: "Intense relative deprivation in an age of rising expectations is the stuff out of which revolutions are made."[3]

The Rise of Direct Action

Before 1960, the traditional civil rights movement was characterized by middle- and upper-class leadership, legal action, efforts to ensure the constitutional rights of black citizens and appeals to white America's sense of fair play and justice. But about this time, however, a different brand of black man was emerging in the South—more confident, less intimidated by white-hooded knights, ready to use his collective strength to reach his own desired ends. Amidst these changes came new tactics and goals aimed at direct and mass action, economic as well as legal issues, and demands based upon the power of the black community. Reflecting this new need, the Rev. Dr. Martin Luther King, Jr., organized the Southern Christian Leadership Conference (SCLC) in 1957, to coordinate direct action in the South. In May 1961, the Congress of Racial Equality (CORE) sent its now-famous "Freedom Riders" into the

South, to test segregationist laws and practices then operative in interstate transportation. The movement gathered steam as other organizations, including the Student Non-Violent Coordinating Committee (SNCC) and the Nashville Student Movement (NSM), staged demonstrations, pickets and sit-ins in the North as well as the South, in lily-white places such as restaurants, theaters, libraries, beaches and hotels. There was some strong white resistance, especially in the South, and police dogs, cattle prods and high-pressure water hoses were used on the marchers. But the movement scored some notable successes. The Civil Rights Act of 1964 and the Voting Rights Act of 1965 were its most outstanding accomplishments.

At the same time, however, many of the younger black activists were becoming increasingly frustrated and disillusioned by the realization that their direct action tactics had not really solved the basic problems of the ghetto. Notwithstanding the movement's rhetoric, blacks still were not "Free by '63" and they had yet to "overcome." In retrospect, perhaps the most significant aspect of the direct action movement was that it paved the way for, or at least foreshadowed, an even more direct, more violent confrontation by the black masses with white America.

Black Consciousness

The cry of "black power" was first heard nationally in 1966, when Stokely Carmichael used the term during the James Meredith March from Memphis to Jackson. Although it started as a hazy, mystical slogan and only later became more of a practical program, black power immediately struck fear into the hearts of many white Americans. Other whites were more skeptical and simply derided Carmichael and his adherents as the creation of the media—a few leaders whose followers consisted largely of *Time* and *Newsweek* magazines.

Looking back, black power was an extremely important new force on the scene—since it encouraged the formation of a new consciousness among many blacks, especially the younger elements. This new consciousness, which antedated and later found expression in the riots, marked an attempt by the black community to define and organize itself around new values and goals. The emphasis was on group solidarity, the development of resources within the ghetto, aggressive community leadership designed to challenge the system and a broadened base of political power. The old civil rights rhetoric was out. "Peaceful progress," "integration," "coalition politics" and "nonviolence" were part of a rejection of "white" methods for alleviating black oppression. This attitude reflected a new racial pride, in addition to greater alienation from the system and doubts about ever achieving meaningful change. Young black activists increasingly denounced white institutions, white leaders and their former allies, white liberals.

This new mood was expressed in various ways. Angry black writers were among the first to opt for separatism. In 1961, Imamu Amiri Baraka (the playwright-activist, formerly known as LeRoi Jones) was already sneering at "white liberalism." On the political front, new organizations such as SNCC were black-led and black-dominated from the start. By 1960 the Black Muslims, under the leadership of Elijah Muhammad, had become a vocal and vigorous religious sect. Remaining aloof from the civil rights movement, the Muslims preached against "white devils," renounced all names that might imply a connection with white America, and stressed self-help and separatism. They were also armed and well-disciplined. When their mosques were raided by the police, the Muslims sometimes fought back, as the Black Panthers did later. The Muslims had at least 50,000 members during the early sixties.

Of course, the most dramatic manifestation of the new black consciousness was found in the riots themselves. The open hostility of the participants toward whites, their extreme distrust of white institutions and their great sense of racial pride, have all been documented in numerous studies. Carmichael and Hamilton forcefully expressed the mood of many rioters:

> Black people in America have no time to play nice, polite parlor games. . . . White people own the society. For black people to adopt *their* methods of relieving *our* oppression is ludicrous. We blacks must respond in our own way, on our own terms, in a manner which fits our temperaments. The definitions of our- selves, the roles we pursue, the goals we seek are *our* responsi- bility.[4]

Growing Dissatisfaction: The Illusion of Equality

In recent years, much has been made of the expanding number of "Negro firsts": the first black Senator in the twentieth century, the first black Supreme Court Justice, the first black woman to seek the presidential nomination, the first black in the United States Navy to be promoted to flag rank, the first black general manager in sports, the first black conductor of the Metropolitan Opera, the first black to make a national television commercial and so on. But, however, comforting these examples may be to white America, many blacks are aware that these and other such "firsts" are essentially isolated events—personal achieve- ments for a lucky or resourceful few—rather than meaning- ful advances for the Negro race itself. A series of newsworthy "firsts," along with some impressive legislative gains, have ironically served to sustain the illusion of equality, obscuring the fact that there has been very little improvement in the lives of the black masses. Despite the rosy picture printed by some social statisticians, millions remain imprisoned in environmental jungles—trapped in a vicious cycle of poverty which perpetuates family disorganization, personal insecurity, a higher incidence of major disease as compared to whites, a higher infant mortality rate and a lower life expectancy.

If anything, the token changes in recent history have increased black perceptions about the elusive nature of equality and resulted in a rising tide of dissatisfaction. One Lemberg Center report documented the feelings among many blacks that the growth of local job opportunities, the pace of racial integration in the schools and efforts to provide opportunities for blacks to live where they want within the city, were all going too slow. The report found: "Large numbers of Negroes in all the cities are clearly disturbed and angry, and these feelings have in them a strong riot potential."[5] The actual survey, completed in 1966 and released publicly in June 1967 before the tremendous onslaught of violence that summer, concluded somewhat pessimistically: "Though disliking violence and troubled with mixed feelings about its effects, Negroes are shifting to the opinion that only intense forms of social protest can bring relief from social injustice."[6]

The Vietnam War

In the opinion of many behavioral scientists, historians and philosophers, the Vietnam War, more than any previous military conflict, helped foster violence at home. Evidence of the war's impact were public opinion polls indicating that many Americans regarded Lt. William Calley's behavior at Mylai as normal. These surveys suggested that the longest, most divisive war in our history had unleashed a more casual attitude toward violence here at home—including, for example, the increased willingness of blacks to resort to violence.

Other aspects of the war weighed on the racial picture as well. Many blacks regarded the war as racist because we were killing people of a different color than ourselves. Questioning our commitment to the corrupt political regime in Saigon, parallels were drawn between the "imperialist war" abroad and "internal imperialism" at home. At the same time, domestic strains reverberated within our fighting forces overseas. There was a new refusal among blacks to allow the regimentation and isolation of the military to lessen their identification with the black struggle going on in the United States. Vietnam saw the rise of soldier-activists who organized themselves within military units and denounced "double standards" in promotion procedures, job assignments and the dispensation of military justice. Racial incidents were often withheld or covered up by local commanders, but the war had unquestionably intensified racial tensions at home and abroad.

These, then, were the background factors which set the stage for violence. It remained only for more immediate conflicts to trigger disorders in hundreds of communities across the country.

THE NATURE OF THE DISORDERS

In contrast to the pattern found in earlier riot cycles, the disturbances during the sixties were mostly black-dominated and property-oriented, with a notable absence of large-scale clashes between civilians of both races. The Kerner Report correctly described the recent riots as more racial than interracial in character. (Accordingly, we will use broader terms, such as "racial disorders" and "racial disturbances," in this section, rather than "race riots.")

The reasons for the changed nature of the violence do not concern us here. However, the implications regarding the white community's involvement in the disorder process is a relevant issue. For, if whites were largely divorced from these proceedings, then any discussion of rumors within their community would become extraneous.

We must not view the disturbances in a racial vacuum affecting the black community only, with whites able to maintain a business-as-usual attitude, happily removed from the conflict and violence of the day. To begin with, the electronic age would have made such a situation impossible. Widespread television coverage gave the riots tremendous immediacy and impact. If millions of white Americans were not quite eyewitnesses to these dramatic events, they were something more than casual observers. Moreover, in many small but important ways, the lives of whites were directly affected during, or in expectation of, trouble. Baseball and football games and other sporting events were banned in some cities. Merchants boarded up their stores and carted away valuable merchandise. Nervous parents picked up their children at schools, while apprehensive husbands came to get their teacher-wives. Theaters, restaurants and bus service closed down in many business districts. In Raleigh, North Carolina, during a disturbance in 1968, a statewide conference on the Future Homemakers of America was canceled, as was a perform-mance of the Ice Capades. In Chicago, in the midst of serious violence related to the assassination of the Rev. Dr. Martin Luther King, Jr., employers sent workers home early and banks closed, while telephone service was slowed down by the heavy volume of calls. At about the same time in Baltimore, shortly before the ghetto blew up, Baltimore County experienced a sharp rise in gun sales to suburbanites.

In addition, the public authorities—those who had to restore order and contend with volatile situations—were largely white. Local and state officials used their power to close bars and gas stations, order curfews, declare states of emergencies, form grievance committees and negotiate with black leaders. Of course, the police and other law enforcement personnel had the closest contact with the participants. Charged with representing the entire community, but coming from mostly white areas and having to deal with angry, hostile blacks, the policeman's job was, in many ways, an impossible one. Rocky Pomerance, Miami Beach's police chief extraordinaire, once wryly observed that, caught in the social crossfires of the day, the police could not possibly win. The best they could do, he said, was "to lose gracefully." In any event, the presence of the police was bound to have repercussions in *both* the black and white communities.

Finally, we should note that, while the majority of racial disorders involved black participants, whites were not excluded altogether. In fact, the Lemberg Center report cited earlier found a "dramatic decrease" in the proportion of disorders involving *only* black participants— from 77 percent in 1967 to 40 percent by 1969. At the same time, the study also showed a sizable increase in the number of "two-formation events" (open hostility between members of two or more groups, usually both blacks and whites), from 13 percent in 1967 to 33 percent in 1969.[7] A large portion of the increase was associated with the rise in school-related disorders.

In sum, we can see that whites were involved in the interaction process on a variety of levels, ranging from

steps taken to protect themselves, to decision-making
which bore on the outcome of the disorders, to occasional
outright participation. It is clear that any analysis of the
role of rumor in sixties' style disorders should encompass
both the black and white communities.

DATA COLLECTION

The elastic, slippery quality of rumors makes data
collection in this field an extremely risky business.
Intellectual appetite whetted, armed with his or her
research net, the investigator is still at a great disadvantage
in trying to snare the elusive rumor. Adding to his or her
frustration is the knowledge that, no matter what means of
attack is employed, for every rumor "caught," at least
twice as many undoubtedly "got away." It seems safe to
say that there is no "best" means of approaching this task
—but some approaches may be more fruitful than others.
The data used in the historical chapter of this book
point up some of the difficulties involved here. First, the
sample was extremely small; only 11 riots involving rumor
formation were included. Estimates of "The Red Summer"
of 1919 alone have run as many as 25 race riots. However,
largely due to the paucity of available data, rumors were
documented in only four of these riots. The incompleteness of the material was further underscored by the
division of rumors along racial lines. Far fewer rumors
were uncovered among blacks as compared to whites. In
addition, only the larger riots were studied. For example,
many rumors were discerned for the Chicago riot in 1919.
But no information was forthcoming for smaller disturbances such as those in Berkeley, Georgia and Bogalusa,
Louisiana, which occurred in the same year. A final
problem is that the sources were not of a uniform quality.

Thus, our historical material is hardly representative or systematic. While it is very helpful in raising questions, stimulating ideas and serving as a reference for analysis, beyond that its value is limited. Certainly a more comprehensive, more cohesive approach is needed to test the propositions listed at the close of the last chapter.

Toward this end, the writer has drawn upon the resources of the Lemberg Center's Civil Disorder Clearinghouse (CDC). Three different data sources will be used. For analysis purposes, however, each will be kept separate, unlike the various types of historical data—which were lumped together. The decision to draw from several kinds of data stems partly from the recognition that no one given source is entirely satisfactory and that each has its limitations. Also, more than one source will enable us to make occasional comparisons. Taken together, these sources should provide a reasonably precise picture of the nature of rumors and an adequate means of evaluating our propositions.

The three data sources are:

(1) *News clips.* For several years, the CDC received information about racial disturbances from two commercial newspaper clipping services which monitored local daily and weekly newspapers on a nationwide basis. Between January 1967 and October 1969—the period encompassing data collection for this phase of our study—a total of 1,296 definite racial disorders were recorded. Of this figure, 224 disorders made reference to rumors.[8] More than one rumor was reported in some disturbances, for a total of 295 rumors in all. The number of cases involving rumors relative to the incidence of disorder is extremely small (17 percent, or 224 out of 1,296 cases) since reporters covering stories were not usually on the lookout for rumors per se. Nevertheless, in itself, the sum of 224 disorders involving rumors is still a substantial one (compar-

ed, for example, to the 11 cases in the historical chapter) and should be useful for examining thematic content in each race. Moreover, because reporters were frequently at the scene of a disorder, a good percentage of the rumors uncovered involved blacks. Of the total number of usable rumors, those in which both the content and the race were identifiable, nearly 60 percent (124 out of 211 rumors) circulated among blacks.

(2) *Investigative Accounts.* In-depth reports and studies were occasionally made in the aftermath of disorders. Some were of an official nature, involving the police, government commissions, human relations agencies and so on. Others were done by independent groups and individual academics, journalists and citizens' groups. Generally speaking, these narratives are extremely hard to locate. Relatively few of them were compiled in the first place, and those that do exist have not always been made available to the general public. Nevertheless, various documents representing 22 disorders were collected for this study.[9] These accounts span the years 1964 through 1970, although most fall between 1967 and 1969.

Facts, statistics and in-depth interviews have been marshalled in these studies, in order to give an extremely detailed picture of the disorders. A measure of the thoroughness of these studies is the fact that the 22 disorders have furnished us with 166 rumors—an average of 7.5 rumors per disorder. This ratio compares with 224 disorders accounting for 295 rumors via newspapers—an average of only 1.3. Thus, despite the small number of investigative accounts, the yield in terms of rumors is something of a windfall.

These accounts also supply a sizable amount of rumor material from among whites. Whereas close to 60 percent of the usable rumors from news clips were distributed among blacks, the reverse is true here. Slightly more than

60 percent of the rumors from investigative accounts were circulated among whites. Each data source, then, complements the other and affords a good means of substantive comparison.

(3) *Police Survey*. The several hundred cases derived from news clips and investigative accounts can be expected to illuminate the character and quality of rumors, including their content, division along racial lines and relation to the hostile belief system. However, these sources are weak in terms of discerning patterns of rumor formation—especially the quantity of rumors, both their flow and fluctuation. This is because information was collected on an ad hoc basis—a rumor cited here, a rumor mentioned there—but not in any systematic fashion. For example, a reporter filing a story at the time of a disturbance might or might not make reference to clusters of rumors prior to an outbreak, depending on his or her whim or interest; the same holds true (although to a lesser extent) for the academic doing a post-mortem on a disorder. The problem is that neither individual is *specifically* or *necessarily* looking for instances of rumor formation. Consequently, little can be learned about the relationship between rumors and disorders in this way.

So what can an investigator do? The answer is to station a research net at a source which is close to the disorder and which functions as a repository for rumors. On this basis, the most obvious choice is the local police department. The police are, of course, interested and involved in events when their city erupts. But, more important, the neighborhood police department traditionally functions as a central clearinghouse for anxious citizens wishing to check out reports, or simply to notify the police about what they had heard. The fact that many departments keep records of incoming calls as a matter of standard practice adds to the attractiveness of the police as a source of information.

Moreover, the CDC had had considerable contact and cooperation with police departments throughout the country. In 1967, for example, statistical forms were mailed to the police chiefs of the 173 cities which had experienced disorders. These forms were part of an effort to verify certain aspects of the disorders—exact dates, numbers of arrests and casualties, property damage estimates, and so on. Nearly 55 percent of the police departments replied. All these factors made the police a unique and potentially valuable source of information.

That is not to say they were ideal; indeed, numerous problems could be anticipated in advance. In the first place, while there might be an upsurge in rumors at the time of a disorder, there was certainly no guarantee that citizens would be sufficiently motivated to inform or make inquiries of the police in every instance. Bias was another problem. The police are considered to be among the more conservative groups in our society. It was conceivable, or even likely, that their attitudes on race, poverty and social issues in general, might hamper any attempt to probe the relationship between rumors and community conflict.[10] The matter of credibility was closely associated with the bias problem. For, given the black community's deep distrust of the police, it was reasonable to assume a certain reticence on its part to call on them for assistance—even to report or verify rumors. The fact that the police were frequently unable to identify or neglected to record the caller's race was another limitation. And finally, it was by no means certain that any data sample that came by way of the police—or almost any single source, for that matter—would replicate the overall distribution of events.

Fully appreciating the advantages and disadvantages of using the police as a data source, the writer constructed a questionnaire designed to uncover patterns of rumor formation.[11] Along with the annual verification forms, this questionnaire was mailed to the police chiefs of 261 cities which had 569 disturbances in 1968, as recorded by the CDC.[1][2] A total of 73 cities representing 112 disorders replied[1][3]—a response rate of 28 percent for cities and 20 percent for disorders. These percentages were considerably lower than the previous year, when only our statistics were verified. This lower response rate probably stemmed from several factors.

First, many of the cities which exploded in 1968 had experienced disorders in 1967. The burden of doing paperwork a second time around could not have been terribly attractive to overworked police officials. Second, by 1968, government agencies and other research groups were making similar demands on the police, anxious to get facts and figures for their own purposes. Even from an information standpoint, the police were getting it from all sides. Third, our own rumor questionnaire tended to require a fair amount of digging, rather than simple statistics, which usually were more readily available. And finally, the growing criticism of the police for their handling of disorders—particularly from the academic community—served to strain relations between the two groups.

Nevertheless, the reduced response rate from the police was offset by the fact that our data sample compared favorably with the general population—the total number of disorders by the CDC in 1968—on a variety of characteristics. In terms of the disorder rate, 64 percent of the recorded cities had only one outbreak during the year, compared with 70 percent in our survey sample (see Exhibit 5.1). In both cases, "repeat" cities—those with more than one disturbance—occurred about one-third of the time. According to our general population, the average number of disorders per city was 2.2 (261 cities out of 569 disorders), compared with 1.5 in our sample (73 out of 112), a slightly lower figure.

Similarities were also found regarding the apportion-

Exhibit 5.1
DISTRIBUTION OF DISORDERS BY CITY (1968)

Number of Disorders per City	Recorded Disorders		Sample	
	%	No.	%	No.
1	64	167	70	51
2	17	45	11	8
3	7	18	15	11
4 or more	12	31	4	3
Number of Cities Experiencing Disorders	100	261	100	73

Exhibit 5.2
DISTRIBUTION OF DISORDERS BY REGION (1968)[14]

Region of the Country	Recorded Disorders		Sample	
	%	No.	%	No.
East	28	160	15	17
Midwest	27	155	32	36
West	10	59	13	15
Border	14	77	14	16
South	21	118	25	28
TOTAL	100	569	99	112

Exhibit 5.3
DISTRIBUTION OF DISORDERS BY MAGNITUDE (1968)

Magnitude of Disorders	Recorded Disorders		Sample	
	%	No.	%	No.
Minor	68	389	58	65
Medium	25	144	30	34
Serious	5	29	9	10
Major	1	7	3	3
TOTAL	99	569	100	112

ment of disorders throughout the country (see Exhibit 5.2).[14] For example, the total North/South breakdown for recorded disorders (considering the East, Midwest and West to comprise the "North") was a top-heavy 65 to 35 percent; for the survey sample is was 60 to 39 percent. Thus, the clear concentration of disturbances in the North was very definitely reflected in our smaller sample.

Parallels were also discerned when it came to ranking disorders by magnitude (see Exhibit 5.3). A rough order of magnitude was calculated on the basis of three variables: duration of the disorder in terms of hours, number of participants and amount of property damage (in dollars). Each disturbance was then classified in terms of one of four possible categories: minor, medium, serious and major.[15] Using these measures, we determined that more than one-half the disturbances were minor—68 percent of the disorder population, 58 percent for the disorder sample. Furthermore, only a small fraction of disorders in both distributions qualified as either serious or major—6 percent of the recorded disorders, 11 percent of the sample.

Thus, on a series of key variables—disorder rate, regional apportionment and magnitude—our sample approximates the larger distribution of disorders. As a data source, the police survey is both systematic and representative, and gives us some basis from which to generalize about disorders as part of our analysis of rumors. Let us therefore turn to the important matter of testing our propositions concerning the process model of rumor formation.

PROPOSITIONS

The series of propositions which follow can be divided into two separate groupings. The first set focuses on the relationship between rumors and racial disorders. Discussion and analysis will center around the incidence of rumors—when and how rumors are formed. Here we will rely mainly on the findings from our police survey questionnaire. The second set is concerned with the relationship between rumors and the hostile belief system. These hypotheses involve the nature of rumors, their character and content—in other words, what they are about. At this stage, we will draw heavily from our news clips and investigative accounts.

PROPOSITIONS: RUMORS AND RACIAL DISORDERS

1. *Most racial disorders are characterized by rumor formation.*

At first glance the notion that rumors and riots somehow go together must sound about as profound as saying that blind people have trouble seeing. Closer inspection, however, reveals that most such statements concerning rumors have *assumed* such a relationship, based on very little documentation. Part of the problem is that past research efforts in the areas of rumors and riots have concentrated on one or the other, almost exclusively. The historian looking at a particular riot has tended to devote some, but not terribly much, space to rumors. On the other hand, the social psychologist investigating rumors has tended to give short shrift to the phenomenon of riots. The result has been a hodgepodge of unverified statements about a connection between the two, in which an untested assumption eventually came to approach the status of a natural law.

Indeed, it is easy to trace the evolution of this "law." We begin with the small number of studies about riots in the twentieth century, some of which were made before World War II. Numerous references to rumors may have existed in those accounts, but there was virtually no attempt made to posit a general relationship between rumors and riots.

Race Riot, by sociologists Lee and Humphrey, represented an important and, in some ways, an unfortunate departure from earlier studies of this kind. The book is essentially a case study of the massive riot occurring in Detroit in 1943, published in that same year. However, the authors did not confine themselves to a chronology and assessment of what had happened in their city. Using Detroit as their model (with a sprinkling of information about the riots in Harlem and Los Angeles that took place around the same time), they proceeded to generalize about the nature of riots, as well as rumors. Eight areas were discerned as "symptoms of the riot virus." Rumors, or "the verbal milling process," as they were termed, qualified as one of the eight. Setting aside the many variations of the famous "bridge" rumors and other unsubstantiated charges disseminated *after* the riot, fewer than a dozen specific rumors were cited in the actual text of the book. However, this apparent lack of information did not deter the authors from making a slew of generalizations.

> Rumors symptomatic of race riots generally go through three chief stages. . . . as racial tensions mount, the rumors that circulate take on a nastier and more purposive character.
> While he [the rioter] is an unstable person easily seized upon by emotion and hysteria, it usually takes an actual clash or a lurid story to drive him across the line into anti-social mob activity. . . . on the eve of race riots, rumors frequently bear the earmarks of artificial creation and abnormally rapid dissemination.[16]

By the time they had finished their discussion, Lee and Humphrey had managed to touch upon a great many facets of rumor development, including number, character, tone, speed, even the personality traits of the rumor-prone rioters—all this on the basis of a handful of examples taken essentially from one riot.

Gordon W. Allport and Leo Postman's *The Psychology of Rumor* was published several years later, and is considered by many to be the definitive work in this area. It included a six-page discussion of rumors and riots, in which the authors state their now-famous "law of social psychology":

> the evidence at hand is so convincing that we may advance it as a law of social psychology that *no riot ever occurs without rumors to incite, accompany, and intensify the violence.*[17]

Unfortunately, the "evidence at hand" which was found "so convincing" seems to have consisted largely of Lee and Humphrey themselves. The ideas which Allport and Postman set forth, their line of inquiry, even their language all bear a striking resemblance to passages from *Race Riot,* as the following excerpts demonstrate.

Lee and Humphrey	*Allport and Postman*
Rumors symptomatic of race riots generally go through three chief stages:	Ordinarily four stages in the process are discernible.
1. They begin with tales of alleged insults and discriminations, frequently traceable to subversive groups.	1. For a period of time before an outbreak there are murmurs of unrest. These murmurs may take the form of stories featuring discrimination, insults, or misdeeds ascribed by each group to its opponent.

2. Then come stories of imminent violence, of arming by the other race, of the need to protect one's home and loved ones, of invasion from another city.

2. Danger is indicated when the rumors assume a specifically threatening form. ... Sometimes the stories may ascribe impending violence to the opposing camp: 'The bastards have been saving up guns for a month.'

3. Finally one hears the crisis rumors, the inflammatory accounts of sexual assaults, beatings, and murders.

3. Often, though not invariably, the spark that ignites the powder keg is itself an inflammatory rumor.

4. These rumor symptoms circulate with increasing rapidity.[18]

4. During the heat of a riot rumors fly faster than ever. ... Tortures, rapes, murders are recounted in a frenzied manner.[19]

We need not discuss rumors with respect to content or to the different phases of the disorder here; all this will be treated later. Our purpose at this point is merely to emphasize the fact that Allport and Postman's often cited "law of social psychology" rests on shaky, meager evidence consisting largely of one very questionable source.

Once started, however, even rumors about rumors are hard to stop. Largely because a presumed relationship between rumors and riots had been laid down as "law" by two distinguished social psychologists, theirs became the final word on the subject. In its manual called *Prevention and Control of Mobs and Riots,* the FBI makes some observations which may have a familiar ring:

> In fact, some writers go so far as to state that no riot ever takes place without a build-up through rumor. ... Rumors start out as stories of insults, progress to stories of impending trouble, and finally become inflammatory accounts of intolerable acts such as beating, etc.[20]

A year later, *Parade* magazine ran an article which declared: "Last summer and this spring, in Detroit, Tampa, Cincinnati, Washington, *Wherever riots have occurred or threatened,* rumor has played an ugly, insidious role."[2 1] Predictably, this author went on to cite Allport and Postman's immutable "law."

More recently, the National Advisory Commission on Civil Disorders (the so-called "Kerner Commission") undertook an intensive investigation of 24 racial disturbances, which included a brief, but valuable, look at rumors. In a statement frequently cited in establishing rumor control centers, the Commission report asserted that: "Rumors significantly aggravated tension and disorder in more than 65 percent of the disorders studied by the Commission."[2 2] The Commission's findings are important on two counts: first, it took a fresh look at the issue of rumors and riots, not being content to rely on traditional sources; and second, it attempted to apply some precise measure to the question, without resorting to nebulous "laws" or shaky generalizations.

There is, however, at least one important criticism of its findings—involving methodology. In classifying 164 disorders recorded in 1967 according to magnitude, 75 percent of them (123 out of 164) were said to be "minor." Nevertheless, in selecting the 24 disorders to be used for analysis, only one-third were in this category. In other words, the data sample was heavily weighted in favor of the larger disorders, and it therefore was not representative of those collected by the Commission. As a consequence, their findings have to be qualified as pertaining to the bigger disturbances alone. Let us therefore pick up where the Kerner Commission began, using our own sample, which *is* generally representative.

In our survey questionnaire, police officials were asked a series of questions pertaining to an increase in rumors at three stages in time: the pre-disorder period, the precipitating event and during the outbreak itself.[23] In the vast majority of cases—78 percent, or 87 out of 112 disorders—the respondents noted an increase in rumors at one or more of these stages. Moreover, the association of rumors was extremely strong for disorders of all sizes, just slightly less so for the smaller disturbances (see Exhibit 5.4). An increase in rumors was reported for all disorders classified as serious or major (100 percent, or 13 out of 13); for minor disorders the percentage was 71 (46 out of 65 cases).

Thus, our findings lend support to our proposition that most racial disorders are characterized by rumor formation; furthermore, as a generalization, this appears to hold true for disturbances of every size.

2. *As a disorder becomes imminent, the number of race-related rumors in the community will tend to increase.*

Exhibit 5.4
DISTRIBUTION OF REPORTED RUMOR INCREASE BY
MAGNITUDE OF DISORDERS

Reported Rumor Increase	Minor %	Minor No.	Medium %	Medium No.	Serious %	Serious No.	Major %	Major No.	TOTAL %	TOTAL No.
No	25	16	18	6	0	0	0	0	20	22
Yes	71	46	82	28	100	10	100	3	78	87
Unclear[a]	5	3	0	0	0	0	0	0	3	3
TOTAL	101	65	100	34	100	10	100	3	101	112

[a]The respondent said the information was not available or left blanks for *all* the relevant questions.

Let us preface our discussion here with some remarks about the data. As stated earlier, our sample from our police survey consists of 112 cases of disorder. Of these,

38 took place within a week of the assassination of the Rev. Dr. Martin Luther King, Jr. (April 4, 1968) and, in most cases, were directly related to the civil rights leader's death. The King disorders are different from the others, in a number of respects. First, the precipitant was a national, not a local, event. Few such events have ever been communicated as quickly and widely. Most of the disorders that followed took place hundreds, if not thousands, of miles from the site of the assassination, Memphis, Tennessee. In addition, there tended to be an unusually long time-lapse between the triggering incident and the outbreak itself. With most disorders, the outbreak follows the precipitating event immediately—often within a matter of hours, sometimes only minutes. By contrast, most of the King disorders listed in our sample erupted a full day later, in many cases several days later.

Given the unusual nature of the King disorders, some confusion on the part of police respondents was quite understandable. Therefore, in order to avoid biasing the data in any way, our sample will be divided into King and non-King disorders, for questions involving the pre-disorder period or precipitating event. Findings for the King disorders will be presented but, unless otherwise noted, they will be given less weight than the non-King disorders. At the same time, we should stress that the division of our sample into two smaller distributions does not seriously affect the representativeness of the data, either in terms of magnitude or regional apportionment. Indeed, if anything, the 74 non-King disorders more nearly approximate the total number of recorded disorders in 1968.[24]

Turning to the business at hand, our second hypothesis really involves two questions: first, was there an increase in rumors reported prior to the disorders; and second, if so, when? Regarding the first issue, the police were asked the following:

Prior to the disorder, do your records show any noticeable increase in rumors reflecting racial tension? (Yes or No)

If this information was not recorded, do you *recall* that there was a noticeable increase in rumors of this kind prior to the disorder? (Yes or No)[25]

Nearly 60 percent of the respondents for the non-King disorders (44 out of 74 cases) reported an increase in rumors during this time (see Exhibit 5.5). Not surprisingly, an even higher percentage (74) was found for the King disorders (28 out of 38 cases). By combining the two samples, the percentage becomes 64. Thus, a sizable number of disorders—between 59 and 64 percent—had an upsurge of race-related rumors prior to any sort of outbreak. The significance of this finding is increased when we consider that we are dealing with increases in rumors *reported to the police*, as opposed to actual rumor increases per se, and that our figures are therefore likely to be on the conservative side.

In order to get a more precise picture of when pre-disorder rumors are likely to surface, the question was asked:

If there was an increase in rumors prior to the disorder, how far in advance of the disorder did the rumors begin?[26]

The police were given six choices, ranging from "over a year" to "the day of the disorder" (but before the outbreak), and asked to check one. The overwhelming majority of disorders for which a rumor increase was reported showed a clustering extremely close to the initial outbreak (see Exhibit 5.6). In nearly 70 percent of the pertinent non-King disorders (30 out of 44 cases), the rumors began within a few days or on the very day of the disorder itself; the corresponding percentage for the King

Exhibit 5.5
REPORTED RUMOR INCREASE (BEFORE OUTBREAK)
BY KING VS. NON-KING DISORDERS

Reported Rumor Increase	Non-King		King		Sample Total	
	%	No.	%	No.	%	No.
No (not recorded or recalled)	35	26	24	9	31	35
Yes (recalled)	23	17	24	9	23	26
Yes (recorded)	36	27	50	19	41	46
Unclear[a]	5	4	3	1	4	5
TOTAL	99	74	101	38	99	112

[a]Respondent left both questions blank or said information was not available.

Exhibit 5.6
TIME OF REPORTED RUMOR INCREASE
BY KING VS. NON-KING DISORDERS[a]

Period of Reported Rumor Increase	Non-King		King		Sample Total	
	%	No.	%	No.	%	No.
Over a year	2	1	0	0	1	1
More than 6 months	2	1	0	0	1	1
A few months	11	5	11	3	11	8
A few weeks	11	5	11	3	11	8
A few days	46	20	39	11	43	31
The day of the disorder	23	10	39	11	30	21
Unclear[b]	5	2	0	0	3	2
TOTAL	100	44	100	28	100	72

[a]Only for cases that reported an increase in rumors.

[b]Respondent left the question blank or said information was not available.

disorders was 78 (22 out of 28 cases). Thus, in at least 69 and as much as 73 percent of the relevant cases, rumors were found to have arisen within a couple of days of the disorder.

Our findings support our proposition that there is a tendency for rumors to escalate before a disorder and that they are most likely to occur at the brink of the outburst.

> 3. *This increase in race-related rumors during the pre-disorder period tends to be associated with immediate conflicts in the community—more specifically, pending issues or events of a racial nature.*

Setting aside the King disturbances for the moment, approximately 60 percent of the non-King disorders had a reported rumor increase. For these disorders, the following question was asked:

> Prior to the disorder, were there specific issues or events in the community which seem to give rise to the rumors? (Yes or No)[27]

A total of 66 percent (29 out of 44 cases) answered in the affirmative. Certainly, the police are not generally regarded as having their finger on the social pulse of the community to the extent of, say, a human relations commission or grass-roots organization. Therefore, added significance must be attached to our finding that, in two-thirds of the cases, this particular group felt the rumors were tied to conflicts facing the community. Furthermore, six additional instances of conflict can be pinpointed by going to our CDC news-clip files.[28] Our findings indicate that, in a minimum of two-thirds and perhaps as high as 80 percent of our cases, a reported rumor increase prior to disorders was strongly associated with immediate conflicts in the community.

In an attempt to define these conflicts more clearly, the

police who answered "yes" to the previous question were asked to check one or more of four categories listed in the questionnaire.[29] In 21 out of the 29 relevant cases, respondents checked one category only; in six cases two were checked; and in one instance three were identified. Because respondents checked the category marked "other" approximately one-fourth of the time, the categories were rearranged slightly. The breakdown of specific conflicts totalling 36 was as follows: schools (11), living conditions (9), police (7), alleged discriminatory practices (6) and other (3).[30]

Two points ought to be made here. First, there is some evidence to suggest that, as an issue, the police were under-represented in our sample. For instance, a disturbance in Syracuse (September 8-12, 1968) marked by a rise in rumors before the outbreak also coincided with growing criticism of "overpolicing" the black community (according to our CDC files). However, the police chief filling out our questionnaire failed to check the appropriate category.[31] Nevertheless, the slight bias in responses here is not a major problem—which brings us to our second point. The panorama of issues and events can be expected to change somewhat over time. In 1968, for example, schools had become major centers of unrest. Reflecting this trend, schools were the issue cited most often in our survey. It is unlikely that we would have gotten the same results if our questionnaire had been administered, for example, at the time of the first World War. Thus, the division of conflicts into particular categories is not really crucial.

The important thing is that we have been able to document our contention that an increase in rumors prior to disorders tends to be related to the incidence of *definite* and *specific* conflicts pending in the community. Moreover, besides bearing out our proposition, our findings also provide the opportunity for additional analysis and interpretation.

Thus far, we have demonstrated that a rumor increase before a disorder is tied to the presence of immediate conflicts within the community; and that these issues and events, in the words of our questionnaire, "seemed to give rise" to the rumors. But did they, in fact do so? Is there more evidence to suggest that the two are causally related?

The King disorders may help us in this regard. True, these disorders were atypical in some ways. At the same time, however, their unique qualities enable us to look at the same event (i.e., King's assassination) from the standpoint of rumors in many different settings—namely, 38 communities which had disorders.

Earlier we noted a reported rumor increase prior to the outbreak in 78 percent of the King disorders (28 out of 38 cases). Concerning the 28 cases of rumor formation, two questions emerge: first, to what extent were the rumors clustered around Dr. King's assassination; and second, what percent were associated with other pending issues and conflicts in the community? (See Exhibit 5.7). Our figures indicate that 79 percent of the rumors (22 out of 28 cases) were grouped around the time of the assassination, occurring on the same day or within a few days of the disorder. Of these 22 cases, 18 did not seem to be related to local issues or events. This finding is in direct and striking contrast to our sample of non-King disorders, in which between two-thirds and 80 percent *were* attributable to immediate conflicts in the community.

Since most of the rumors for the non-King disorders were identified with immediate, local conflicts, and since we were not able to determine the same for the King disorders in the vast majority of cases, the conclusion is unavoidable that the rumors and assassination were causally related and that the assassination itself was the event which gave rise to the rumors.[32] Furthermore, as a generalization, it would appear that rumors springing up before disorders are causally related to pending issues and events

Exhibit 5.7
KING DISORDERS:
ISSUES OR EVENTS BY TIME OF REPORTED RUMOR INCREASE

Issues or Events in Community	Over a year		More than 6 months		A few months		A few weeks		A few days		Day of disorder		Total	
	%	No.	%	No.	%	No.	%	No.	%	No.	%	No.	%	No.
No	0	0	0	0	33	1	67	2	73	8	91	10	75	21
Yes	0	0	0	0	67	2	33	1	27	3	9	1	25	7
TOTAL	0	0	0	0	100	3	100	3	100	11	100	11	100	28

and are therefore both an *extension* and *expression* of these conflicts.

4. *Since the event that triggers the racial disorder arises at a peak of community conflict, and since increasing numbers of rumors are tied to community conflict, rumors tend to be associated with precipitating events.*

In its discussion of the "riot process," which was based on an investigation of 24 disorders, the Kerner Commission suggested that the violence occurred at the height of tensions in the community:

> We found that violence was generated by an increasingly disturbed social atmosphere, in which typically not one, but a series of incidents occurred over a period of weeks or months prior to the outbreak of disorders. . . . As we see it, the prior incidents and the reservoir of underlying grievances contributed to a cumulative process of mounting tension that spilled over into violence when the final incident occurred.[33]

Our own findings have demonstrated that increasing numbers of rumors in the pre-disorder period are related to these conflicts and are most likely to occur just before the outbreak. Therefore, is it not logical that rumors should be linked frequently with the precipitating event—that small, but significant, fragment of conflict?

In order to test this assumption, participants in our survey were asked if the disorder was started by an actual incident; and, if it was, whether the incident was intensified by a rumor(s)?[34] Close to 90 percent of the respondents for the non-King disorders (64 out of 74 cases) answered "yes."[35] The remainder left blanks or said such information was not available. Regarding the affirmative cases, rumors were found to accompany the precipitating event one-third of the time. Clearly, this finding does not represent a high degree of rumor formation. Why is our proposition concerning rumors and precipitating events not substantiated by this data?

Two different explanations are possible. One concerns the reliability of the data. As a general rule, many more facts are known about disorders which involve hundreds of people and last several days than about half-hour melees among a dozen or so individuals. Viewed in this light, it is interesting to look at the distribution of disorders by magnitude where rumors accompanied the precipitating event (see Exhibit 5.8). In only 26 percent of the minor disturbances were rumors reported in connection with the triggering incident; by contrast, the figure zoomed to 67 percent for serious disorders. Thus, rumors linked to the precipitating events of smaller disorders may have been under-represented in our data. Since the largest part of our sample was comprised of minor outbreaks, this problem conceivably could have affected our findings.

Exhibit 5.8
DISTRIBUTION OF RUMORS WITH PRECIPITATING EVENT
BY MAGNITUDE (FOR NON-KING DISORDERS)

Rumors with Precipitating Event	Minor %	No.	Medium %	No.	Serious %	No.	Total %	No.
No	61	23	40	8	17	1	50	32
Yes	26	10	40	8	67	4	34	22
Unclear[a]	13	5	20	4	17	1	16	10
TOTAL	100	38	100	20	101	6	100	64

[a]Respondent left the question blank or said information was not available.

But let us look at the issue another way, assuming that our sample is fair and essentially accurate. If this is the case, an entirely different interpretation emerges. Few would question the notion, documented by the Kerner Commission and others, that disturbances generally occur at a peak of community conflict. Indeed, our own study has shown a surge of rumors just before the outbreak. Given this tinderbox situation, the precipitant becomes the match which ignites the disorder. Thus, from a functional standpoint, rumors may at times accompany this incident, but they are not absolutely necessary to bring on the actual outbreak.

This argument is strengthened when we consider that precipitating events and rumors share many characteristics. As noted in the previous chapter, both are tied to the hostile belief system, crystallizing, confirming, intensifying and frequently symbolizing these beliefs. It is significant that the police, exemplifying the belief commonly held among blacks that white authorities frequently abuse their power, have been the principals of many precipitating incidents and rumors as well. Previously, we stated that the hostile beliefs common among the members of each race are a kind of warning system signalling danger. In the same way that rumors help set off this alarm, precipitating events appear to be a similar device which also triggers it at a certain time.

Nonetheless, while rumors are not an essential part of the triggering mechanism, they do occur on occasion. Furthermore, there is some reason to believe that this may be the most critical (as opposed to the most frequent) stage for their appearance. In this connection, let us return to Exhibit 5.8, which shows the distribution of rumors which accompanied precipitating events tabulated according to the size of the disorder. This time, however, let us assume that the data are correct. Once again, the reader will note the clear trend of such rumors among the larger disorders. Of the minor disturbances, only 26 percent had rumors; for medium-sized ones, the figure rose to 40 percent; while the percentage for the larger disorders skyrocketed to 67.

The historical record provides additional support for these findings. In our earlier chapter which examined riots between the two World Wars—most of which were on a large scale—nine out of the 11 cases studied had rumors which accompanied precipitating events. The same point holds for the biggest riots of the sixties. In Watts, immediately following a series of arrests, word spread that a young woman who had just been arrested (who happened to be wearing a smock) was pregnant and had been abused by the police. Erroneous reports also spread concerning the other individuals arrested. In Newark, fresh on the heels of the taxicab driver's arrest came stories that the man had been beaten to death. And in Detroit, a barrage of rumors followed the police raid on a "blind pig" (an after-hours drinking club), including reports that the police had manhandled a woman prisoner and pushed a youth down some stairs.

The strong association of rumors with precipitating events in relation to large-scale disorders suggests that the effects of rumor formation at this time are extremely serious, with important implications for the whole inter-action process: enlarging the inflammatory quality of the precipitating event; affecting the number of people on the scene; the rate at which crowds gather; changes in their mood; and finally, the response of the police and other civil authorities. At the same time, however, it should be emphasized that we are not talking about causes, implying that rumors at this stage necessarily increase the likelihood of bigger disturbances. The point is simply that, given the explosiveness of a situation, which is governed by many factors, rumors which accompany precipitating events can have devastating consequences. It's like throwing an additional match into the powder keg.

This line of argument is reinforced by studies of specific riots. For example, the reader may recall that the riot in Chicago began with the drowning of a black youth. Rumors followed that the boy had died after having been hit by stones thrown by a white person, and that a policeman had refused to arrest the murderer. The commission investigating the riot indicated that the rumor about the policeman's conduct was crucial to the sequence of events. It noted that whites were not altogether hostile in helping to retrieve the body, and added: "There was every possibility that the clash, without the further stimulus of reports of the policeman's conduct, would have quieted down."[36] The Dowling Report on Detroit's 1943 riot made even stronger statements about the calamitous effect of rumors in the precipitating context. For, in the aftermath of fist fights in the Belle Isle area, a rumor was unleashed among a nearby nightclub audience as a black man took to the microphone, urging retaliation for the alleged murder of a black woman and her baby who had supposedly been thrown from a bridge. According to the report, "pandemonium" erupted at once. Marking this episode as the "principal cause" of the ensuing tragedy, the study went so far as to suggest that, were it not for the rumor emanating from the nightclub, the massive riot might have been averted:

> Had the disturbance ended with the incidents at Belle Isle and the bridge approach, none of the deaths occurring in the riot would have resulted. More than 98% of the injuries would have been avoided; upwards of 95% of the reported property damage resulting from the rioting would never have been suffered; less than 3% of the reported law violations would have existed; less than 3% of the arrests made incident to the rioting would have been made.[37]

Even allowing for the Dowling Report's obvious hyperbole, both studies showed an appreciation for the seriousness of rumors at this time.

Our findings and conclusions can be summarized as follows. The proposition that rumors tend to be associated with precipitating events was not supported by our data. Two different interpretations were advanced as possibilities for this lack of confirmation. The first rested on the assumption that fewer such rumors are reported for minor disorders. Since minor disturbances comprised the majority of cases, our findings may have been biased accordingly. The second explanation assumed that there was nothing basically wrong with the data and that our proposition itself was simply off-target. The reason for this might be that precipitating events, sharing many characteristics with rumors, are ordinarily sufficient to trigger a disorder. But, while rumors may not occur at this stage very often, there were also indications that this might be the most critical point for their appearance.

    5. *Since community conflict reaches a new peak during the course of the disorder, the volume of rumors increases at this time.*

Police officials said there was a reported increase in rumors during the disorder for at least 56 percent of the cases (63 out of 112).[38] The true figure is probably even higher, since information was unavailable or blanks were left in 11 percent of the sample. We should also re-emphasize the fact that our figures refer to rumors *reported to the police*, rather than actual rumors per se. Even so, 56 percent represents a majority of the cases and thus supports our proposition.

RUMORS AND THE HOSTILE BELIEF SYSTEM: RATIONALE

As mentioned earlier, two data sources have been used for the purpose of probing the content and character of rumors: first, news stories—most of them from local areas—which provided 295 cases of rumors connected with 224 disorders; and second, 166 cases relating to 22 disorders derived from investigative accounts. In some instances a given source noted the existence of a rumor, but failed to explain what it was about or who was spreading it. This problem was encountered in 28 percent of the rumors cited in news clips and 11 percent of the investigative reports. These cases have been discarded, so that we are left with reduced totals of 211 rumors (representing 181 disorders) from news-clips and 148 rumors (from 22 disorders) via investigative studies. These latter figures are the ones we will use to test our propositions.

In outlining the "process model," we noted that the hostile belief system gives rumors their special character and force, arguing that the content of rumors was largely determined or programmed by these beliefs. As part of the rationale for the ensuing series of propositions, the rumors collected from news clips and investigative accounts have been classified in a manner that is consistent with the hostile belief system (see Exhibits 5.9 and 5.10).

Exhibit 5.9
RUMOR CONTENT AMONG BLACKS BY TYPES OF DATA SOURCE

Rumor Content	News Clips		Invest. Accts.		Total	
	%	No.	%	No.	%	No.
Predictions of violence	7	9	21	12	12	21
Police brutality	46	57	37	21	43	78
White brutality	27	34	14	8	23	42
Conspiracy (by whites)	15	19	25	14	18	33
Other	4	5	4	2	4	7
TOTAL	99	124	101	57	100	181

Exhibit 5.10
RUMOR CONTENT AMONG WHITES BY TYPES OF DATA SOURCE

Rumor Content	News Clips		Invest. Accts.		Total	
	%	No.	%	No.	%	No.
Predictions of violence	36	31	30	27	33	58
Exaggeration or distortion of violence	17	15	27	25	22	40
Black brutality	18	16	7	6	12	22
Conspiracy (by blacks)	21	18	33	30	27	48
Other	8	7	3	3	6	10
TOTAL	100	87	100	91	100	178

Paralleling hostile beliefs, these rumors divide along racial lines in the sense that they tend to arise and circulate among each group about the other. Moreover, underscoring the hostile qualities of the beliefs, these rumors vilify the adversary group—violence perpetrated by blacks is predicted among whites, blacks charge police brutality and so forth. Thus, there appear to be two separate rumor networks; the so-called ghetto grapevine or telegraph is, in effect, matched by a suburban one among whites.

But more important, these data illustrate the functional aspects of rumors in relation to the hostile belief system. First, the rumors are concrete and concise representations —crystallizations—of the beliefs held by each race (see Exhibits 5.11 and 5.12).

Exhibit 5.11
CRYSTALLIZATION FUNCTION
RUMORS AMONG BLACKS

Disorder Place (Date)	Rumor (Category)	Hostile Belief(s)	Source
1. Chicago, Ill. (11/21-24/67)	Black who fell in front of an elevated train was push by white boys. (White brutality)	1. Whites inherently violent.	Chicago *Tribune*, 11/24.
2. Chicago, Ill. (2/21/68)	Black coed beaten up by black students when she went into a cafeteria "reserved" for whites. (White brutality)	1. Whites inherently violent. 2. White people wish to deny blacks their rightful place.	Chicago *Daily Defender*, 2/21.
3. Denver, Col. (6/22-24/68)	Black, wounded in shooting incident with policeman, had carried a plastic toy gun instead of a real one. (Police brutality)	1. Whites inherently violent. 2. Police, symbolizing white authority, abuse their power.	Denver *Post*, 6/23.

Exhibit 5.12
CRYSTALLIZATION FUNCTION
RUMORS AMONG WHITES

Disorder Place (Date)	Rumor (Category)	Hostile Belief(s)	Source
1. Watts, L.A. (8/11-14/65)	Rioters were arming themselves with machine guns. (Exaggeration of violence)	1. Blacks inherently violent.	*Rivers of Blood*[a]
2. Painesville, Ohio (8/16-18/67)	What happened in Newark and Detroit "could happen here" (Prediction of violence)	1. Blacks inherently violent.	Cleveland *Plain Dealer*, 8/27.
3. Orangeburg, S.C. (2/5-8/68)	Black Power people have plans to do away with town's waterworks, lights, gas and telephone service. (Conspiracy)	1. Blacks constantly conspire to undermine the system.	*The Orangeburg Massacre*[b]

[a]Robert Conot, *Rivers of Blood, Years of Darkness, The Unforgettable Classic Account of the Watts Riot* (New York: William Morrow, 1968), p. 218.

[b]Jack Nelson and Jack Bass, *The Orangeburg Massacre* (New York: World, 1970), p. 63.

We should emphasize here that only the most salient of the hostile beliefs have been listed. Virtually every one of the rumors among whites contains the implicit belief that blacks are pushing too hard—that they are taking deadly aim at the position of whites and that therefore *the status quo must be maintained.* The opposite holds true for blacks, who believe the system is oppressive—that whites wish to deprive them of their rightful place as equals and that therefore *the existing order must be altered.*

Symbols remain an important feature of rumors and can be viewed as part of rumor's crystallizing function. Among blacks, the police, representing white authority, are the most obvious symbol. In both our news clip and investigative account samples, police brutality rumors ranked first among blacks, with 46 and 37 percent of the totals respectively. Examples of such rumors include: a shooting incident in Lorain, Ohio, in which a white bartender fatally shot a young black and which was followed by a rumor that the police had arrested the white man and then let him go; during a disturbance in Detroit, the police were accused of beating black students with baseball bats; and in Orangeburg, S.C., the police reportedly had orders to "shoot the long-haired niggers first."

Other symbols were found in rumors among blacks. Just before a protest rally in Houston, word spread that a member of the Ku Klux Klan—that venerable symbol of militant white resistance—had shot a black child. And stirring black fears in Jackson, Miss., was a story that Charles Evers and his wife had been gunned down in Natchez. Evers is, of course, a prominent Southern figure in the civil rights movement and the brother of the slain activist Medgar.

But symbols are by no means the exclusive property of blacks. For example, a story reverberated through the white community in Tampa that Stokely Carmichael,

personifying black power, was en route to the city and had
reserved a room at the Sheraton Hotel. Two symbols for
the price of one rumor were embodied in a tale that
floated through Richmond, California. At the time of a
disorder there, it was said that Black Panthers (representing violence and radical change) planned to burn down city
hall (the seat of the white power structure). The latter is
something of an investigator's dream rumor, since it is such
a perfect illustration of a fancied assault on the established
order and the crystallization of so many hostile beliefs
held by whites.

We contended earlier that rumors affected closure
between a hostile belief(s) and its embodiment as a "fact."
This confirming function was readily apparent in the data
collected. Take, for example, the conspiracy rumor that
circulated in Detroit's suburbs at the time of King's
assassination, i.e., that blacks planned to systematically kill
children in white neighborhoods. This rumor confirmed
the belief that black people are naturally violent, forever
plotting against whites and simply will not stay in their
place in the ghetto. Each justified the other: the rumor
"proved" the beliefs, while the beliefs explained the
rumor. Clearly, rumors are not simply a refinement or
crystallization of hostile beliefs, but a realization of them
as well—a kind of corroboration attesting to their truth
and validity.

Rumors also serve to reinforce hostile beliefs, making
them stronger and more acute. For example, the many
rumors among whites that fall into the category of
"exaggeration or distortion of violence" demonstrate this
intensification function. Overstatement or the twisting of
reality is a common means by which intensification takes
place: in Watts, a couple of drunks were perceived as
ominous snipers; in Camden, New Jersey, an interracial
brawl between some students aroused fears that "hun-

dreds" were involved in racial plots; and in another New Jersey town called Piscataway, a few fist fights were transformed into rumors of a "race riot." On August 27, 1967, the Cleveland *Plain Dealer* ran a news story about a disturbance in Lorain, Ohio, which contained a perfect illustration of the intensification function of rumors at work:

> A Greyhound bus with one Negro passenger aboard became a busload of troublemakers. A car with a Negro family in it became a car full of outsiders looking for trouble. The family was from New York and stopped in the city to eat lunch. To others a patrol car in a Negro neighborhood meant that police were increasing patrols and were on the alert for trouble.

As part of this function, rumors sometimes express the paranoid fantasies of a group. For example, feelings of persecution can be discerned in horror or atrocity stories—the more details, the more credible the story. The rather elaborate rumor that follows frightened many white people in the environs of Philadelphia shortly before a riot that occurred there in 1964. The tale was told that the Black Brothers, a radical black nationalist cult with its headquarters in New York City, had intended to send secret agents into Philadelphia "to create a holocaust." Six well-dressed blacks reportedly had circulated through the slums of North Central and South Philadelphia for over a month, trying to engineer a teenage rumble on the last Saturday in August. These sinister, albeit mythical, characters even distributed liquor for the purpose of stirring up trouble.[39]

Age and sex factors are often an important dimension of these fantasies, for criminal acts committed against those less able to handle themselves physically are especially reprehensible. This explains why old people, women and children are the subject of so many rumors. Black citizens in Detroit, for example, were enraged by a report that police on horseback had trampled an elderly woman to death; in Philadelphia following the arrest of a quarreling couple who were intoxicated, word spread that a pregnant black woman had been beaten to death by a white policeman; in Tampa, Florida, after a gambling raid in a black neighborhood, it was said that the police had shot and killed a two-month-old black baby; and in Buffalo, New York, there was a story that blacks had mutilated an eight-year-old white boy.

At times, such rumors may have an eerie, wild, fantastic quality about them. In Watts, rioters were reputed to have sucked out eggshells and filled them with gasoline to make innocent-looking Molotov cocktails. Not to be out-fantasized by whites, many blacks were convinced that white citizens were going to drop bombs on them from the air. Meanwhile, at the time of Detroit's major riot in 1967, rumor had it that a number of persons had been killed and stuffed down sewers. The latter example is reminiscent of the Bubbly Creek rumors that circulated around the time of the Chicago riot of 1919, when people thought that numerous bodies—none of which was ever recovered—had been dumped into the water.

It may be difficult to accept the notion that more or less well-balanced people could succumb to some of these rumors. Certainly, it would be easier to attribute them to the work of a few disturbed or demented individuals. But, ultimately, the key to understanding all this can be found within our social system. The tragic fact is that the inequities within this system have significantly colored, perhaps warped, our perceptions. Given the nature of things, some exaggerations and distortions of reality are to be expected as part of the "normal" course of events, whereby the incredible becomes credible; the unbelievable, believable; the nonsensical, "sensical."

Previously, the point was made that rumors are almost always preceded by an event of some kind. This event was broadly defined as an incident, issue, grievance, complaint or happening. Challenging the traditional view of this event as insignificant, we argued that the event was conflict-inducing—an expression or outgrowth of existing racial discord. An inspection of the data seems to support our judgment that these events represent an element of conflict—small, perhaps, but significant—and that rumors link hostile beliefs to this kind of event (see Exhibits 5.13 and 5.14).

This perspective is not meant to dismiss all other factors. In particular, we must acknowledge that some degree of ambiguity is present in many situations. For example, the setting in Tampa (exhibit 5.14), in which a group of black construction workers happened on the scene of a disorder, could easily have been interpreted as a menacing mob. However, we must also bear in mind that the transformation of an innocent group of construction workers into club-wielding rioters is thoroughly consistent with white perceptions about blacks. Indeed, our finding that "black brutality" is a common theme in rumors among whites suggests that certain constants are at work—in this case, hostile beliefs. The point, then, is not to dismiss outright other factors such as ambiguity, but to emphasize that, by themselves, they are not sufficient to explain the content of rumors in connection with racial disorders.

Having attempted to provide a framework for rumors and hostile beliefs, let us move to the testing of our second and final set of propositions.

6. *Due to the complementary aspect of hostile beliefs held by the white group and black group, there will be some overlap in terms of thematic content for rumors circulating among both groups.*

Exhibit 5.13
LINKAGE FUNCTION
RUMORS AMONG BLACKS

Disorder	Hostile Belief(s)	Rumor (Category)	Event	Source
1. Washington, D.C. 10/8/68	Police, symbolizing white authority, abuse their power.	Man had been shot for jaywalking. (Police brutality)	Black man fatally shot by policeman after apparent attack on officer.	*The Washington Post,* 10/9.
2. Swanquarter, N.C. 11/11/68	System forever conspiring against blacks.	Black students would still be in segregated classes when they attended a white school. (Conspiracy)	Federally imposed school integration plan.	Norfolk *Virginian-Pilot,* 11/12.
3. Ithaca, N.Y. 4/12-20/69	System forever conspiring against blacks. Whites inherently violent.	Armed vigilante groups preparing to mount an attack. (Conspiracy)	Unknown persons threw burning cross on the porch of black women's university cooperative.	*The New York Times,* 4/20, 27.

Exhibit 5.14
LINKAGE FUNCTION
RUMORS AMONG WHITES

Disorder	Hostile Belief(s)	Rumor (Category)	Event	Source
1. Tampa, Fla. 6/11-16/67	Blacks inherently violent.	20 Negro males massing with clubs wearing levis, no shirts. (Black brutality)	Construction workers on the job during disorder.	After-Action Report[a]
2. Orangeburg, S.C. 2/5-8/68	Blacks constantly conspire to undermine the system.	Militants would kill the bowling alley's owner and son. (Conspiracy)	Protests over a segregated bowling alley.	The Orangeburg Massacre[b]
3. Augusta, Ga. 5/11-12/70	Blacks inherently violent. Blacks have a definite place. The status quo must be maintained.	Threats against Gary Player and property of Augusta National course. (Prediction of violence)	Masters golf tournament including participation of South African golfer Gary Player.	Augusta, Ga. and Jackson State University[c]

[a]Tampa Police Department, *After-Action Report*, Pt. 1 (mimeo), p. 11.

[b]Nelson and Bass, *The Orangeburg Massacre*, p. 63.

[c]William Winn with D.L. Inman, *Augusta, Georgia and Jackson State University: Southern Episodes in a National Tragedy* (Southern Regional Council, June 1970), p. 17.

Throughout this book we have maintained that rumors are an expression of hostile beliefs and, furthermore, that each belief set is one of two completing parts reflecting parallel or similar concerns. If these assumptions are correct, some similarity of themes should be found in the rumors common among both races.

To test this propostion, the rumors collected from our news clips and investigative accounts were combined and fitted into categories by race, giving us two samples: 181 for blacks, 178 for whites (see Exhibit 5.15).

A few words about the categories are in order here. In the majority of cases, the placement of rumors into individual categories was a simple task. Nevertheless, we should note that the categories themselves are not entirely mutually exclusive—there were times when a particular rumor contained elements of more than one category. For example, the report that blacks planned to systematically kill children in white neighborhoods contained several themes, including prediction of violence, black or civilian brutality and conspiracy. With this kind of case, the writer simply determined which theme seemed most salient. Many of the rumors falling into the category "prediction of violence" were of a general nature ("trouble is in the air," "our town is going to be hit next," and so on). Brutality rumors usually referred to a related act or event that had already taken place. At the same time, the conspiracy theme was readily apparent in the notion that a plot was under way. Therefore, this particular rumor (and ones like it) were placed in the conspiracy category. The point, then, is to notify the reader that the categories are not completely exclusive of one another and that, at times, some degree of subjective judgment was required in assigning rumors to a particular category.

Looking at Exhibit 5.15 we see five distinct rumor categories. Of these, three are present in varying degrees

Exhibit 5.15
RUMOR CONTENT BY RACE

Rumor Content	Blacks		Whites		Total	
	%	No.	%	No.	%	No.
Police brutality	43	78	0	0	22	78
Exaggeration or distortion of violence	0	1	22	40	11	41
Predictions of violence	12	21	33	58	22	79
Civilian brutality[a]	23	42	12	22	18	64
Conspiracy	18	33	27	48	23	81
Other	3	6	6	10	4	16
TOTAL	99	181	100	178	100	359

[a]For blacks, civilian brutality refers to specifically harmful acts allegedly committed by whites; the opposite holds true for whites.

among both racial groups: predictions of violence, civilian brutality and conspiracy. Police brutality (as rumored among blacks) and exaggeration or distortion of violence (among whites) were the only types of rumors confined to one group.[40] These findings, therefore, confirm our proposition concerning an overlap in themes.

But let us not stop with the verification of our proposition, for some interesting and important questions are raised by these data. First, why were two of the themes restricted to a single group? Why were corresponding themes distributed so differently among each race? For example, can we account for our finding that predictions of violence showed up least often among blacks (12 percent) and most often among whites (33 percent)? Finally, are there any qualitative differences in those rumors that are common to both races? For example, does a conspiracy rumor mean the same thing to a black person as it does to someone who is white?

To answer these questions, we must return to the beginning—to the fact of an inequitable system, with whites occupying the superior, and blacks the inferior position. The imbalance within our system has given rise to two central preoccupations which translate more formally into separate guiding principles: for whites, it is order; for blacks, justice. These principles are the distinguishing ingredients which make up the beliefs of each race. As such, they have implications for the type and manner of rumors operating within each group.

Given the interest of whites, it is logical that themes reflecting their concerns about order should predominate in their widely held rumors. A fear of imminent violence, a tendency to magnify the amount of violence (such as property damage) that occurs and an almost incessant emphasis on conspiracy are all in keeping with perceived threats against the social order. Such rumors accounted for over 80 percent of the total among whites. Similarly, as an aggrieved minority trying to break through the wall of oppression, it is understandable that two-thirds of the rumors among blacks involved the theme of "brutality." Civilian brutality (white against black) rumors alone were found nearly twice as often as compared to those among whites—23 to 12 percent.

If blacks are "hung up" on the police, whites are equally fixated on property ("the blacks are coming to our suburbs, etc."). It is all—or, primarily— a matter of personal interest. However, we must be careful not to oversimplify, at the expense of our point. In particular, the matter of immediate reality merits some consideration. For example, the intense preoccupation of whites with "order" themes during the most recent cycle of *dis*order, was only natural; after all, blacks *were* the main perpetrators in this case. Moreover, during crisis situations people have a tendency to brace themselves for the worst—hence the unverified reports of more violence, more looting, more sniping, more property damage, etc. Therefore, let us recognize that the salience of rumor themes is, at least to some extent, also influenced by the immediate circumstances involved.

Thus far, we have attempted to explain the presence and prominence of rumor themes, three of which were found among both races. But are there any qualitative differences within the themes that overlap? If so, can they be interpreted in the same way?

A closer inspection of the data indicates important distinctions for two of the themes. First, conspiracy. Let us begin by noting that conspiracy rumors among both races had some common characteristics. By definition, there was always a sense of planned activity or action intended to inflict harm on some person or group. The antagonists were invariably the same—i.e., members of the opposite race. Sometimes, the alleged conspirators were ordinary citizens. At other times, they were comprised of quasi-organized groups, such as gangs. Or, they were part of a formal organization: the Ku Klux Klan, the Minutemen, the John Birch Society, on one side; the Black Panthers, the Black Muslims, SNCC, the Communists, on the other. Some notion of the size of the conspiracy was occasionally reinforced by citing specific numbers. A force of 2,000 white men was supposed to march into Watts; "hundreds" of blacks were reportedly involved in a racial plot in Camden, New Jersey. The same feeling for size was conveyed by references to "busloads," car loads," even "truckloads" of the enemy on its way. Moreover, the threatening quality of these rumors was enhanced at times by allusions to violent means of destruction: through the use of guns, ammunition, dynamite, as well as talk of "race *wars.*"

But these similarities were predictable. Far more important was the different emphasis in rumor content stemming, once again, from the basic concern of each group. Whites were extremely afraid that the existing order was in danger—so, danger might be signalled to them in a vague, hazy sort of way: through reports of plans by blacks to stir up trouble, engineer rumbles and cause disturbances. But frequently, more specific targets were mentioned. These targets tended to focus on property, that important symbol of white power. Hence, various plots were attributed to blacks involving plans to destroy downtown business areas; ransack suburban shopping centers; invade white neighborhoods; do away with vital services (electricity, gas telephone, etc.); even burn entire cities.

There were also fears among blacks about armed vigilantes and car loads of whites "coming to get" *them*. But, more often than not, their attention centered on alleged acts by whites which, in the eyes of blacks, were profoundly insulting, insensitive or unjust. For example, at the time of disturbance in Wilkinsburg, Pennsylvania, black students were angered by a report that some young whites had banded together to form an organization called the ANA—Anti-Negro Association. In Louisville, Kentucky, Stokely Carmichael's failure to appear at a rally was cited as "another honky trick." Many blacks were convinced that whites were preventing his airplane from landing, an unverified rumor which helped set off a disturbance.

A large portion of the conspiracy rumors common among blacks might be subtitled "official brutality," for they involved acts or policies by the system and its representatives regarded as discriminatory and unfair. As an example, young blacks in San Francisco charged that the school administration had rigged the homecoming queen elections. In Swanquarter, North Carolina, a federally imposed integration plan was followed by a rumor that there would be segregated classes in a white school. And, in the aftermath of the fatal shooting of three students by the police in Orangeburg, South Carolina, black adults gave serious consideration to a theory that a deliberate effort had been made to kill Cleveland Sellers, a frequent visitor to the campus, who was popular with a black power-oriented student organization. They cited as circumstantial evidence the similarities in physical size, clothing, or hair style among the fatalities to those characteristics of Mr. Sellers. In fact, 61 percent of the conspiracy rumors among blacks (20 out of 33 cases) also fall under the heading of "official brutality."

The term "outside agitator" further underlines the difference in conspiracy rumors by race. Not one such reference was found in the rumors among blacks, whereas the term was frequently employed by whites to describe the conspirators. Each word is significant. "Outside" suggests a kind of boundary; one gets a feeling of exclusiveness, of not belonging, of distance. "Agitation" refers to turbulent, violent action. Putting the words together, we get a picture of a group which does not belong, which is out to upset the existing arrangement—a picture which, as we have seen, is thoroughly consistent with white perceptions about blacks.

There was also some notion of "agitation" by whites against blacks, in rumors among the latter. But, significantly, as a general rule, the culprits simply came from another part of the same town—whereas, among whites, "outside" frequently meant out-of-town, out-of-state, even out-of-country. The more "outside" the agitator, the more menacing-sounding the rumor. Thus, in Paterson, New Jersey, a carload of blacks were reportedly on their way from New York; in Tampa, busloads were supposedly coming all the way from Alabama; while in Orangeburg, South Carolina, white citizens stopped the police chief wherever he went to tell him that black militants were fast moving in "from other states."

There is a certain irony, as well as logic, in the fact that the in-group in our society should be so preoccupied with those on the outside. But that is part of the price whites have traditionally paid to retain their favored position. In any event, it is clear that the guiding principles of "order" vs. "justice" have been brought into play once again, and serve to explain the differences in conspiracy rumors between the races.

Earlier we found that predictive rumors of violence flowed through the black and white communities alike, although they appear to be more common among whites. An examination of the specific content of this type of rumor reveals another qualitative difference.

Whites almost always (in 57 out of 58 cases) perceived themselves as the objects of violence, with blacks as the aggressors. Fear was the hallmark of these rumors: fear that this store would be hit and that shop burned; fear that school children would be harmed and neighborhoods stormed; fear of "more unruly demonstrations," "more rowdyism" and "more explosions."

The reverse of this pattern did not generally hold for blacks. Only 19 percent of such predictive rumors among blacks involved imminent attacks by whites (4 out of 21 cases). Instead, more than half the rumors—52 percent— centered around threats of violence by *blacks against whites*. To illustrate: following an attack by 200 whites, most of them off-duty policemen, on Black Panthers inside a Brooklyn courthouse, the black community bristled with rumors of "retribution." A police communications lieutenant said that an anonymous phone call had warned of 700 blacks converging together to shoot policemen in retaliation for the incident. No further violence occurred, however. In Washington, D.C., rumor was piled upon rumor when a report that soul singer James Brown had been assassinated was followed by another having to do with "getting even with Whitey." In this case, the latter rumor proved to be true, when violence erupted for several days.

The remaining cases of rumors among blacks (29 percent) fell into a more general category of trouble-brewing, with implicit overtones that blacks would soon act ("Something's gonna happen tonight," "We'll burn the whole town this weekend," and so on). Thus, more than half and possibly as much as 80 percent of the predictive rumors of violence by blacks had whites or the white community as their principal target.

While fear was the distinguishing feature of such rumors among whites, anger mainly charcterized those held among blacks. The reason for this is not difficult to fathom. Indeed, we need look no farther than the context of the disorders themselves, for the riots were an overt expression of tremendous hostility and resentment on the part of blacks. Mixed in with these feelings was a demand for retribution—a desire to pay back whites for all the years of oppression by them. In 1963, the year which marked the inception of a new cycle of disorders, a black-owned motel in Birmingham and the home of Martin Luther King's brother, were bombed. Two days later in Chicago, a couple of black youths assaulted the mayor's eighteen-year-old nephew, shouting: "This is for Birmingham." In recounting the incident in their book, Carmichael and Hamilton add significantly: "It was for Birmingham, true, but it was for three hundred and fifty years of history before Birmingham as well."[41] Similarly, the attitude of many blacks was expressed in Conot's account of the Watts riot:

> and the word had spread from door to door with the rapidity of a jungle telegraph that Watts was going to be hit next; that Watts was going to be hit next because Whitey . . . must be driven out; because this was the day of reckoning with *the man,* the day of retribution when the soul folk would pay him back for all the years of anguish.[42]

This "anguish" felt by blacks was expressed in actual violence, as well as many predictions of violence—predictions which were not always borne out or substantiated. Besides reflecting the new assertiveness of blacks, these rumors were another way of confronting Whitey, although not necessarily on the conscious level—daring him, baiting him, challenging him, punishing him. The open anger of blacks had its counterpart in the aroused fears among whites of imminent violence, frequently disproportionate to the amount which actually occurred. Therefore, the different focus of predictive rumors of violence among each race has as its origin their immediate historical context.

In this section, we have verified our proposition that some rumor themes are complementary and therefore occur among both races. We also found quantitative, as well as qualitative, differences in these themes. Finally, in order to interpret these differences, we examined a variety of factors, principally group interest, historical context and immediate setting.

7. *Because rumors are tied to the hostile belief system, the salience of themes common among each race does not differ markedly at different stages of the disorder.*

In assuming that rumors are related to the hostile belief system, we would expect the distribution of themes among the races to be roughly the same, regardless of the stage of the disorder. For example, police brutality rumors, comprising 43 percent of the rumors among blacks, should logically appear in approximately the same proportion before the disorder, in connection with precipitating events[43] and during the actual outbreak. To test this proposition, the data were divided into two samples by race, while each rumor was designated according to its first known appearance on the scene (see Exhibits 5.16 and 5.17).

Exhibit 5.16
RUMOR CONTENT BY DISORDER STAGE (AMONG BLACKS)

Rumor Content	Before		Precip. Event		During		Total	
	%	No.	%	No.	%	No.	%	No.
Predictions of violence	11	4	2	1	19	16	12	21
Police brutality	20	7	61	38	39	33	43	78
White brutality	23	8	27	17	20	17	23	42
Conspiracy	37	13	10	6	17	14	18	33
Other	9	3	0	0	4	4	4	7
TOTAL	100	35	100	62	99	84	100	181

Exhibit 5.17
RUMOR CONTENT BY DISORDER STAGE (AMONG WHITES) [a]

Rumor Content	Before		Precip. Event		During		Total	
	%	No.	%	No.	%	No.	%	No.
Predictions of violence	50	13	25	1	30	44	33	58
Exaggeration or distortion of violence	0	0	0	0	27	40	22	40
Black brutality	0	0	75	3	13	19	12	22
Conspiracy	42	11	0	0	25	37	27	48
Other	8	2	0	0	5	8	6	10
TOTAL	100	26	100	4	100	148	100	178

[a]There were relatively few disorders during the sixties in which an incident precipitated a disorderly or violent response by whites and even fewer instances where rumors were found to accompany the event. The number in our rumor sample was 4, compared with 62 among blacks. Therefore, because of the small number of such cases, we will confine our discussion of rumors and disorder stages among whites to two, not three, time periods.

The reader will note that, for both samples, the actual number of cases was weighted in favor of rumors occurring "during" the disorder. This situation is understandable when we consider that more information from news sources and investigative accounts was available for the actual, rather than pre-disorder, period. However, there is no reason to believe our findings will be affected by this, since we are dealing essentially with percentages, not real numbers per se.

Turning our attention to the figures themselves, major differences are immediately apparent. Among blacks, police brutality rumors comprised 20 percent of the rumors in the pre-disorder period, skyrocketing to just over 60 of those associated with precipitating events, and falling to about 40 percent during the outbreak itself. Conspiracy rumors among blacks did not fare much better, with percentages of 37, 10 and 17, respectively. The only consistency found was for white brutality rumors, where all the figures were in the vicinity of 23 percent.

The statistics for whites were equally varied. Predictive rumors of violence accounted for 50 percent of those reported in the period before the disorder, but fell to 30 during the outbreak itself. No black brutality rumors showed up initially, although they amounted to 13 percent of the total, during the final stage. Conspiracy rumors started at 42 percent, but then dropped to 25.

Thus, no real consistencies in the distribution of rumor themes by stage emerged among either race. The jigsaw quality of these figures makes it glaringly evident that our proposition has not been borne out.

In searching for an explanation, two primary factors emerge. One is the subject population, a contextual factor. During the latest cycle of disorders, with some notable exceptions already mentioned, blacks were the active participants, with whites playing a more passive or reactive role. In the period leading up to the disorder, blacks were usually the ones who "made" an issue—of schools, the police, the welfare system, living conditions and the like. And, of course, they were the main initiators of the disorder itself. It seems fair to say that, were there no blacks, in most cases, nobody would have showed up for the riot. (Of course, there is a great deal of truth in the corollary that, in the ultimate sense, were there no whites, there would not have been a riot to come to.) This is not to imply that whites had no grievances. Busing, for example, was probably more of an issue among whites than blacks. But, on the whole, whites were less inclined to take the initiative in articulating and acting upon their concerns. On this occasion at least, blacks did indeed seize the time.

The different roles of these two groups had definite implications for rumor formation by stage. Since blacks were the group most directly involved in these events, rumors among them appeared on a wide-ranging basis at all times. Every kind of rumor was present among blacks, to some degree, at every state of the disorder (see Exhibit 5.16).

This was not the case with whites; because of their less active role, rumors occurred among them in a more limited way. During the pre-disorder period, when whites were least involved, only two of the four kinds of rumors appeared: predictions of violence and conspiracy. However, by the time the actual disorder broke out, a different picture had emerged. Because of the impact of the news media and the disruption of their normal routine along with occasionally active participation, whites were more directly engaged in what was happening. As their role was altered, they apparently became susceptible to a greater variety of rumors. Significantly, all four rumor themes were operative at this stage (see Exhibit 5.17). Therefore, it seems that the degree to which a group is involved in the disorder situation has some bearing on when and what kinds of rumors will emerge.

Time is the other major factor. On one level, time is important in the sense of the circumstance or opportunity of a given moment. To take the most obvious example, rumors which exaggerated or distorted the nature or amount of violence could not very well have appeared *before* there was any disorder. All such rumors had to emerge in the final stage, during the outbreak itself.

That police brutality rumors might be affected by time is less obvious. The reader will recall that police brutality rumors ranked first among blacks, with an overall percentage of 43. This finding underscored the intensity of feelings which blacks have toward the police; indeed, over the years the police—their practices, policies and behavior —have been a continuing source of friction within the community. In our own survey, police officials themselves cited "the police" as a key source of conflict prior to the disorders. Thus, the solid figure of 20 percent representing police brutality rumors in the first stage (before the disorder) is consistent with our previous findings and all that we know about traditional relationships between the two groups. But why did the figures jump so dramatically at the other two stages, to 61 and 39 percent? The answer seems to bring us back to circumstance and opportunity. First of all, many precipitating events involved police actions. In 12 out of the 24 disturbances investigated by the Kerner Commission, the police were involved in the final incident preceding the actual disorder. It is therefore logical to assume that, on those occasions where rumors arose in the precipitating context, the police would frequently be their subject. The same point holds true for the last stage, when the interaction between civilians and civil authorities often continued. Thus, the increased prominence of police brutality rumors corresponds to more direct contact between blacks and the police at these particular stages in time.

Time intrudes in another way as well. The interval between an actual event and the emergence of a rumor concerning that event may vary. Conspiracy rumors, in particular, are a way of explaining or interpreting an event(s) which requires time—time to consider what will happen; time to ponder what has happened; time to think about why something has happened. In this sense, the time factor seems to explain why conspiracy rumors rarely show up in the precipitating context (only 10 percent among blacks), when the chain of events often occurs incredibly fast. It is also noteworthy that conspiracy rumors among both whites and blacks ranked first in the pre-disorder period, but fell to third and last place respectively during the disorder itself, which frequently had a more frenzied pace.

Thus our findings indicate that, despite our proposition, content does indeed vary by stage. But these findings do not deny the essential relationship between rumors and hostile beliefs. The interpretation of the data suggest that other factors—contextual and temporal—must be recognized alongside this relationship as influencing the distribution of rumor themes at different points.

8. *Owing to the perseverence of the hostile belief system, within each race thematic content is similar for disorders—both past and present-day.*

We have already pointed out that our social system is not completely static—conditions have changed, anti-Negro attitudes held by whites have been modified, while the actual status of the blacks has improved. But all of these developments are more in the nature of dents, rather than real blows, to a system which, by and large, has remained intact. As it is, the barriers between the races—economic, social, political, psychological—continue to be enormous; both groups have yet to "overcome." Given this situation, the hostile belief system is still a potent force, retaining a large measure of its strength and resilience down through the years. If this assessment is correct, especially in reference to the hostile belief system, we can anticipate that rumor themes within each race should be basically the same, regardless of time.

To test this proposition, we will compare rumors from past and more recent riots. One set of data pertains to riots during World Wars I and II. The reader will recall from Chapter 2 that most of our information about rumors during the earlier cycles came from comprehensive studies, either of an official nature (the Chicago Commission on Race Relations, the LaGuardia Commission, the Dowling Committee) or in the form of independent works (Rudwick on the East St. Louis riot, Waskow's general treatment of World War I riots, and so on. Primary sources were used sparingly and, more often than note, merely verified details from these larger studies. Thus, in the interests of maintaining the comparability of the data, we will omit our newspaper sample in regard to 1960s disorders, relying on our in-depth accounts—at least for analytic purposes.

Despite the different time periods, the two sets of data share some important characteristics. Both represent a small number of disorders: 11 cases for World Wars I and II combined, 22 for the sixties;[44] both yield similar amounts of usable rumors per disorder—6.1 rumors for past disorders (11 disorders, 67 rumors),[45] compared to 6.7 for the recent ones (22 disorders, 148 rumors); both encompass disorders from every section of the country; and finally, both are weighted in favor of the larger disorders. On this last point, we might add that the largest riots in history are included in the data: East St. Louis

(1917), Chicago (1919), Detroit (1943), Watts (1965), Newark (1967) and Detroit (1967). In fact, by applying our ranking scheme to our recent sample, 14 out of 22 disorders qualify as serious or major.

The bias of our data regarding magnitude raises the issue of our ability to generalize about rumor themes for disorders of all sizes. After all, most disorders that occurred during the sixties (and in all probability those during the previous cycles) were on a relatively small scale. Our newspaper sample is therefore highly useful in this respect. Applying the ranking scheme used earlier to this sample, the breakdown of disorders is as follows: 57 percent, minor; 29 percent, medium; 11 percent, serious; and 3 percent, major. It is clear that, in keeping with the actual trend of the 1960s, smaller disturbances are most heavily represented. Moreover, if we refer to Exhibits 5.9 and 5.10, which demonstrate rumor themes among the races by data source, two findings are immediately apparent. One is that the rumors fit into precisely the same categories, regardless of the source. The same themes widespread among blacks via news stories were the same ones that showed up in investigative accounts; this was also true for whites. Secondly, where percentages were concerned, there were only a few, minor differences in the distribution of themes. Among blacks, police brutality rumors ranked first in the news clip and investigative account samples alike. Predictions of violence and conspiracy rumors among whites held either the number one or two position in both samples. In fact, in dealing with the total number of themes among both races (8), with a single exception, each theme ranked within one place of itself in the other data. For example, black brutality rumors finished third in the news clip sample and fourth in the investigative accounts. Exaggeration or distortion of violence rumors were third in the investigative accounts and fourth in the news clip sample. The only real difference was in terms of white brutality rumors, which occupied the number two spot in the news clips, but wound up last in the investigative accounts.

An examination of the data, then, suggests that the size of the disorder has no bearing on the emergence of themes; nor does it seem to affect the distribution of themes in any significant way. Let us therefore turn our attention to the business at hand—namely, a comparison of rumor content for past and present-day disorders.

For this purpose, we have taken each set of data, listing all of the various categories or themes by race. Next, individual rumors were alternately counted and given a percentage number within each sample.[46] For instance, predictions of violence among whites appeared four times, accounting for 10 percent of the sample of earlier disorders. This same kind of rumor compared with 27 cases representing 30 percent of the more recent sample. The results of these tabulations appear as Exhibits 5.18 and 5.19:

Exhibit 5.18
RUMOR CONTENT BY HISTORICAL PERIOD (AMONG BLACKS)

Rumor Content	World Wars I & II		1960s	
	%	No.	%	No.
White brutality	38	10	14	8
Police brutality	23	6	37	21
Predictions of violence	8	2	21	12
Conspiracy	23	6	25	14
Other	8	2	4	2
TOTAL	100	26	101	57

Exhibit 5.19
RUMOR CONTENT BY HISTORICAL PERIOD (AMONG WHITES)

Rumor Content	World Wars I & II		1960s	
	%	No.	%	No.
Rape	20	8	0	0
Black brutality	29	12	7	6
Predictions of violence	10	4	30	27
Exaggeration or distortion of violence	12	5	27	25
Conspiracy	27	11	33	30
Other	2	1	3	3
TOTAL	100	41	100	91

The reader will note that every one of the four themes common among blacks was found in past and present-day riots alike—although not to the same degree. But for rape rumors, the same was true for whites regarding three out of four rumor themes. In almost every instance, then, a given type of rumor known to have occurred in earlier riot cycles was repeated in the most recent one, thereby confirming our hypothesis.

While verifying our proposition, these findings raise two related issues. First, why did one rumor theme fail to show up in our recent data? Rumors of sexual assaults against white women ranked second in our sample of earlier riots with 20 percent, but failed to show up at all in our more recent sample. Out of 91 cases, not one such rumor was uncovered. The second issue involves the distribution of rumor themes. While the presence of certain themes among both races was essentially the same in both samples, their percentages varied greatly. White brutality rumors, for example, comprised 38 percent of the World War I and II rumors, but made up only 14 percent of those reported for the 1960s. How can we account for these differences?

With regard to the first issue, there are at least three possible explanations. The first two explanations, assuming the existence of rape rumors, relate directly to the data. The problems of data collection, given the elusiveness of rumors, were mentioned earlier. It is therefore quite conceivable that this type of rumor simply failed to come to the attention of researchers. This argument, however, is not terribly convincing in light of evidence from our other data source—i.e., our news clips. Consulting this sample among whites, we did find two rumors involving rape. During a 1968 disturbance in Trenton, New Jersey, a local newspaper reported that hundreds of young whites began moving downtown when an unfounded rumor was spread that a white girl had been raped by 15 black youths. A year later, a Providence paper ran a story in which a local official speculated that a disorder there might have been the outraged reaction to a false report that two white girls had been assaulted and threatened with rape.[47]

Nevertheless, these rumors accounted for only two out of 87 cases, and thus appear to have been little more than isolated events. Were we to combine our news clip and investigative account samples, the grand total of rape rumors would stand at two out of 178. Therefore, the argument that rape rumors failed to appear in not one, but two, data sources, simply because of chance, does not carry too much weight.

There is, however, another, more plausible explanation pertaining to the data, which involves the subject matter itself. In the past, crimes of violence, including rape, were generally synonymous with blacks in the public mind and the press bore an important responsibility for this—all too often engaging in needless sensationalism, distortion and misreporting. At the same time, in recent years the press has displayed greater sensitivity in this area, which has resulted in more balanced reporting. A by-product of the increased responsibility of the press has been an under-standable reluctance to devote much newspaper space to reports of rape—particularly if they have not yet been confirmed. The same point would undoubtedly hold true for those persons engaged in more detailed accounts of disorders. Thus, rape rumors might well have flourished among whites during the disorders of the 1960s, but still be absent from the data, given the explosiveness of the subject and more recent thinking about how to handle it.

A final alternative is that our findings *were* correct and that rape rumors have all but disappeared from the scene. If this were the case, the validity of one hostile belief would be open to serious question. The reader may recall from Chapter 4 that many whites believe that blacks are unusually promiscuous. Rape rumors would be consistent with this belief. However, we also cited some evidence suggesting that this particular belief had weakened in recent years, although it was difficult to gauge just how much. Thus, we must seriously consider—or at least raise the possibility of—a slight modification in our notion of the hostile belief system, which would explain the virtual disappearance of one type of rumor.

At this point, we can simply say that, out of eight themes found among the races, only one failed to show up in past and present-day disorders alike and that several different explanations were offered as possibilities for this phenomenon.

The issue of how (as opposed to which) rumor themes were distributed goes beyond our hypothesis, since our immediate objective was to demonstrate similarities in thematic content for disorders from a historical perspective. Thus, strictly speaking, the frequency with which themes show up in a given period is not relevant here. Nevertheless, the availability of figures affords us the opportunity to explore what factors, if any, govern the prominence—not merely the presence—of themes. Therefore, let us turn our attention to this issue.

Returning once again to Exhibits 5.18 and 5.19 on rumor content by historical period, we see that among both races the conspiracy theme showed a good deal of consistency. The percentage of these rumors among blacks in the sample of World War I and II disorders was 23; for the sixties it was 25. Among whites, the percentages were somewhat higher—27 and 33 percent, respectively—but there was still only a six-point spread. However, the consistency of figures began and ended here.

The remainder of themes among both races were a kind of crazy quilt—a patchwork of numbers with no apparent meaning. For blacks, white brutality rumors were 38 percent of the earlier sample, but only 14 percent of the later one; police brutality rumors were 23 and 37 percent, respectively; predictions of violence were 8 compared with 21 percent (see Exhibit 5.18). The statistical picture among whites appeared just as confused. Exaggeration or distortion of violence rumors were pegged at 12 percent on one sample and 27 on the other; the figures for black brutality rumors stood at 29 and 7; predictions of violence were 10 and 30 percent, respectively (see Exhibit 5.19).

A more critical appraisal, however, shows that these figures are actually quite logical. The key to understanding the prominence of themes lies in recognizing situational factors—that is, who was doing what at a given time. As mentioned earlier, the prototypical riots of the two World Wars featured bloodly clashes between the races. In contrast, the style of disorders in the 1960s more frequently involved action by blacks against symbols of the white establishment—authority figures and property—rather than white persons.[48]

The nature of disorders—past vs. present-day—had definite implications for the salience of rumor themes at different times. Reflecting the largely interracial character of disorders in the past, a large chunk of rumors among *both* races during the World War I and II riots seemed to revolve around persons. Fifty-one percent of the rumors among blacks from our earlier sample involved white or police brutality. Similarly, rape and black brutality accounted for 49 percent of the rumors among whites during the same time period.

The picture for disorders in the 1960s was different in certain ways. In both historical samples involving blacks, themes of brutality—practiced on blacks by white people or police—accounted for over half the rumors. However, within each sample, the emphasis was reversed. Rumors in the sixties' disorders pertaining to the police—the most conspicuous symbol of white authority—rose dramatically, from 23 to 37 percent. At the same time, white brutality rumors plummeted from 38 to 14 percent—evidence of decreased contact with whites.[49]

In turn, the aggressive stance of blacks during the sixties sent waves of fear running through the white communities of this nation—fears about the established order and fears about their property. Certain types of rumors became more conspicuous among whites: predictions of violence (by blacks against whites) tripled, from 10 to 30 percent; exaggeration or distortion of violence more than doubled going from 12 to 27 percent; meanwhile, black brutality rumors—once again signalling the relative lack of interracial contact—plummeted from 29 to a mere 7 percent.[50]

The evidence before us suggests that the types of rumors

to appear are largely determined by the hostile belief system, but their salience during one period vs. another is related to the nature of the disorders themselves.

Thus far we have been on a lengthy journey—confronting a maze of assumptions, facts and figures—which undoubtedly taxed the reader's patience at times. Having completed the testing of our propositions, this may be an appropriate place to pause and review our findings, laying the groundwork for the concluding chapter.

As the basis of the process model of rumor formation, we made eight propositions centered in two areas. One was the relationship between rumors and racial disorders, both of which were seen as part of the same process. Using the results of a survey questionnaire administered to police officials whose cities had experienced disturbances in 1968, discussion and analysis revolved around when and how rumors are formed.

In four out of five cases, our expectations were confirmed. Specifically, our findings showed that, in line with conventional wisdom, most racial disorders were indeed characterized by rumor formation. In the vast majority of cases—78 percent—an increase in rumors was reported at one or more stages of the disorder. This association was extremely strong for disorders of every size, although a shade less so for the smaller ones. Our findings also demonstrated that a sizable number of disorders—between 59 and 64 percent—had an upsurge of race-related rumors prior to any outbreak. In about 70 percent of the relevant cases, the clustering of rumors occurred within a couple of days of the disorder. Furthermore, a minimum of two-thirds of the cases with pre-disorder rumors were found to be tied to immediate racial conflicts pending in the community. Finally, an increase in the volume of rumors was discerned during the actual outbreak, representing a new peak of conflict, in more than half the cases (56 percent).

The relationship between rumors and the hostile belief system was the second area to command our attention. Here the focus was on the nature of rumors—their character and content—or, more simply, what they were about. Using news clips and investigative accounts of disorders spanning the years 1964 to 1970, we were able to classify a total of 359 rumors in a manner consistent with hostile beliefs. The rumors divided along racial lines (181 for blacks, 178 for whites), in the sense that different rumors arose and circulated within each group about the other. Underscoring the hostile nature of these beliefs, the rumors identified the adversary group involved. Moreover, the various functions of rumor were illustrated: the crystallization, confirmation and intensification of hostile beliefs, along with their linkage to actual events. We also used the data to explore related phenomena: the role of symbols, paranoid fancies on a group level, the intrinsic importance of the events to which rumors are tied, as well as the place of ambiguity.

Finally, and most important, we examined three propositions pertaining to the hostile belief system, two of which were verified. In particular, we found considerable overlap of thematic content for rumors circulating among both races, thereby supporting our assumption about the complementarity of hostile beliefs. Out of five possible categories, three were present among both blacks and whites. We also found that thematic content for disorders —past vs. present-day—has largely remained intact, thereby underlining our assumption about the perseverance of these beliefs. In almost every instance (rape rumors being the single exception), a given type of rumor known to have occurred in earlier riot cycles was repeated in the most recent one.

In sum, six of our eight propositions were substantiated by the data, thus providing a strong basis of support for the process model as a whole. The two which were not borne out were: the fourth, which presumed a tendency for rumors to be associated with precipitating events; and the seventh, which had as its premise the salience of the same themes, irrespective of the stage of the disorder. In the first instance, it was not clear whether our negative findings were due to the nature of the data or to the possibility that rumors were not necessarily functional at the time of the triggering incident. The failure to confirm the other proposition was explained by recognizing the intrusion of other factors—contextual and temporal—alongside the essential relationship of rumors and hostile beliefs.

Within the confines of testing the process model, there were additional finding which, while not directly related, provide us with other valuable insights into the emergence of rumors. These findings can be summarized as follows:

Causal relationship between rumors and immediate conflicts. We demonstrated that an increase in race-related rumors prior to the disorder was tied to the presence of immediate conflicts in the community. Going beyond this finding, there was also some indication that the two were causally related. The King disorders—those occurring around the time of the assassination of the Rev. Dr. Martin Luther King, Jr.—were the basis for this conclusion. These disorders permitted us to examine the same conflict-inducing event—i.e., the assassination of a revered civil rights leader—in 38 different settings or communities. A reported rumor increase prior to the outbreak was found in 78 percent of the cases. Furthermore, 79 percent of these rumors were bunched within a few days of the disorder. Most important, a huge percentage of the cases (82) did not seem related to local issues or events—a finding that stood in direct and striking contrast to the non-King disorders in which most (between two-thirds and 80 percent) *were* attributable to some immediate conflict(s) in the community. Thus, while acknowledging that the King disorders were atypical in some respects, we concluded that our data, at least, suggested that: the rumors and the assassination were causally related, with the assassination being the event which gave rise to the rumors; and rumors springing up prior to outbreaks are causally related to pending issues or events in the community and are therefore an *extension* as well as *expression* of these conflicts.

Qualitative differences in rumor themes. Three out of five rumor themes were found to occur among both races in our recent sample (proposition 6). Nevertheless, we also detected qualitative differences for two of the overlapping themes. The typical conspiracy rumor among whites featured plots—either general or specific—by blacks to undermine the system. There was a heavy emphasis on property, a common symbol of white power, and on the notion of "outside agitators," as well. But if the hallmark of conspiracy rumors among whites was order, then brutality marked those among blacks. Here the rumors focused on insulting, insensitive, unjust acts perceived as deliberately instigated by whites, often with official complicity. The nature of these rumors among blacks appeared symptomatic of the widespread feeling that the system and its representatives are out to oppress them.

Substantive differences were also discerned for predictive rumors of violence. Whites almost always saw themselves as the objects of attack; whereas the majority of such rumors among blacks centered around threats against whites. The differences in these rumors were mostly attributed to the nature of 1960s-style disorders, in which blacks played the more active (aggressive) role and whites, the more reactive (passive) one.

Quantitative differences in rumor themes. During the course of our analysis, rumor content was examined in three different ways: by race, by disorder stage and, finally, by historical period. Each time, certain themes were more prominent than others. For example, in comparing themes among the races in our sample of disorders during the 1960s, civilian brutality rumors occurred almost twice as often among blacks as whites (see Exhibit 5.15). Similarly, there were marked differences in the salience of rumors according to the stage of the disorder (see Exhibits 5.16 and 5.17). To illustrate: police brutality rumors comprised 20 percent of the rumors in the pre-disorder period, but jumped to about 40 percent during the outbreak itself. When it came to comparing rumor content for past and present-day disorders (see Exhibits 5.18 and 5.19), once again the percentages varied greatly. For example, among whites rumors exaggerating or distorting violence were pegged at 12 percent on the earlier sample, more than doubling to 27 percent on the later one; whereas the figures for black brutality originally stood at 29 percent, but dropped to a paltry 7 percent on the later sample.

The implication of these findings is that, despite the importance of the hostile belief system in determining rumor themes, there are other factors which govern their prominence at various times. The three principal "other" factors are as follows.

1. *Structural.* Setting aside the immediate, underlying strains within our social system, we are still left with one fundamental reality: an unequal social structure, with whites in the superior and blacks, the subordinate, position. This state of affairs has long been a source of agony for both races. Whites have been faced with the defense of their position (in effect, the prevailing social order), as blacks have tried to alter theirs in favor of a more equitable system. Thus, each group has tended to be guided by a set of different, often conflicting, interests: for whites, order; for blacks, justice. These interests can be

seen at work in the emergence of rumors, affecting the distribution of themes among each race.

Taking our sample from disorders in the 1960s, the structural factor helps explain: first, why predictions of violence, the magnification of violence and conspiracy charges—all representing threats against the established order—accounted for 80 percent of the rumors among whites; and second, why 77 percent of the rumors among blacks had to do with brutality or injustice—on the part of whites (civilians), the police and other officials.[51]

Returning to our earlier historical sample, predictably we find that brutality rumors stand out among blacks. Whites (civilians) and the police alone were the subject of 61 percent of the rumors. Nevertheless, an interesting situation was presented in the rumor sample among whites. For, while order themes dominated the later sample, this trend was not as clear-cut for the earlier period. Themes relating to violations of order vs. justice (brutality) were split exactly, each at 49 percent—a finding which brings us to a second factor.

2. *Situational.* Immediate circumstances also have an important bearing on the prominence of themes. The prototypical riot of the two World Wars featured inter-racial clashes—active participation by both groups, white persons against black persons. As expected, brutality rumors were the most conspicuous among blacks. At the same time, white people, seeing themselves in immediate danger, were made more susceptible to brutality rumors—thereby mitigating somewhat against order themes. Hence, the even split of such rumors.

In the same way, the changed picture of disorders during the 1960s represented a new and different situation. No longer was it white persons against black persons, so much as blacks against white property and white authority. This new set of circumstances helped account for a relative increase in order themes and a decrease in brutality and injustice among whites.

3. *Temporal.* Time is another factor which is especially important for the disorder stage. On one hand, time involves the circumstance or opportunity of a given moment. For example, as evidence of the poor relations between the police and the black community, police brutality rumors accounted for a solid 20 percent in the pre-disorder period. Nevertheless, this same type of rumor virtually doubled during the outbreak itself (39 percent). This jump in figures may be attributed to the more direct contact blacks had with the police during the actual disorder.

But time is also important in that the interval between the event and the emergence of a certain type of rumor sometimes varies. Conspiracy rumors, for example, require time to ponder, consider and interpret; thus they probably should not show up strongly in the precipitating context, given the usually swift flow of events. According to our findings, in fact, they don't appear very often at this point.

IMPLICATIONS FOR FURTHER RESEARCH

We have spent the better part of this chapter trying to answer questions but, in finding solutions for some of these, still other questions have surfaced. Some new questions arose as a consequence of our data's limitations. For example, it is not clear whether rape rumors are more common than is indicated by the information at hand. The same point applies to other rumors of a sexual nature. In an interesting essay, Marilyn Rosenthal has noted: "The castration rumor seems to erupt at many times of crisis in and should be posed with regard to personality traits. After all, a black (or white) person is not only a member of a particular race, but an individual as well. Admittedly, our study has, of necessity, focused on the former, neglecting the latter. Therefore, any attempt to rectify the imbalance here would be most welcome.

But, while raising questions which may generate additional research in this area, there is at least one issue raised by our findings which merits more immediate attention. For, having demonstrated that race-related rumors are part of the whole disorder process, we know something about when they are likely to appear. Similarly, having constructed a typology of rumors, we also know what kinds of rumors are likely to occur.

When a data-gathering venture such as the preceding is completed, the researcher always has at least two alternatives. One is to pack up his research gear and go home, secure in the feeling that he or she has added to humankind's knowledge. The other—a bit more mundane —is to apply what has been learned and develop policies to cope with similar situations. The latter is, of course, the critical test of the long-range value of any research; and for that reason, we have elected to take this study one step further. The final chapter, then, will explore the implications of our model for public policy.

history"; whereupon she refers to one such st
"common rumor" in the Detroit area by late
1968.[52] Two or three castration rumors did sho
our news clips and investigative accounts (a
included in the civilian brutality category)—but
all. Further testing would be needed to ascertain
how abundant these rumors are. Similarly, o
showed a strong association between rumors and p
ting events for the larger, but not the smaller, distu
A closer look at the relationship between rumors
cipitating events might also yield some significant

Going beyond the immediate scope of our stud
questions are raised. One involves the issue of race
rumors during "peacetime"—those periods lacking
disorder. It is noteworthy that nearly 70 percent
respondents in our police survey said that, g
speaking, rumors reported to their or a related dep
involved the matter of race *frequently, if not m
ten.*[53] Do such "peacetime" rumors fit the typol
structed in our study; are some more common than
and if so, why?

In addition, we need to learn more about the
networks. Our data suggested the existence of a
grapevine or telegraph which was, in effect, match
suburban one among whites. But are these n
completely separate? At what points, if any, d
converge? For example, does a given rumor which
in the black community—say, one predicting vio
somehow make its way into the white community?
so, how? To answer these questions, it might be hel
examine a day in the life of a single rumor—tra
path, while assessing its impact on the community(i

Finally, there is the issue of to what extent
variables—age, sex, class, education, etc.—affec
group's susceptibility to rumors. A similar questi

6. THE ROLE OF FORMAL GROUPS: IMPLICATIONS FOR PUBLIC POLICY

On April 11, 1968, the following story appeared in the Cleveland *Plain Dealer:*

COLUMBUS: Wild rumors of possible violence at Ohio State University yesterday resulted in the mobilization of 900 National Guardsmen and the sending of 100 state highway patrolmen to the campus here. . . .

The rumors which first swept the campus Tuesday centered on a scheduled noon rally yesterday. . . .

One wild report had it that the OSU administration building would be attacked by flamethrowers after the rally. A calmer rumor simply suggested that the building would be burned down.

Sponsors of the rally contending that the OSU administration purposely was minimizing the rumors in order to keep students away, canceled the rally later Tuesday.

Despite the announced cancellation, the rally was held after all—without incident. Richard Zimmerman, the reporter who covered the story for the *Plain Dealer,* noted that there was virtually no violence, except for a minor scuffle in front of a flagpole and a fight between two dogs. Since so much had been made of so little, Zimmerman wrote facetiously: "The mongrel appeared to be an outside agitator, while the Doberman was kept under control by what appeared to be a bona fide student."

Wild rumors; the mustering of 1,000 law enforcement officers; charges that the university administration had used the rumors for its own ends; an ensuing news story about the episode. This affair serves to remind us that, when it comes to rumors and racial disorders, the cast of characters includes not only ordinary citizens—both black and white—but also those who must act in a more formal or official capacity. Accordingly, we will devote this final chapter to a critical appraisal of three such groups: the police, the civil authorities and the news media. The final section will examine something that many members of these groups have advocated—namely, so-called "rumor control centers."

Before venturing into this new territory, however, we ought to clarify one point. An underlying theme of this book—which began as an assumption and was subsequently borne out by our data—has been that, rather than an isolated phenomenon, race-related rumors are an essential part of the whole disorder process. If we can agree that most such rumors serve no constructive purpose and simply add to racial polarization, then we must also recognize and affirm that any attempt to contain or prevent these rumors, without dealing with the other "root causes" of disorder—namely, the inequities within our social system—is doomed to certain failure.

Even the most casual observer can see that something is wrong in our society; the evidence is all around us. But, while long on description, we have been short on prescription—if, indeed, a perfect one exists. For when a real inequity exists, the remedy is never easy, nor is it likely to be agreeable to all. Therefore, in discussing the policy implications of rumors, without presenting our own "prescription" for change, let us remember that any suggestions made here must be placed within the larger context of the continuing search for solutions.

THE ROLE OF THE POLICE

In a report to the attorney general of the United States made in 1968, the International Association of Chiefs of Police spoke of the need on the part of public officials for information which is both accurate and reliable, especially during times of crisis:

> A community's ability to act effectively and appropriately in the face of a mounting or on-going disorder depends in large measure upon the quality and quantity of information available to those who must direct the allocation of resources. Beyond this obvious command system need for valid information relating to current situations is the role which information plays in stimulating or quieting the citizens in the disorder area.[1]

In relation to this point, police officials from eight cities participating in the study conducted by the IACP were asked to rank various intelligence sources in terms of their reliability. These sources, totalling 15, included police informants, citizens on the scene, officers on the scene, the news media and rumors. Significantly, rumors ranked at the bottom of the list.

Nevertheless, despite the findings and pronouncements of the IACP, we find that, as a group, the police tend to be extremely susceptible to rumors. Earlier we indicated that the police were important receptors of rumors; indeed, a substantial part of our research and analysis was based on information received from the police. However, the role of the police with respect to rumors is not always so limited. There are many instances—indeed, too many—in which the police, as "rumor carriers," initiate or transmit unverified reports and, perhaps more to the point, stand ready, willing and able to act according to them. Witness the following examples.

In 1968, a rumor panic gripped the Detroit area, throwing a number of police departments into confusion. One police official in suburban Livonia indicated that only a few rumors were widespread—black snipers would kill a white child on each block, burn shopping centers and poison water supplies. "We tell people flat out that these rumors are full of hot air," he said. At the same time, however, he hastened to add: "but any Negroes coming down Plymouth Road [a major Livonia thoroughfare] will be shot."[2] At the time of the tragedy at Jackson State College in 1970, highway patrol investigators reported to the Mississippi governor that officers were the targets of a "constant barrage of flying missiles." Nevertheless, the President's Commission on Campus Unrest (the so-called Scranton Commission) found that only a "small number" of rocks, bottles and bricks were thrown.[3] When the nation's capital erupted into violence after the King assassination, the police in Fairmont Heights, Maryland, reported that they were fired upon from a car carrying three Washington Negroes. But no gun was found when the

car's occupants were arrested. Ray Girardin, former commissioner of the Detroit Police Department, has given a
candid assessment of the problem: "I'm sorry to have to
say that many police, without realizing that they carry
such authority, do pass on these rumors. The average
policeman doesn't stop to weigh what he says."[4]

This failure to "weigh" or evaluate what is heard and
said can have grave consequences. For a rumor that
predicts a particular event can easily become a destructive
self-fulfilling prophesy contributing to its own outcome.
All of us know that, if enough depositors believe their
bank is going to fold, their panic-stricken withdrawals can
result in the actual insolvency of the bank, even if it had
been in perfectly sound, financial shape. In the same way,
rumors can become an integral part of a situation and
affect subsequent events. Initially, these rumors may be
false; but by eliciting the expected behavior they become
true.

The recent history of racial disorders in this country
abounds in examples of this vicious cycle, whereby police
respond to false rumors, and only exacerbate the situation,
sometimes with tragic results. During an outbreak of violence in Richmond, California, in 1968, rumors concerning
the possible activities of the Black Panthers and other militant groups were accepted at face value and acted upon.
One rumor stated that the Panthers planned to burn some
temporary wooden school structures and even city hall
itself. On the basis of this rumor and others like it, increased numbers of police were sent out, while roadblocks
were set up at specific points in anticipation of acts which
never occurred. An independent investigation of the incident offered the following assessment:

> the presence of large numbers of police on the streets aroused
> among blacks at least as much disgust and anger as terrified
> compliance. By increasing tension in the community, massive

police presence may have served to mobilize groups who otherwise would have remained uncommitted.[5]

Earlier, when former commissioner Ray Girardin acknowledged that the police were highly prone to circulating rumors, he went on to attribute this behavior to "just the process of people talking to each other and, without thinking, enlarging on what they have heard"—or seen, we might add. But is the problem simply one of absent-mindedness or poor judgment? A closer look suggests that the problem is considerably more complicated, and that we must examine the policeman's life on at least three different levels—as an individual, as a person doing a job and finally, as part of a particular social situation.

First let us examine the policeman as an individual. Surprisingly little research has been done on the policeman's personality. However, the Law Enforcement Assistance Administration (LEAA) sponsored one such study in 1972, the findings of which have not yet been released. The 1972 Democratic National Convention Training Report, as it was called, was part of the training police officers received as the city of Miami Beach prepared for what turned out to be two national political conventions. One key finding was that, while the average policeman tends to be factually oriented, he is also inclined to over react in problematic situations. On the one hand, this means that there is much validity to the Sergeant Friday stereotype, with his no-nonsense, just-the-facts-Ma'am approach. However, the same finding also suggests that, in a confused, stressful situation, Sergeant Friday might well lose his cool.

The study could not determine whether police work attracted or developed this particular personality type. However, it did imply that in difficult situations—such as civil disorders—because of the swift onrush of events and the lack of a clear, calm perspective, the police were inclined to substitute rumors for facts.

The policeman's tendency to spread and act upon rumors can also be explained in terms of the nature of his job. By now the reader is well aware that, in times of crisis and disorder, the local police department literally becomes a rumor warehouse, as hundreds of reports from anxious citizens jam the switchboards. These reports are at once abundant, contradictory and frightening, creating problems on two fronts. First, at a time when he is probably tired and tense, the policeman's exposure to so many rumors—echoing the same themes over and over—may increase his willingness to accept them at face value. Despite his factual orientation, stress may temporarily impair his critical judgment, and give the rumors a built-in credibility they might not have ordinarily.

A second dimension of the problem has to do with the need to check rumors. Ninety-nine out of a hundred bomb threats fail to materialize; nevertheless, the police cannot afford to ignore such warnings. The same applies to most rumors connected with racial disorders. Verification is a necessary, but frequently monotonous, task which may involve a frenzy of activity leading to one dead end after another. As an example, a police chronology of events during a 1966 disturbance in San Francisco noted:

> Reports of serious incidents, allegedly possession of guns by juveniles, were received and checked for verification. In all but one or two cases these reports proved false, but the requirement to check on their accuracy kept the patrol personnel constantly utilized.[6]

A vast expenditure of time and energy on the part of the police with little in the way of return (i.e., something positive to report) inevitably results in a certain amount of frustration. This frustration may take the form of wish-ful-

fillment—an unconscious desire to believe that the rumors
are really true. For, if indeed young hoodlums *are* cooking
up trouble; if snipers *are* holed up in rooftops; if armed
Black Panthers *are* headed for the suburbs, then otherwise
dull, routine work takes on new significance and purpose.
In other words, the increased willingness of the police to
accept and even act upon rumors serves to relieve the
frustration bound up with the drearier aspects of police
work.

A final problem related to the job itself is that the policeman, like the fisherman, has a tendency to exaggerate
the magnitude of the catch, particularly when he is still
fresh from the battle. This fact helps to explain the en-
largements policemen often make of crowd size, the nature
and amount of destruction and generally speaking, the extent of the danger involved in a given situation. More realistic appraisals of the situation invariably occur in the aftermath of a disorder, when emotions have begun to cool.

But the average policeman is not only an individual with
a particular job to do; he is also generally white, and as
such, shares the attitudes and beliefs of his fellow white
citizens. He is therefore extremely open to rumors
emanating from the white community—because he lives
there. A glance at the specific rumors attributed to
policemen earlier in this chapter indicates that they are
precisely the same kinds of rumors common to other
whites. The rumor in Livonia, Michigan, that blacks may
have been headed for a busy suburban thoroughfare was a
prediction of violence; the alleged gunfire directed at the
police in Fairmont, Maryland, from a car carrying blacks
was a black brutality rumor; while plans attributed to the
Black Panthers in Richmond, California, to burn down
some school structures and city hall itself echoed the
familiar theme of conspiracy. Needless to say, we do not
find many rumors of police brutality among the police.

That last remark was not meant to be entirely facetious. For the policeman's authority is another important factor in the social setting of rumors. He is the one charged with enforcing the law and maintaining order—and he is extremely conscious of this responsibility. In an essay on police brutality, Reiss addresses himself to the policeman's need to feel he is "in charge":

> Often he seems threatened by a simple refusal to acquiesce to his own authority. A policeman beat a handcuffed offender because, when told to sit, the offender did not sit down. One Negro woman was soundly slapped for her refusal to approach the police car and identify herself. . . .

> The important issue seems to be whether the policeman manages to assert his authority despite the threat to it. I suspect that policemen are more likely to respond with excessive force when they define the situation as one in which there remains a questions as to who is 'in charge.'[7]

If a policeman over reacted to the failure of a handcuffed prisoner to sit down, we can well imagine his feelings about the situations that occurred so often during the 1960s, in which blacks consistently flaunted the law and were the frequent initiators of disorder.

If we take the negative attitudes about blacks which the policeman shares with other white citizens, and add to this his own sense of the erosion of his authority, we are led to speculate as follows: the average policeman is even more firmly committed to the set of hostile beliefs commonly held among whites than is the average white citizen; therefore, when it comes to race-related rumors which spring from these beliefs, the policeman is that much more vulnerable.

But, while the policeman is charged with enforcing the law, he is by no means above it. Fortunately, this responsibility carries with it a measure of accountability to the public. Thus, in the aftermath of a disorder, the police are frequently placed in the position of explaining their actions. Why were patrols beefed up in the community prior to the outbreak? Was tear gas really necessary? Was the force used against the dissidents excessive? Why did the police fire into a crowd? And so on.

For the policeman fresh from the heat of battle—angry, tired and shaken—this can be an uncomfortable situation, particularly when there are indications or allegations of over reaction on his part. Faced with the defense of actions which are not always defensible, the police have a tendency to lapse into rumors. The shooting at Jackson State College (1970) was justified partly on the grounds that the police had been bombarded with flying missiles and were all but overwhelmed by a surging crowd. Similarly, police gunfire resulting in the deaths of three persons at Orangeburg State (1968) and six persons at Augusta (1970) was said to have come only after snipers had initiated the shooting.

Moreover, in trying to explain the cause of the outbreak itself, the police have often reverted to that old bugaboo, the imagined conspiracy. Two points ought to be made here. First, while police talk of will-o'-the-wisp snipers, urban guerrillas and national conspiracies represents a serious problem in general, it seems to be more common among the cop on the beat than his superiors. In 1968, the Lemberg Center conducted a study of 25 disorders containing alleged sniping against the police. Significantly, we found that 14 out of 19 police chiefs or other high-ranking officials expressing a view on the matter said there was no evidence of prior planning.[8] Second, while contending that the police elevate rumor above fact on far too many occasions, we are not suggesting a deliberate ploy on their part to deceive the public. Police cover-ups utilizing rumors do occur every now and then; but much more often, their resort to rumors seems, on the one hand, part of an honest reflection of the sentiments of many whites; and, on the other, part of an unconscious effort to justify their behavior, particularly under controversial circumstances.

RECOMMENDATIONS

By virtue of his personality, his job, his race and his authority, the policeman is highly susceptible to rumors—all too often accepting or transmitting reports which have not been verified. This problem has hampered his overall effectiveness in making rational, intelligent decisions and acting in a responsible manner, especially during times of crisis.

In order to minimize the policeman's proneness to rumors and, at the same time, maximize his ability to handle them, the following recommendations are suggested:

1. *The supply of information.* Since, as the IACP stated a community's response to civil disorder depends partly on "the quality and quantity of information available," and since rumor is generally a poor source, there is an important need for the police to develop and incorporate new and better procedures—procedures which speed the flow and increase the reliability of information. Improved communications in the form of planning and equipment are essential in achieving these goals. For example, through the use of miniaturized transceivers, communications could be maintained with all police officers, even when they have left their cars.

Turning from technical to human resources, the establishment of a nerve center that gathers reliable information for police and government officials should be planned and ready to activate when a disturbance reaches a predetermined level of intensity. The purpose of the center, to be located at police headquarters or city hall, would be to supplement eyewitness reporting and to supply information about official actions. There should also be greater utilization of community leaders, agencies and organizations within the ghetto. Citizen security patrols, for instance, have been found to be extremely effective in checking erroneous rumors during disorders.[9]

2. *The selection of personnel.* We have already noted the policeman's tendency to over react when confronted with problematic situations and personal affronts to his authority, and we have observed how this increases his susceptibility to rumors. As this is certainly not a desirable quality for a policeman to have in difficult, volatile situations, more careful screening procedures would be helpful in rooting out less stable applicants for police work. No police department should admit any person into public service unless his background has been thoroughly investigated. Properly administered tests can eliminate many of the emotionally unfit; some police departments already conduct psychological and psychiatric examinations of all their applicants. Between 1953 and 1957, 11 percent of the applicants to the Los Angeles Police Department were rejected as not meeting the required psychiatric qualifications. Such tests ought to become standard practice for police departments everywhere.

Finally, the police ought to move away from their "macho" mentality, which extols toughness, power and the use of physical force. (Note the unduly restrictive requirements on physical stature and condition.) Despite the increasing involvement of the police in social matters, the important characteristics which relate directly to their ability to perform more delicate functions—including the handling of inflammatory rumors—namely, sensitivity, intelligence and maturity, have been neglected.

3. *Training procedures.* While much progress has been made during recent years in the development of training programs for police officers, the total training effort, when compared to modern law enforcement needs, remains "grossly inadequate"—according to the President's Commission on Law Enforcement and Administration of Justice. Current training programs are fragmented, sporadic and generally poor. The overhaul of police training requires, among other things, better instructional materials and techniques which place a greater emphasis on the social context in which the police must carry on their work.

In their manuals and reports, the FBI, the IACP and other law enforcement organizations have demonstrated a commendable awareness of the potentially dangerous effects of rumors. But as part of their training, the police themselves must become more rumor-conscious—more sensitive to their *own* role with respect to rumors. This can be accomplished by increasing their understanding of the connection between rumors and civil disorders, the kinds of rumors which commonly occur among each race and finally, by instilling in them a keener appreciation of the part the police play as "rumor carriers."

4. *Police-community relations.* The susceptibility of the police to rumors in the white community, which are invariably pointed against blacks, and the high incidence of police brutality rumors among blacks, which are of course pointed against the police, provide simple proof—if any were needed—of the sorry relations between these two groups. Like so many other social problems, this one is inclined to continue on in a vicious cycle. As one observer said:

> Blacks hate cops because they beat them up in the past and still do, and because they represent America's unpaid debts and empty promises for social progress. Cops hate blacks because they

(the cops) have inherited the hatred from the racist traditions of the profession, and because as one policeman put it, 'When somebody hates you, you get to hate them.'[10]

Obviously, any attempt to reduce antagonistic rumors between the police and blacks must be tied to the larger issue of reducing general antagonism. Toward this end, we urge the following "first steps": the development of meaningful community relations—not public relations—programs within police departments; more active involvement of the black community in matters of mutual concern to both parties; more effective procedures for handling complaints of police brutality and other charges of official misconduct; the recruitment of younger, better-educated whites who generally hold less racist attitudes; along with the addition of young blacks, who may have less education, but a greater knowledge of the ghetto. Attorney General Ramsey Clark, in an off-the-record talk to police chiefs and mayors in 1968, summed up the long-term problem in this way:

> Police community relations is . . . the most difficult and important police problem of the next ten to twenty years . . . and in the long run . . . the very function of police work in a free society. It has to be, for otherwise it is war and unending opposition. . . . You can't handle a situation indefinitely with an army or with occupation.

THE ROLE OF PUBLIC OFFICIALS

When violence breaks out, the police are usually the most conspicuous officials on the scene. However, they are by no means the only officials involved. The leadership and support of the civil authorities is equally, if not more, important—since public officials bear the final responsibility for whatever action is taken. As the Kerner Report points out: "Civil disorders are fundamental governmental problems, not simply police matters." Public officials must grapple with an appropriate strategy of response, which includes: attempted resolution of issues and grievances by political means, negotiations with community leaders, the dissemination of information to the public at large via the news media and finally, cooperation and coordination with various law enforcement agencies.

Because of the broad responsibilities of public officials, their role with respect to rumors merits close scrutiny. Looking at this role, we find essentially the same syndrome that operates among the police. The basic elements are as follows: acceptance and transmission of the types of rumors associated with the white community; response to rumors at face value; the use of rumors to justify immediate action; the use of rumors to explain the disorder and its causes.

In order to understand this syndrome better, let us take the 1971 uprising at Attica state prison as a case in point. Several factors were involved in the selection of our subject. First, rumors were an extremely important and overt part of the disorder context—before, during and even after the outbreak. Second, because of an exhaustive amount of subsequent investigation, analysis and reflection, we can get a detailed look at both the rumors themselves and the way in which they engaged the attention of those public officials closest to the situation. Finally, along with a few other disorders, "Attica," as it has come to be called, symbolizes America's ongoing tragedy. The hostages and inmates who lost their lives were all victims—victims of tragic circumstances and tragic choices.

At the same time, however, the reader should be

cautioned. For, in using the case study approach, we must recognize that no two officials in public life are susceptible to the rumor syndrome we are about to present to the same degree; nor does the entire syndrome necessarily operate in all situations.

Attica: The Setting

In many ways, the uprising at Attica Correctional Facility in upstate New York followed the general scenario of other disorders in the 1960s. Two months before the trouble, deepening tensions were reported between the inmates and prison administration. At the start of July, a statement of 27 demands was drawn up by a group of inmates and sent to the new Commissioner of Corrections, Russell G. Oswald. Complaints centered around diet, censorship, medical care, working conditions, parole procedures and religious expression.

On Wednesday, September 8—one day before the rebellion—a misunderstanding in the exercise yard led to an intense confrontation between officers and inmates, at which time a lieutenant was struck by an inmate. Two inmates involved were taken to a special disciplinary housing unit, amid the anguished protests of their fellow inmates. A corrections officer was later struck in the head by a full soup can thrown by an inmate, who was also taken away, further intensifying the situation. By breakfast the next morning, a rumor spread that the two inmates taken to "the box" had been beaten. Meanwhile, the inmate involved in the soup can incident was released by his fellow inmates, and the uprising was underway. By 10:30 A.M. and inmates had seized control of four cell blocks and all the yards and tunnels, as more than a thousand inmates gathered in D Yard holding over 40 correctional employees as hostages.

Rising tensions, anxiety and frustration surrounded frantic attempts to resolve the crisis during the next four days. Commissioner Oswald, at considerable personal risk, met with the inmates three times; a Citizens Observers Committee, which included such luminaries as journalist Tom Wicker, Congressman Herman Badillo, lawyer William Kunstler and Clarence Jones, the publisher of the *Amsterdam News,* was set up to act as an arbitrator between the inmates and prison officials; a list of 28 proposals was drawn up as the basis of a settlement and rejected by the inmates; numerous appeals were made for Governor Nelson A. Rockefeller to come to Attica, all of them unsuccessful. Finally, in what Commissioner Oswald termed "an agonizing decision" for him, the state police mounted an assault of D Yard on Monday morning, September 13. When the shooting stopped, 10 hostages and 29 inmates were dead or dying of bullet wounds inflicted by the authorities,[11] while many others had been injured. Except for the Indian massacres of the late nineteenth century, it was, in the words of the New York State Special Commission on Attica (the so-called McKay Commission) "the bloodiest one-day encounter between Americans since the Civil War."

But these are only the barest outlines of the tragedy. Let us now examine the role of the public officials involved, with respect to rumors.

1. *Acceptance of white community-type rumors.* In his book, *Attica—My Story,*[12] Commissioner Oswald goes to some length to deny the racial overtones of the uprising. "In no way . . . was Attica a white massacre of blacks," he says (p. 18). After assuring the reader of his firm belief in equality on page 17 (". . . I have never viewed a black man as any less nor any more than a white man."), he points out that 20 black prisoners were killed, along with 12 whites. In fact, 4 of the 12 "whites" were Puerto Ricans.

Moreover, the state policemen, every one of them white, were reminded before launching their offensive that all the hostages were also white. And, in the aftermath, a number of troopers openly declaimed the triumph of "white power." Thus, while Attica was in some ways a massacre of all races, the uprising also had racial overtones which cannot and should not be ignored.

For our immediate purpose, it is important to remember that Oswald and almost all of his associates were white. Theirs was a white viewpoint, based on a white experience and a white perspective, which had a profound influence on their thinking and lent a certain inevitability to the subsequent actions, as we shall see. Like other white citizens, they were strongly committed to the standard set of hostile beliefs directed against blacks—including the ones that blacks were naturally violent (a belief which was undoubtedly accentuated by the prison setting); that they were pushing too hard and too fast for change, all the while conspiring to topple the system. From a psychological standpoint, these beliefs—however unconscious—would come in very handy when it came time to assign responsibility for what had happened.

More to the point, by adhering to these hostile beliefs, the public officials at Attica became susceptible to the same types of rumors we have previously identified with the white community: predictions of violence (by blacks), black brutality, conspiracy and exaggeration or distortion of the violence. The fact that correctional officials—like the police—often relied on "tips" and "informers" for information meant that they were particularly rumor-prone to begin with.

Long before the uprising there were constant warnings of violence, based largely on hearsay. Word reached Oswald and his associates via an inmate at Attica that a riot would occur there sometime between late August and

September. From an inmate at another institution, they learned that the date was November 2 and that the whole thing was somehow tied to California, where Angela Davis was being held on murder charges. In his book, Oswald reports he found these details "highly convincing." He also notes that corrections officials in New York state believed that "outside groups" supporting revolutionaries were going to seize control of a prison, by killing the corrections officers in the towers and bringing in guns and explosives. While Oswald appeared skeptical of these reports, he said the situation at Attica became "critical" in August, following the fatal attempt by George Jackson to escape from San Quentin Prison in California. According to Oswald, about one week after Jackson's death, three times the usual number of men arrived on sick call at A Block, asking only for aspirins or laxatives. Oswald cites this as "impressive evidence" of "effective planning."[13]

During the uprising, there were many brutality rumors which were widely believed by prison officials. Each day brought new stories of atrocities committed against the hostages. On the stairs leading up to the second floor in A Block, corrections officers pointed out the bloodstains of William Quinn.[14] One rumor said he had been thrown down the stairs; another that his skull had been crushed. Both were untrue. A sick inmate who was released from the Yard reported that inmates there were building a gallows to hang the hostages—another false tale. Rumors continued to circulate even after the assault. One report specified falsely that a hostage had been castrated. According to another version, a dead hostage had had his testicles cut off and stuffed into his mouth. But, without question, the rumor that the hostages had died by having their throats cut turned out to be the most widely circulated, and significant report.[15]

2. *Transmission of white community-type rumors.*

These and other rumors reaching the ears of this or that official were invariably communicated to his other associates. For example, confronted with the ominous "sick call incident," Oswald told Governor Rockefeller in his monthly report:

> While it is not characteristic of me to 'cry wolf,' the recent tragedy at San Quentin has made it all too apparent that anything can happen in dealing with the kind of idealists and fanatics housed in our facilities.[16]

During the ensuing crisis, Dr. Warren Hanson, a surgeon who had been making daily visits to D Yard, heard on Saturday night (September 11) that inmates had forced two hostages into a bathroom, thrown wood in after them and set the place on fire. The report came from Robert Douglass, Governor Rockefeller's representative, Commissioner Oswald and his Deputy, Walter Dunbar. One of the cooler heads at the time, Dr. Hanson told them the story was "nonsense"—which it was.

Immediately after the assault on Monday morning, distraught corrections personnel filed in and out of Superintendent Vincent Mancusi's office, which was functioning as a command post, with fresh reports of dead hostages. Some of these reports were embellished by rumors. For example, Deputy Superintendent Leon J. Vincent repeated to Mancusi the widely accepted, but untrue, story that some hostages appeared to have been killed before the assault.

The rumors went far beyond the prison walls of Attica, as high officials reported the atrocity stories as facts to the news media, without waiting for authoritative verification (such as the autopsy reports). The lead article in the *New York Times* on Tuesday, September 14, said:

> In this worst of American prison tragedies, several of the

hostages—prison guards and civilian workers—died when convicts slashed their throats with knives. Others were stabbed and beaten with clubs and lengths of pipes.

. . . a deputy director of correction, Walter Dunbar, said that two of the hostages had been killed 'before today' and that one had been stabbed and emasculated.

News stories similar to those in the *Times* were published around the world.

3. *Response to rumors at face value.* Ominous-sounding rumors which, if true, can affect the community frequently require some sort of response on the part of public officials. Whether it is a rumored plot to assassinate some government figure or word of an imminent riot, the investigation of these reports is a necessity for those persons entrusted with the safety and security of the community. Indeed, verification should be the first order of business in formulating such a response—precisely because so many rumors prove to be false. Admittedly, a lack of time may impede the verification process—in which case officials may be forced to rely on their experience, judgment and luck. However, our concern here is to point to the need—whenever and wherever possible—to confirm incoming reports which are not substantiated. For the impulsive, automatic acceptance of reports at face value—independent of verification—can lead to hasty, questionable, even self-defeating, actions.

The problem concerning public officials, even during crisis situations, is frequently not the actual lack of time, but rather the failure to make sufficient time available. Such was the case at Attica, where many reports went unverified, were acted upon and later figured in the turn of events. Unchecked rumors of imminent violence, brutality and atrocity by the inmates served to reinforce the belief among officials that the hostages' lives were in immediate danger and that, since negotiations had not borne fruit, a strong show of force by the state was the only available alternative. While they were certainly not the dominant factor in the decision to mount an assault, rumors did contribute to the emotional climate in which that decision was made. For, if lives were at stake, so the reasoning went, the failure to send in troops would surely jeopardize those lives even further. Later, testifying before the McKay Commission, Commissioner Oswald listed a number of different factors which influenced his decision and, according to the Commission report, "referred particularly" to a note he received from Tom Soto, a member of the Citizen Observer Committee, as he entered the prison Sunday morning. The note, which was apparently written by an inmate, read: "Only among ourselves—they have a gun, Molotov cocktail, gas gun, knives, and some other weapons. Destroy after reading this." However, the McKay Commission found: "There was no evidence that the inmates had a gun other than the two gas guns they had captured on Thursday.[17] But, like so many other fragmented reports received at the time, this one too was accepted and treated as fact.

Moreover, stories about dead hostages and untrue atrocity stories told following the assault increased the likelihood of revenge on the part of the police. The desire to "get even," in this case, was enhanced by the conviction that the inmates were guilty of widespread "murder" and "mutilation" of the hostages. But, instead of seeking to track down these rumors, the general official response was merely to circulate them and thus, in effect, to sanction the reprisals made by state troopers. Widespread beatings and kickings of inmates, as well as vicious racial and sexual slurs occurred under the myopic eyes of those who represented legal order at Attica. The hours following the assault were filled with continuing rumors, reprisals and official silence. Most corrections officials subsequently refused to acknowledge, or accept the responsibility for what took place.

We are not suggesting here that, had there been no rumors, there would have been no "Attica." The point is that the ready acceptance of rumors by everyone involved impaired the decision-making process and played a significant part in the tragic outcome of the situation.

3. *The use of rumors to justify immediate action.* Immediately following the assault, a number of questions were directed at state officials. Was the use of force and that amount of force by the state warranted? Why weren't the inmates warned that their refusal to release the hostages would result in gunfire being used against them? Would a personal appearance by Governor Rockefeller have altered the outcome? The answers to these and other questions were not immediately apparent. What was clear was that, when the uprising was over, 39 men were dead—including 10 hostages—and more than 80 others wounded. Already some were calling the attack by the state police a "massacre."

Some answers were forthcoming from officials, in the form of rumors which placed the immediate burden of responsibility on the inmates. For example, on the same day as the assault Walter Dunbar, the Executive Deputy Commissioner, took members of the press and legislators on a tour, providing them with vivid accounts of the hostages' deaths and mutilations, all of which proved untrue. Legislators were shown one naked inmate lying on a table with a football under his chin, who Dunbar introduced as the "castrator" of a hostage. According to Assemblyman Arthur O. Eve and Congressman Herman Badillo, two of the legislators present, Dunbar said that the "castration" had been filmed from a helicopter as well as observed from a rifle's telescopic sights. The same official also informed the press that some hostages had been killed before the attack and repeated the story that the hostages had died from slashed throats.

The resort to rumors by Dunbar and other corrections officials, while not necessarily justified, was understandable in some respects. The four-day ordeal had taken its toll on those in charge, leaving them extremely tired, confused and no doubt ambivalent about having to explain themselves to others. Moreover, the "facts" issued to the press and public were compatible with their hostile beliefs toward blacks—all of which suggested a strong and serious commitment to their initial version of what happened.

However, the corrections officials' quick acceptance of Monday's rumors contrasted with their dogged resistance to Tuesday's facts—and now raised questions about their motivation. For, following the autopsy reports which showed that all of the hostages died of gunshot wounds— from the guns of the authorities, their ostensible protectors—officials still clung to their original version of events. The McKay reports states: "When autopsies proved those reports [of atrocities] to be false, the first reaction of some officials was to search for ways to question or discredit the medical examiners, rather than to face up to their own mistake."[18] Some went so far as to try to manage the news.

But the attempt by state officials to dispute the autopsy reports was more than a device for avoiding public embarrassment; it was also a way of diverting attention away from their own behavior and onto that of the inmates. For if the inmates had actually built gallows and then killed hostages by castrating them and slashing their throats as suggested, it would be extremely difficult to quarrel with the state's assault—on any grounds. In this sense, rumors served to justify official actions at the time.

4. *The use of rumors to explain the cause of disorder.*

Within hours after the assault, Governor Rockefeller issued a statement charging that the tragedy had been brought about by "the highly organized, revolutionary tactics of militants," and hinted strongly about the activities of certain "outside forces." When asked whether there was any proof regarding a militant plot or who the "outside forces" might be, the Governor's press secretary only said that there would be no elaboration at the time. Similarly, without citing any real evidence, Commissioner Oswald stated that the rebellious inmates at Attica "had fought the swiftest and most skillful revolutionary offensive since the 1968 Tet attack in South Vietnam."[19]

An entirely different and much more convincing picture emerged from the report of the McKay Commission, a special investigative body appointed by the state government. After exhaustive interviews with inmates, corrections officials, administrators, observers and experts, the Commission concluded as follows:

> Rather than being revolutionary conspirators bent only on destruction, the Attica rebels were part of a new breed of younger, more aware inmates, largely black, who came to prison full of deep feelings of alienation and hostility against the established institutions of law and government . . . and an unwillingness to accept the petty humiliations and racism that characterize prison life.

> Like the urban ghetto disturbances of the 1960s, the Attica uprising was the product of frustrated hopes and unfulfilled expectations, after their efforts to bring about meaningful change had failed.

> The uprising began as a spontaneous burst of violent anger and was not planned or organized in advance.[20]

Where public officials are concerned, we generally associate the casual blaming of disorders on plots—out of

ignorance, habit or design—with those on the conservative
side, politically. We are not surprised when Lester Maddox
and Sam Yorty rant and rave about the Commies or
Black Panthers in their midst. But Commissioner Oswald
and Governor Rockefeller can hardly be placed in the same
category. Oswald is regarded as a decent, honest, well-in-
tentioned man who has spent his entire professional life in
social work and correctional service. Governor Rockefeller
has had a long and generally distinguished career in public
service. Both have addressed themselves on various occasions to the need for changes within the corrections
system. Thus, it is all the more disturbing and perplexing
when men of this caliber misguidedly point their fingers at
imagined conspirators, rather than existing conditions.

Without knowing the personal thoughts and motivations
of either man at the time, we can at least offer several
tentative explanations of why they did this. First, in
echoing a point made earlier, Oswald and Rockefeller were
both white and, therefore, shared the views, values and
beliefs of their fellow white citizens—who also formed the
basis of their constituencies. Thus charges of conspiracy—
even if they were not documented—fell on the friendly
ears of the dominant majority, who already believed that
blacks were plotting against the system.

The fact that both Oswald and Rockefeller were public
servants added another dimension. Despite certain reform-
ist leanings, both men were still representatives of the
system they sought to change. And, caught in the
immediate social crunch of a prison uprising, they opted
for the system against its detractors, now labelled "conspirators," "outside forces" and "revolutionaries." For to
put the blame squarely on the system would be, in part, an
admission of personal responsibility—placing both men in
an uncomfortable, perhaps untenable, position before the
public. It may be too cynical to accuse these two men and

other officials involved at the time of crying "plot" to save their own political skins. But, at the same time, they must certainly have been aware that attributing the cause of the uprising to "outsiders" deflected attention away from their own role as "insiders" within the system. Intentional or not, their conspiratorial view helped buttress their position, in the face of mounting criticism and a growing national debate about prison conditions and inmate grievances.

Another factor was their belief that Attica was a direct challenge to their authority. Convinced as they were that their power had been severely compromised by the uprising, they proceeded to paint the conflict in the grandest of strokes. It was not rebellion but revolution they were up against; it was a contest between the forces of good and evil; Attica was a test case for a broader conspiracy by the enemies of the Establishment:

> On the eve of Attica, then, the disinherited and the villainous, the alienated and the pawns, the flotsam and jetsam of society, and a new generation of revolutionary leaders focused on the prisons as their point of leverage. Here was where the Establishment could be made to buckle. . . .[21]

In their view, the nation's very survival could be at stake. For as Attica went, so went the rest of the country. According to Oswald, a major reason for Governor Rockefeller's decision not to go to Attica was his fear that other prisoners in other states might riot and demand the presence of their chief executives, whereupon "the whole prison system of the United States might be thrown into turmoil—not for prison reform, but as the trigger point of a national revolution."[22]

Thus, a complex mix of race and politics, tinged with personal prestige and power, influenced the way in which officials viewed and sought to explain the tragedy in conspiratorial terms. In the wake of the uprising, perhaps the most telling remark was made by State Comptroller Arthur Levitt, who asked: "If the 28 demands at Attica [representing a broad reform package] were acceptable by the state immediately, then why the hell could this have not been done before?"

Recommendations

This, then, represents the rumor syndrome as it functioned among public officials at Attica. Because this syndrome—either in part or as a whole—is applicable to so many situations, we make the following recommendations:

1. *The importance of verification.* At first glance, our pointing to the need for public officials to verify potentially important reports must sound rather elementary. It is. But, while simple and obvious, the point has too often been ignored by or lost on public officials—sometimes at serious cost. One of the lessons of Attica is that official reliance on faulty reports impaired their perspective and harmed, to some extent, the decision-making process. If Oswald and his associates had not readily accepted as true the terrible atrocity stories about the hostages, would they have acted differently? Perhaps not. The McKay Commission contended that the fundamental question was really the authority of the state, not the lives of the hostages. But even if this is so, if more accurate and complete information had been available—if corrections officials had taken the time to investigate the rumors—the issues might not have seemed quite so cut and dried, and the situation not so desperate. Greater thought might have been given to alternative, less drastic types of action—such as cutting off the inmates' food and water supply.

2. *Responsibility to the public.* When public officials

disseminate rumors to the people—whether it be the knee-jerk or political hat trick variety—there may be immediate political gains in terms of making their case before the public. At the same time, however, serious long-range problems may occur. The atrocity rumors which officials at Attica passed along to the press and public were exposed as false as soon as the autopsy reports were released. The result was a monstrous credibility gap and justifiable loss of public confidence in the officials involved. The damage done in terms of increasing racial animosity was even more serious. For, since the word of public officials is generally regarded as "authoritative," hammering home misinformation to the public in the form of anti-black rumors of brutality, conspiracy and the like could only serve to reinforce the hostile beliefs and racist attitudes of whites, while alienating blacks from the system even more.

This kind of behavior on the part of public officials presents something of a dilemma. After all, the ostensible role of public officials is to lead, to educate and to inform the public. If these individuals have difficulty in meeting their commitments and responsibilities, to whom can we turn to lead our leaders, educate our educators and inform out "informers"? From a long-range standpoint, the answer lies in attracting more young people into public service—people who are better educated, more sophisticated, more sensitive to racial and other social issues and, thus, less prone to picking up or playing upon white community-type rumors.

In the meantime, we need to search for ways of broadening the views of those who currently bear the public trust. One approach might be increased contact between politicians and professors—two groups which have a great deal in common, but who have been much too isolated from one another. For example, there ought to be more exchange programs in which public officials would receive university appointments, while academics would be "loaned out" to the government. For the public official, given more time to think, reflect and study, the experience would at least hold the promise of a new perspective regarding his or her responsibilities.

3. *Accountability.* Given their awesome responsibilities and power, public officials ought to be more directly accountable to the public and news media. When, for example, an official lapses into the familiar song-and-dance of "conspiracy," he or she ought to be expected to explain what is, after all, a serious charge. Greater accountability also requires greater responsibility on the part of the news media and the public.

When Governor Rockefeller made his charge of organized activity at Attica, the *New York Times* dutifully carried a front-page story the next day (September 14, 1971), headlined: "Governor Contends Uprising Was Work Of Revolutionaries." The fact that his press secretary failed to provide an ounce of evidence—indeed even refused to elaborate—was buried in the story. Did a story apparently based on hearsay—even from the governor of New York—really rate front-page coverage? Wouldn't a more appropriate headline have been: "Governor Accuses Revolutionaries—No Evidence Offered"? But no voices arose from the community to question the governor's claim. William J. Vanden Heuvel, chairman of a citizens' advisory group on corrections, could only say: "The word of riot spreads like the whirlwind to other prisons," warning that other inmates "may erupt at any time."

As we have stated, public officials have an obligation to inform the public and speak their mind. But, because of their position, their statements and actions ought to be subject to far more rigorous discussion and review by the public and press alike.

of provocative actions by the police actually triggered the disorder.

The parallels between the two cases are indeed striking: armed confrontations between blacks and police precipitating large-scale riots; early press reports placing the responsibility on blacks, faulting them as the aggressors, asserting that they had planned the violence; and subsequent evidence which showed the press was in error. Because the riots are so far apart in time—1917 vs. 1968—a question arises as to why the misreporting occurred in each instance. Is the answer to be found in the context of the immediate situation? Were the errors simply due to sloppy reporting by a few newspapermen or to the prevailing chaos of the moment? Or did the errors stem from more fundamental weaknesses inherent in the system of reporting? Put another way: do East St. Louis and Cleveland represent historical accidents in misreporting, or are they part of a more general pattern of bias which has tended to characterize media coverage of all interracial conflict?

A natural inclination to sensationalize the news may provide a partial answer to these questions, for any picture of murderers, plotters or other criminals is almost guaranteed to whet the appetite of the average viewer. The difficulty, however, is that this explanation begs the question of why blacks rather than whites have continually been the object of such attention. After all, there is no reason to suppose that the image of whites engaging in these same violent activities would not prove just as exciting and stimulating to the media audience. Thus sensationalism appears to be only a partial explanation.

The notion of a conspiracy by the news media—despite the widespread currency of this view among many activists today—is equally unsatisfactory. No hard evidence exists to support this view, and the picture of a bunch of "media barons" meeting secretly to devise ways of keeping blacks

THE ROLE OF THE NEWS MEDIA

Earlier we noted that a 1917 riot in East St. Lc
Illinois, was triggered by a faulty news account
Chapter 2). Some 50 years later a riot took plac
Cleveland, Ohio, under circumstances that were surpri
ly similar. On July 23, 1968, in response to intellig
reports (later shown to be rather shaky) that some b
were about to stage an armed uprising, the police
several unmarked cars to the area. A few hours la
group of armed blacks emerged from one of the h
under surveillance. Almost at once, an intense gun
broke out between the police and the black men, fo
by several days of disorder. At least nine person
killed, while the property damage losses were put ;
million.

Immediately, the Cleveland tragedy was describ
deliberate plot against the police and was said to
new phase in the course of racial conflict. The *C*
Press (July 24, 1968) compared the violence in C
to guerrilla activity in Saigon, and noted: "It did
to be a Watts, or a Detroit, or a Newark. Or even
of two years ago. No, this tragic night seemed to b
a plan." A reporter writing in the *New York Tir*
28, 1968) stated: "It marks perhaps the first do
case in recent history of black, armed, and
violence against the police." Investigations lat
taken by a task force of the National Commissi
Causes and Prevention of Violence, the Lemb
for the Study of Violence, and the *New Y*
(which had reversed its position) cast serious do
initial press reports, while revealing that the sit
far more complicated than had originally bee
The investigations suggested that, in all probabi

down, is no more plausible than the view of blacks continually conspiring against whites. Moreover, it is important that we draw a distinction here between cause and effect. While the kind of misreporting just cited may well have helped to maintain the status quo, that does not necessarily mean that the news media have pursued such a course as a matter of conscious policy. The media have been woefully irresponsible at times, but not inherently evil. If the latter diagnosis were correct, then the bad guys could simply be exposed by Nader's Raiders and sent to a special home for wayward journalists. (Or better yet, they could all be exiled to the New York *Daily News*.) As it is, the conspiratorial view remains an overly sinister and simplistic explanation.

We contend that many of the deficiencies of the media—including their dissemination of race-related rumors—lie in their very structure. For when we speak of the news media (newspapers, news magazines, radio and television), we are really speaking about the white media—white-owned, white-controlled, white-operated, white-dominated, and geared to an almost exclusively white audience. Throughout their history, the media have been comprised of thousands of individuals who, by and large, come from and represent the mainstream of American life. Therefore, aren't we likely to find the media expressing the prevailing sentiments of the dominant majority?

The white man's picture of the black individual—as aggressive, promiscuous, violent, criminal, influenced by agitators—should have a familiar ring to the reader. Public opinion surveys indicate how pervasive these negative and stereotyped white views about blacks are and suggest that the media have mirrored these views, sharing the perceptions of the larger society. But the media's role has not been entirely passive. Like actors before their audience, longing to please, the media have not been above playing to *their* audience—pandering to the fears, frustrations and hostilities of the general public. In this sense, the media stand highly accountable for their misreporting.

True, there have been some perceptible changes within the news media, not only as compared with the previous cycles of violence, but also during the later stages of the most recent wave. The media today are generally more sympathetic and more sensitive toward blacks. Guidelines for handling disorders have become standard operating procedure. And today, the media are better informed on the dangers of "rumor-reporting."

But serious problems remain.[23] For example, many guidelines specifically call for greater accuracy, the elimination of rumors and the avoidance of unverified statements. Unfortunately, in practice the media have paid little more than lip service to their own pronouncements and have continued to indulge in reporting rumors as fact—especially those emanating from the white community. These rumors are not only confined to the story itself, but are also contained in the words, pictures, headlines, and wire service reports, not to mention the media's interpretation of events. Let us therefore take a concrete look at how rumors manifest themselves in each of these areas.

The Story

When the Attica throat-slashing story reached the general public, only to be repudiated by the autopsy reports, there was disagreement about who bore the responsibility for this error. The McKay Report hit hard at corrections officials such as Walter Dunbar, for handing out unverified information to the news media. On the

other hand, Commissioner Oswald defended Dunbar as
having been "completely exhausted," blaming the news
media instead. ("The reporters, for their part, did not
check out these stories nor attribute the sources of other
stories.") While Oswald's explanation was, on one level, an
obvious case of buck-passing, it may surprise the reader to
learn that many within the ranks of the media agreed with
him. *St. Louis Journalism Review* (December 1971) called
the news coverage of the Attica uprising "sloppy and
incomplete." *Chicago Journalism Review* (December
1971) charged the media with gullibility: "Once again, the
press bought a false official report." But perhaps the best
and final word came from the editors of *Columbia
Journalism Review* (November/December 1971). Noting
that the confusion of the moment and the eagerness to file
a comprehensive story were both factors, they added:
"But there was something more, perhaps, at work to lend
credibility: the stereotypes [of blacks] that remained
printed on journalists' minds. . . ."

It is clear that, insofar as the "white" version of events
found a ready acceptance at Attica, the media bear a heavy
responsibility for misinforming the public.

Headlines

If it is true that one headline is worth a thousand words,
then headlines have a tremendous potential—one that is
too often realized—for telescoping rumors. Disparities
between headlines and news stories have been a continual
problem—often, much less occurs in a story than the
rumor-laden headline indicates. Take, for example, the
following headlines from successive editions of the St.
Louis *Post-Dispatch,* on July 17, 1970:

RIGHTS MILITANTS
TAKE OVER MEETING
(City Edition)
MILITANTS TAKE OVER
MEETING ON RIGHTS
(Second Edition)
ACTIVISTS ARE HEARD
AT RIGHTS MEETINGS
(Final Edition)

The headlines from the first two editions conjure up visions of Black Panthers storming into a meeting and seizing the microphones by force. But those who took the trouble to read the story carefully, and those who actually attended the meeting, knew that the "militants" had been granted time to speak prior to the conference. Only after the reporter who wrote the story complained was the headline finally changed, to reflect more accurately what had actually taken place.

A similar situation occurred in 1969, when some concerned parents in Jacksonville, Florida, removed their children from a local junior high school after a local radio station had broadcast an exaggerated report of a fight between black and white students. The school principal later indicated that "classes continued and there was no panic." Nevertheless, the Miami *Herald* headlined its story on April 25: "Moms Mob School After Riot 'News.'" Sometimes no violence occurs in the story, dramatic headlines to the contrary. A story appearing in the Boston *Globe* on May 10, 1969, told of a peaceful rally by a small group of students at a local theological seminary. According to the *Globe,* the rally was "brief and orderly." But the headline above the story read "Newton Campus Erupts." Conspiracy rumors are often condensed into fallacious headlines such as these:

'Outsiders' Linked to Omaha Rioting
(*Arkansas Gazette,* June 27, 1969)

Agitators Cited in Bladensburg Turmoil
(Washington, D.C. *Star,* November 19, 1969)

Organized Violence Suspected in Houston
(Dallas *Morning News,* September 28, 1970)

Carbondale Gunfight Linked to Panthers
(St. Louis *Globe-Democrat,* November 13, 1970)

In each case the charge was either unattributed or else incorrectly attributed in the story.

Words

The very words used in stories and headlines may be a subtle form of rumor. By themselves or strung together, words can convey a distorted impression of events, not based on verified fact. The Kerner Commission and others have documented the strong protest character of racial disorders in the 1960s as expressions of rage, anger and frustration by blacks. These studies have shown that the riot participants were even more dissatisfied with their condition than non-participants; the studies also failed to show that a disproportionate number of "criminal elements" were involved.

Certainly, these findings were applicable to the massive outburst of violence triggered by the assassination of Martin Luther King. How did the media handle the disorders? How did they describe the activities of the participants? The two following newspaper stories typify the coverage of these outbreaks at the time.

The Buffalo *News* ran this story on April 9, 1968, the day of Dr. King's funeral:

An uneasy calm enveloped Buffalo today—the day of Dr. Martin Luther King's funeral—after an evening of burning, rock throwing and looting by gangs of Negro youths. . . .

Roving gangs seemed to concentrate on [one] area, sweeping it from one end to the other several times. Gangs regrouped as soon as police moved on to other trouble spots.

The rampage seemed to swiftly gain in intensity from 7:30 to 9:30 PM, when reported vandalism started to slack off, finally dying out by 1 AM today. . . .

As the roving gangs began to concentrate on the Jefferson Ave. stores, police shut off all traffic along Jefferson between Best and East Ferry. . . .

Shortly after 7 PM Mayor Sedita sent about 40 volunteers, mostly Negroes, into the embattled neighborhoods to try to pacify the rampaging youths.

One day later, the Trenton *Times-Advertiser* ran this story:

Trenton was in a state of emergency today, reeling from the effects of a night of terror and worrying about the threat of more to come tonight.

The orgy of destruction and looting that broke over the city about 7:30 last night continued out of control until about 1:30 this morning. . . .

Of the more than 300 youths who rampaged through the downtown and Battle Monument areas last night, 108 were in the county jail today. . . .

The riot gained momentum quickly soon after 6:30 PM when gangs of youths began roaming the downtown area and some incidents were reported. But by 7:30, it was in full swing. . . .

The marauders literally ran the police in circles. . . . All along the way, there was the sound of broken display windows to mark the movement of the vandals.

> For the most part, the rioters appeared to be on a gay holiday. But the gaiety was punctuated by sudden flareups of tension between police and rioters.

Value-laden words receive unusual emphasis. Who are the participants? They are young and black. That much is clear. But we are also told that they are "marauders," not men; that they travel in "gangs," not groups. What do they do? They go around "roaming," "roving," and "rampaging." What is it like to engage in the violence? It's a "gay holiday," an "orgy," "in full swing." As described in these stories, the participants behave in a wild, crazy manner which is thoroughly consistent with the prevailing view of disorders as meaningless and irrational.

The terms "gangs" and "marauders," along with others such as "hoodlums," "toughs," "troublemakers" and "rowdies," are among the words most commonly used by the media. The problem is that we have all grown so used to viewing blacks as stereotyped criminals that it is difficult to imagine them in any other role. Thus we encounter such phrases as "roving gangs," "roving gangs of hoodlum youths," "roving gangs of rampaging teenagers," or (for variety) "a window-smashing rampage by roving gangs of Negro youths." The *New York Times'* assertion on July 1, 1969, that "roving bands of ruffians" were involved in a disturbance in Middletown, Connecticut, seems somewhat feeble by comparison.

Pictures

Rumors may also crop up in the form of pictures. Toward the end of a disturbance in York, Pennsylvania, in mid-July 1968, a photographer took a picture of a motorcyclist with an ammunition belt around his waist and a rifle strapped across his back. A small object dangled from the rifle. On July 18, the picture reached the nation's press. The *Washington Post* said:

> ARMED RIDER—Unidentified motorcyclist drives through heart of York, Pa., Negro district, which was quiet for the first time in six days of sporadic disorders.

The Baltimore *Sun* used the same picture and a similar caption:

> QUIET, BUT ... An unidentified motorcycle rider, armed with a rifle and carrying a belt of ammunition, was among those in the heart of York, Pa., Negro district last night. The area was quiet for the first time in six days.

The implication of this photograph was clear: the "armed rider" was a sniper. But since when do snipers travel openly in daylight completely armed? Also, isn't there something incongruous about photographing a sniper, presumably "on his way to work," when, according to the caption, the city was "quiet"? Actually the "armed rider" was a 16-year-old boy who happened to be fond of hunting groundhogs—a skill he had learned as a small child. On July 16, as was his custom, the young man had put on his ammo belt and strapped a rifle across his back, letting a hunting license dangle so that all would know he was hunting animals, not people. Off he went on his motorcycle headed for the woods, the fields, the groundhogs— and the place reserved for him in the nation's press.

The Wire Services

The picture of the "armed rider" in York, which reached readers in Baltimore and Washington, was actually furnished by a stringer from the UPI office in Harrisburg, Pennsylvania. The wire services are probably the most under-examined segment of the media, although well over half the news in a given newspaper or newscast on a particular day probably comes from the wires. Since one error in a wire service report from one city may be repeated and communicated to hundreds of communities across the country, the wire services are a powerful tool in the spreading of rumors.

On October 24, 1970, for example, United Press International and the Associated Press—the two major wire services—issued releases about a supposed raid on a police station in the racially beleaguered town of Cairo, Illinois, by "squads of armed Negro men" (UPI) or 19 to 20 "rifle-wielding blacks in army fatigue uniforms" (AP). Hundreds of rounds of ammunition were reportedly fired in what appeared to be a deliberate, unprovoked attack on the police. The story made its way into scores of newspapers across the country, ranging from the *New York Times* and the *Washington Post,* to the Milwaukee *Journal* and the Ann Arbor *News*; to *Newsweek* magazine; to countless radio and television newscasts. Omitted from the story was the fact that a black-owned tavern, a church used for meetings by blacks, and the offices of a civil rights lawyer were all riddled with bullets at about the same time of the alleged raid by blacks.

This story was not only misleading; it was inaccurate as well. A skeptical *Times* reporter (Seth S. King) who took the trouble to do a follow-up story for his newspaper could only find 17 pockmarks on the police station which "could" have been caused by gunfire that night. *Chicago Journalism Review* (December 1970) has gone so far as to suggest that the alleged raid never took place. But these follow-up stories could do little to offset the initial damage done by the earlier wire service reports.

Martin Hayden of the Detroit *News* has suggested "an

almost mathematical relationship between the level of exaggeration and the distance of news transmission." Edwin Guthman of the Los Angeles *Times* maintains that the early wire service report "is at the crux of the news media's problem." Our own research indicates that misreporting by way of rumors remains a problem at *every* media level, although its effects are usually more widespread in the hands of the wire services.

Interpretation

No law says that the media have to interpret, and not simply report, the news. But, having assumed this responsibility, they have an obligation to make reasonable judgments, based on careful analysis and research. Unfortunately, journalistic attempts in the direction of social science have not only been rather amateurish; they have also been biased against blacks, particularly where new trends and patterns are concerned. For example, following the Cleveland "shootout" in 1968, disorders in which shots may have been fired were immediately suspected by the media of being part of a "wave" of black-instigated violence. A series of rumors involving a handful of cities became the basis of a myth—that the pattern of violence in 1968 had changed from spontaneous to premeditated outbreaks. Few of the nationally known newspapers, news magazines or news networks attempted to verify sniping reports coming out of the cities and over the wire services; few were willing to undertake independent investigations; and far too many were overly zealous in their assertions of a new "trend," based on limited and unconfirmed evidence. Heaping one rumor on top of another, the national media had constructed a scenario of full-scale armed uprisings.

Although they have more time to check and verify reports than daily newspapers, the news magazines were even more vocal in their assertions of a "new pattern." On September 13, 1968, *Time* took note of an "ominous trend" and declared that the violence "appears to be changing from the spontaneous combustion of a mob to the premeditated shoot-outs of a far-out few." The story went on to indicate that "many battles" had begun with "well-planned sniping at police." Nearly a year later, on June 27, 1969—long after the misreporting had been exposed—*Time* was still talking about the possibilities of a "guerrilla summer" and reminding its readers of the time in Cleveland when "police were lured into an ambush." Once started, rumors are always difficult to extinguish.

Recommendations

Press reports of throat-slashings by blacks; an imagined black sniper perched on a motorcycle; an alleged raid by armed blacks against a police station; continual suggestions of black conspiracies. These and other examples, including the historical ones mentioned in Chapter 2, are not simply errors in reporting. They are also evidence of a pattern of bias—more specifically, an enormous susceptibility on the part of the white-dominated media to the types of rumors found in the white community. From the standpoint of rumor-reporting alone, it is clear that blacks have continually received a raw deal from the American news media. In a broader sense, the media have borne an important responsibility for needlessly increasing racial tensions—tensions which, in combination with other factors, have often created a climate conducive to violence. When violence has occurred, the media have frequently presented a distorted view of reality, seeming to justify rather than explain events. Finally, and most important, they have all too often appealed—consciously or not—to the baser instincts of their predominantly white audience, building walls instead of bridges between the races.

These pessimistic conclusions are even more striking because the news media are one of the most powerful institutions in the country. If the media are not exactly "alive, well—and kicking like mad," as Katharine Graham, publisher of the *Washington Post,* stated recently, nevertheless we must proceed on the assumption that they have a potential for change.

Therefore, while realizing that any attempt to make the media less rumor-prone must be considered part of a more general reduction of bias against blacks—and believing that both are in the realm of possibility, the following recommendations are offered:

1. *Enforcement of guidelines.* Updating its guidelines for reporting racial disorders in March 1968, the Associated Press stated:

We don't rush out with rumors of impending trouble.

We don't rush out with a story about a disturbance on the basis of a single telephone call.

Check and double check.

But AP, and the rest of the media, still do not follow these guidelines consistently. Because they have not been seriously enforced thus far, the guidelines have been little more than window dressing designed to appease critics of the media. Frequently the average reporter—the man or woman on the beat who actually covers the disorder—is not even acquainted with these guidelines.

In principle, the existence of guidelines indicates a growing awareness of the media's responsibilities; but they are of no real value unless translated into practice. The AP guidelines say: "We have three rules: (1) ACCURACY. (2) ACCURACY. (3) ACCURACY." To which we suggest two additional sets of rules: VERIFY. VERIFY. VERIFY; and, ENFORCE. ENFORCE. ENFORCE THE GUIDELINES.

2. *Exposing rumors*. Hand in hand with the media's responsibility to refrain from reporting rumors is its obligation to expose those rumors making the rounds of the community. On July 27, 1967, the South Bend *Tribune* ran an editorial which serves as a model of this important function and is reproduced here in its entirety:

TALKING UP TROUBLE

If there had been no civil disturbance in South Bend the last two nights, a lot of residents would have been disappointed.

It was not that they desired trouble. It was simply that they had convinced themselves, primarily through groundless rumors, that trouble was imminent.

Rumors were rampant in the community all day Tuesday, and residents were all too willing to believe anything they heard. Wednesday was worse.

There were reports of a Sunday night disturbance which was 'kept quiet.' The reports had no truth, but they circulated and grew through the day nevertheless.

When a batch of Army helicopters landed at St. Joseph County Airport Tuesday afternoon, two sets of rumors started flying. One was that the helicopters contained federal troops which had come to put down riots variously described as already under way, or expected during the night. The other set of rumors was that the helicopters had brought 'outside agitators' in to start trouble.

Many of the rumor mongers implied that the news media were 'covering up' whatever it was the mongers were spreading. And the community, nervously watching the eruptions in neighboring

> Michigan, was all too ready to accept every back-fence or
> telephone rumor as truth.
>
> It is hard to document a cause-and-effect connection between
> rumors and events which follow them. But there are always a few
> hotheads willing to oblige those who believe the worst, and the
> more generally trouble is expected, the more likely it is to come.
>
> We hope that this community has got a grip on itself by now,
> and that the rumor mongers will be treated with the skepticism
> that common sense suggests.

This editorial was valuable on several counts. First, it
singled out and detailed the most troublesome rumors
afflicting the public—at least, the white public; second, it
drew a clear distinction between fact and fiction; and
finally, it called attention to the responsibilities of the
community with regard to such rumors.

We are not saying here that a single editorial had the
capacity to nip the rumors in the bud, or that they
necessarily had a calming influence during a difficult time.
All along we have maintained that race-related rumors are
less the product of immediate circumstances than the
result of the deeply ingrained beliefs of the people. But if
there were more news stories and editorials like the one in
the *Tribune,* given the media's role as a trusted authority,
the eventual effect would be a subtle but significant assault
on those hostile beliefs which are the major source of
racially divisive rumors.

The media's obligation to root out rumors also extends
to the domain of public officials. In particular, the media
must begin to report more critically news handed out by
public officials—especially news in the form of unverified
statements. When Governor Rockefeller made his charge of
"revolutionaries" at Attica and failed to document it, the
media's responsibility went beyond reporting his statement

in robot-like fashion. Attention should also have been focused on his glaring lack of supporting evidence, along with a challenge that such information be supplied to the public. In this way, the burden of proof would have been placed on the accuser, where it rightly belonged, rather than on the accused—in this case the inmates, who were hardly in a position to defend or speak for themselves.

Better yet, when such answers from public officials are not forthcoming, the media should be more aggressive in seeking the answers themselves. Immediately after the shootout between the New Orleans police and a sniper or snipers at a Howard Johnson's Motor Lodge in 1973, Louisiana's Attorney General said he was convinced that there was a "nationwide conspiracy" to murder policemen, and promptly demanded a Justice Department investigation. For days his statement received enormous play in both the electronic and print media. But, once again, the media's role was essentially passive, merely reporting what the official had said, with little interest or inclination to initiate investigations of their own.

In the sensitive area of racial conflict, the media must assert themselves more vigorously in holding our public officials responsible for their statements and actions. To fail to do so is to risk their own highly valued independence and integrity, to ally themselves with the official rather than the public interest, and to forfeit their opportunity and obligation to make public officials themselves more rumor-conscious.

As we stated earlier, decreasing the degree of rumor-reporting ultimately depends on a reduction of a more general media bias. Therefore, let us turn to some recommendations aimed at the larger issue of bias.

3. *Pressuring the traditional media.* Over the last few years some important news developments have occurred which have the potential for dramatically altering the

system of reporting, making it more responsive to the
needs of society. One of these developments is the rise of
the alternative or "underground" press. Seven years ago,
the underground press was practically nonexistent. Today,
practically every urban region of the country supports at
least one such publication.[24] Moreover, there are a
number of radio stations on FM bands, such as WBCN in
Boston, WBAI in New York and KSAN in San Francisco,
which also fall into the "alternative" category.

Given their excesses and considering the shoestring
quality of most of their operations, there is some question
as to whether the alternative media have much of a future.[25] But even if they should fade in time, they have a
remarkable list of accomplishments to their credit. First,
they have demonstrated a consistent ability to attract and
hold the interest of young people, something the regular
media have been unable to do. Second, they have been
able to gain access to the dissenters. If black students take
over a building, chances are the establishment media will
talk first and frequently last to the local police chief, the
mayor and other white officials. Opting for the black, as
opposed to the white version of events, the alternative
media will go directly to the students inside the building.
Third, they have shown themselves more responsive to
social issues—more sensitive and better able to anticipate
them, often demonstrating a firmer grip on reality than the
standard media. Stories within the alternative media on the
subject of "white racism" appeared far in advance of the
Kerner Report, which then legitimized the term and made
it respectable for the Establishment media to use. The
Berkeley *Barb* warned about the potentially dangerous
effects of chemical Mace months before the Establishment
press took note of it. Similarly, while the traditional media
swallowed the white version of events and misrepresented
a supposed raid on a police station in Cairo, Illinois, the

Guardian ran a series of incisive reports on the veritable race war going on in the town—more than three months before the *New York Times* gave the story any real coverage in its Sunday magazine.

Finally, whether or not it has been their intention, the "underground" media have succeeded in forcing the Establishment media to take stock of itself. Indeed, the signs of ferment are visible all around us. Between 1968 and December 1972, at least a dozen journalism reviews have cropped up, including ones in Baltimore, Chicago, Denver, Holyoke, Mass., Honolulu, Houston, Los Angeles, New York City, Philadelphia, Providence, San Francisco, St. Louis and St. Paul/Minneapolis. New reviews have also been discussed in such disparate locations as Albany, New York, Washington, D.C. and Anchorage, Alaska. These publications now provide an important forum for working journalists to make important criticisms openly.

There are other signs of change as well. The *Washington Post* now employs an ombudsman who has the power to examine as well as anticipate complaints. A number of newspapers have followed the lead of the *New York Times* and begun an "Op. Ed." page designed to air different points of view. Five years ago, who would have believed that Bobby Seale, Imamu Amiri Baraka and Angela Davis would have by-lines in the *Times*?

Another promising development is the establishment of a national press council. On November 30, 1972, the Twentieth Century Fund announced that a national press council was being formed to monitor the performance of the national media. The council, consisting of 15 members from the press and the public, will accept and investigate complaints from the public about inaccurate or unfair news coverage and issue findings. The council will have no coercive powers.[26]

Predictably, the council has stirred heavy opposition

within some quarters of the media. On January 15, 1973, Arthur Ochs Sulzberger, publisher of the *New York Times,* said his paper would refuse to cooperate with the council, criticizing it as "a form of voluntary regulation in the name of enhancing press freedom."[27]

Despite such opposition, it seems certain that the national council will become a reality. Only time will tell how effective it will be; but even now it is clear that the council idea represents a welcome initiative worthy of the fourth estate.

These developments, then—the rise of alternative media, the burgeoning of journalism reviews, the establishment of a national press council—are evidence of the increasing pressure being exerted on our traditional media. If these and other constructive pressures continue to be applied, we can expect to see a decrease in media's bias (including the tendency to report white community-type rumors), a shortening of their response-time to social issues, and possibly an enlarged view of their role in society.

4. *Racial composition: the dark side of the media.* It comes as no real surprise to find that the media consistently relay lily-white rumors. How could it be otherwise, since the media essentially relay information from and about only one segment of the population—the white community? The media have always reported and written from a white perspective. The problems, the needs and the culture of minority peoples in this country have been almost totally ignored by the press—except for the reporting of crime.

One reason for the distorted stories and inadequate coverage of minority communities is that there are not enough minority journalists involved in the news-gathering process. Even though it has been more than five years since the Kerner Report called the journalistic establishment "shockingly backward" in seeking out, hiring, training and

promoting blacks, the picture today has not really changed—except for a token black face here and there. According to a study undertaken by the Office of Communication
of the United Church of Christ, the results of which were
issued at the end of 1972, 50 percent of this country's
commercial television stations employ *no* members of
racial minority groups in professional capacities. Among
the other findings reported were these:

— 77 percent of commercial stations are "pure white"
  in managerial positions.
— 55 percent employ no minorities as technicians.
— 81 percent hire only whites as sales personnel.

The situation for the print media is no better. The
American Society of Newspaper Editors reported in April
1972 that blacks and other minorities constituted less than
1 percent of all professional newspaper staffs (reporters
and photographers) in the country.

Changing the complexion of the media to more accurately reflect our country's racial composition will not solve
all the media's bias problems. But it will serve as a partial
corrective and draw us a bit closer to the vision of the
media as "makers" and "shakers," as one Florida journalist
put it, rather than "followers."[28]

5. *The wire services.* In April 1971, UPI and AP held
meetings to demonstrate their major new techniques for
speeding the dissemination of news. UPI indicated it was
establishing an automated communications system which
would link its Asian network with domestic and European
circuits. AP showed the nationwide multiplex system,
which uses a leased telegraph circuit broken down into
separate channels and high-speed wires to move sports
news at a rate of 1,050 words a minute and stock market
quotations at 2,000 words a minute. By any standard,
these are important and impressive achievements. But, as
in so many other areas, our human resources have failed to

keep pace with our technological advancements. From a qualitative standpoint, the reporting of these news services has remained about the same.

Wire service blunders, as in the case of Cairo, Illinois, mentioned earlier, illustrate this point. Stringers for both UPI and AP who filed stories about the alleged police raid were from the Cairo area and had close ties with the white power structure. The UPI stringer was a news reporter for a local radio station, whose manager was on the board of directors of the White Hats, a white vigilante group. Significantly, the information used in both press releases was obtained exclusively from the police and the mayor—both of whom were known to be unfriendly to blacks. Two questions arise: first, why did UPI and AP have such individuals in their employ at all?; and, second, why had neither wire service seen fit previously to station less biased, more experienced reporters from some outside area—say, Chicago—in Cairo on a regular basis for what had really been a continuing story of escalating racial conflict for nearly two years?

It is significant that, in the face of this kind of shoddy performance, *AP Review,* an anonymously published sheet, folded after two issues due to fear of management retribution. Given their enormous power, the wire services must become more accountable to the public. The national press council's plan to monitor the major distributors of news, including the national wires, is a step in the right direction. But we need a lot more constructive criticism from both within and without, a general upgrading of staff—along with special attention to hiring more blacks and young whites, in order to really solve this problem.

Finally, the other segments of the media must become more independent and learn to rely less on the wire services. In recent years, the various components of the media have become extremely interdependent. The wire services, the nationally known newspapers, news magazines and television networks feed one another news and information. While the system undoubtedly speeds the flow of news to the public, it has also encouraged a parrot-like character, in which the "different" media segments tend to reproduce rather than examine one another's views. The difference between *Time* and *Newsweek,* Walter Cronkite and John Chancellor, is really the difference between Coke and Pepsi. As it is, the system of reporting ensures that errors of fact and interpretation will be repeated, compounded and reformulated as myths. New initiatives, and less tolerance for the superficial, are vitally needed at every level of the media.

We have all grown so dependent on our news media that the time has come to demand more of it. It is capable of giving much more—and, more important, it is also capable of giving much less than it now does.

RUMOR CONTROL CENTERS: WHAT ROLE?

In recent years, there has been a growing recognition that the dissemination of rumors is a problem of serious proportions. In 1969, Delaware's Governor Russell W. Peterson branded the spreading of unconfirmed stories as "a serious disease," instructing the State Human Relations Commission to "think big" in coming up with proposals to combat the process. The following year in Norfolk, Virginia, at a meeting to discuss ways of averting further school disturbances, the head of the Youth Board said that the real need in the community was for accurate information to combat the "rumor-mongers." "We've got to figure out a way to beat the rumors," he added. "And the police can't do it themselves." Not long ago, the *Police Chief* magazine devoted its lead article to a discussion of explosive rumors. The magazine's cover showed a riot-torn city in ruins. Amid the outlines of flames and huge puffs of smoke was the word "RUMOR!" printed in red, bold-faced type.

"Beating the Rumors"

A variety of approaches have been attempted to find a solution.[29] An Arizona newspaper called the Scottsdale *Progress* has run a column entitled "Rumor Clinic" to find out the answers to questions asked by the public concerning local problems. The Anti-Defamation League of B'nai B'rith uses a film strip as the basis of a "Rumor Clinic" program designed to make individuals more rumor-conscious. As part of a "cool it" effort in 1967, Washington, D.C.'s Urban League conducted a Community Alert Project in which 28 young blacks circulated through their neighborhood, assessing problems, intervening in tense situations and filtering out provocative rumors. The state of Indiana proposed a more controversial program. In 1970, the Indiana Criminal Justice Planning Agency (CJPA) drafted a plan for hiring neighborhood police informers, known as "rumor control monitors," in three or four major Indiana cities. The idea was soon dropped, following the admission by the CJPA director that the plan could lead to a spy network.

So the means for dealing with rumors have been many and varied. But by far the most common attempt has been through establishing a telephone service to combat rumors and provide information to the public, especially during times of stress. Generally this service is called a rumor control center, but other names have been used as well.

Philadelphia has had a "Rumor Central"; Eugene, Oregon, a "Verification Center"; Champaign, Illinois, a "Rumor Clarification Committee"; Portland, Oregon, a "Fact Factory"; while Lawrence, Long Island, instituted a 24-hour telephone service as part of its "Kill a Rumor Today" campaign.

Chicago's Rumor Central, located within the Commission on Human Relations building, has served as a model for other cities. When fully activated, the service consists of ten telephones, personnel to man the telephones, a communications hookup with the police and fire departments as well as other city agencies, and finally, two persons to check out rumors and receive incoming reports from these other groups. This operation can be expanded or decreased, depending on the volume of calls. A large map of the city overlaid with plastic is used to locate trouble areas. Cordoned-off streets are marked in black; alternate bus lines in yellow; sniping areas in blue; while arson spots are colored red.

The rumor control setup is basically simple and inexpensive. A telephone, a few people and some advertising are all that is required to establish a rudimentary operation. Its size is determined by the needs and desires of the city in which it functions. The program in San Bernadino was funded with $40,000; the San Mateo operation was budgeted at just $126 per year (the estimated cost of a single annual phone bill).

There is no way to determine the actual number of cities which have had some sort of rumor control center. However, indications are that the figure is substantial. The National Association of Police Community Relations Officers (NAPCRO) took a survey of rumor control centers in 1970, including every city in the United States with a population of more than 300,000. More than half the cities responding—at least 26 out of 45—indicated that they had experimented with this mechanism. We have been able to document a minimum total of 97 cities—large and small—with these institutions, making rumor control centers something of a national phenomenon.[30] Even the United States Senate, hardly known for its innovative spirit, has been "with it" in this regard. In 1968 a communications service to keep the Senators informed on civil disturbances was quietly installed in senate offices on Capital Hill. Each senator was given a special line connecting his private office with the Capitol Police, where a recording device would give out the latest reports. These "riot phones" were installed to avoid the kind of rumor circulation that swept the Hill during a serious riot after the King assassination.

Background

While the problem of rumor control did not receive widespread attention until the series of race-related emergencies arose in our cities during the 1960s, the idea itself is not new. Previous efforts were concerned with preventing the spread of harmful rumors during the second World War. These efforts took place on the local and national levels, and involved various private and public organizations. The refutation of specific rumors was undertaken by "rumor clinic" columns in newspapers and magazines, and on radio broadcasts as well. Governmental efforts at rumor control included publications of the Office of Facts and Figures. Straddling the line between national security and public insecurity, the Office of War Information (OWI) tried to counter rumors by filling the news gap and improving the quality of news releases. "Security of information" slogans were invented, including such gems as "Zip Your Lip and Save a Ship." (Today's counterpart would probably be "Keep Quiet and Prevent a Riot.")

The most recent impetus for rumor abatement seems to have started with the establishment of a Rumor Central in Chicago in 1967, much heralded by the national media. The findings and recommendations of the Kerner Report proved to be equally important. The Report drew attention to the problem of rumors in the context of racial disorders, stating that rumors were a significant factor in escalating the situation in more than 65 percent of the disturbances studied, and that they made the job of police and community leaders more difficult. Singling out Chicago's Rumor Central for praise, the Commission endorsed rumor control centers as "an innovative method" for the collection, evaluation and counteraction of rumors which could lead to disorders. Lest it seem that the Kerner Report has had no impact outside the academic community, we should point out that cities setting up such centers have invariably cited the relevant passages of this study.

The spin-off effect from Chicago's Rumor Central and the Kerner Commission's strong endorsement of the idea was considerable. Two months after the release of the Kerner Report, the control center idea received an additional airing at a conference held in Chicago by the Community Relations Service of the U.S. Department of Justice. NAPCRO, the group representing policemen involved in community relations, has termed the creation of rumor control centers "a worthwhile municipal endeavor."[31] The International City Managers' Association has pushed the idea, noting: "Rumors are the sparks that ignite and fan many a riot. With modern advances in communications, the spreading of rumors during civil disorders is easier than ever before."[32] Meanwhile, a task force for the National Commission on the Causes and

Prevention of Violence has spoken in favor of "rumor-clearance centers" which would have close ties to the media.[33] Clearly, rumor control centers have been enthusiastically embraced and sanctioned by an impressive array of official groups and agencies.

Evaluation

Assessing rumor control centers in terms of their effectiveness and value to the community is not an easy task. Indeed, the problem of evaluating any social or educational campaign is a perplexing one. Do rumor control centers help to diminish rumors? It is difficult to obtain conclusive evidence on this subject. Regarding rumor control centers, we can probably agree that citing the number of telephone calls per crisis, as has been done by some of the system's proponents, is not an adequate measure. But beyond this, the best we can do is to outline the objectives of these centers as defined by their advocates and architects and, on the basis of our knowledge of rumors and rumor control centers, offer some reasonable judgments.

According to the mass of memorandums, leaflets, and other literature issued by those in charge of rumor control centers, their purposes are:

1. to inhibit and avoid the spread of harmful rumors which feed disorders.
2. to help restore calm during periods of social upheaval, alleviating and quieting the fears and anxieties which accompany rumors.
3. to increase efficiency in handling disorders through better coordination of information needed by city departments and other private agencies.

4. to provide citizens with a central, reliable and official source of information.

5. to make the public more rumor-conscious, putting people on guard against rumors in general.

6. to help bridge the communications gap between the black community and municipal services, while building confidence in our institutions as responsive and "willing to listen."

7. to collect and analyse rumors which lead to racial and other civil disorders.

Thus rumor control centers may be said to have three primary objectives: riot control, riot prevention and the establishment of an information service available to the general public.

If success can be measured by accolades, then rumor control centers have performed their functions well. The confidence displayed by public officials and the news media in such centers has been overwhelming. In establishing a center in Joliet, Illinois, the city manager indicated he considered it "a necessity" in these trying times. Crediting the Los Angeles Rumor Control and Information Center with keeping Watts "cool," the Dallas *Post-Tribune* said, on August 29, 1970: "The pulse of the whole urban crisis beats through the Center as it processes data, coordinates information, investigates issues, monitors activities, and reports emergencies—all for the progress and protection of the community . . . from within and from without." The chairman of the Board of Commissioners in Wayne County, Michigan, issued a claim that "two-thirds or more of the rumors that are circulated can be stopped by means of this device." Meanwhile, the Philadelphia *Bulletin* on October 7, 1969, ran a headline which must have been very reassuring to its readers:

'DON'T WORRY, SWEETIE';
RUMOR CONTROL KEEPS AN
EYE ON TROUBLE

To the extent that rumor control centers have provided the public with quick access to information and eased the burden on the police and other agencies, they have been a useful aid to many cities in distress. On the whole, however, rumor centers have not lived up to their press clippings or promise. We believe that they are of extremely limited value in meeting any, much less all, of their stated objectives; that they have been generally ineffective, both as a riot control technique and as a means of riot prevention; that insofar as they have rendered a public service, they have rendered it to the white community, by and large ignoring the black; that the reasons for their existence are rooted in certain invalid assumptions; and, finally, that they are counterproductive, because they not only treat rumors as an isolated problem, they treat it as *the* problem, with rumor control as *the* solution. Because our own assessment is critical of rumor control—both in concept and as constituted in fact—and because ours is something of a maverick view, let us treat these points in finer detail.

Some of the problems besetting rumor control centers have been of a minor nature. For example, the Chicago Riot Study Committee found that, when the city was in flames after the King assassination, a large number of callers were unable to reach the Rumor Central, due to the agency's overtaxed telephone lines. Because of insufficient phones, some people who called continually received a busy signal and, according to the study, "became panic stricken." South Bend's rumor control service was of no use during a disturbance because no one answered the phone—despite repeated efforts by various citizens to reach the number. At the time of a disorder in the ghetto of Venice, California, crowds gathered when a rumor control staffer from the Los Angeles agency was halted by a policeman with a drawn revolver. But these and other mistakes were understandable; such things were to be expected as part of the process of starting any new operation.

Other problems proved more bothersome and serious. Some rumor control centers—such as those in Boston, Chicago, Detroit and Los Angeles—have been full-time services, operating seven days a week with paid staffs and well-publicized telephone numbers. But the vast majority of these centers have been fly-by-night affairs, arising during disorders, folding in their aftermath. Most rumor control centers are now dormant or have been quietly phased out of existence, which means that their long-term goals—making the public more rumor-conscious, improving communications between the black community and city government, doing data collection and analysis, etc.—were never realized.

But, even in the days when rumor control centers flourished, there was a certain incongruity about them. For, if the centers were designed to aid in the control and prevention of riots, necessity and logic would dictate that they reach those people who were most involved—directly or indirectly—namely, the black community. But this was not the case. Rumor control centers serviced the white community primarily; relatively few calls were received from blacks. The Chicago Riot Study Committee found that the city's Rumor Central, which handled some 40,000 calls at the time of the King disturbance, provided "little service" to the residents of the riot areas, adding: "In the opinion of the employees of the commission [on Human Relations], most of those who telephoned Rumor Central were white, not Negro."[34] Writing about the Urban

League's rumor control center in Washington, D.C., which opened up during the King disorders, columnist William Raspberry noted: "Most of the calls then were from the suburbs and the callers mainly wanted to know whether it was true that the rioters were headed that way, whether specific acts of sabotage were in the works or was it true that snipers were at such and such location."[35] Detroit's Rumor Control Center averaged 132 calls per day prior to the assassination of Dr. King and 915 calls the day after the shooting. During the ensuing three days, over 1,000 calls per day were received. A memo written by the Detroit Commission on Community Relations states specifically: "These calls came mainly from the suburbs surrounding Detroit (mainly white communities)."[36] Nevertheless, the commission reached the somewhat puzzling conclusion: "CCR staff believes a Rumor Control Center is absolutely vital to a community experiencing heightened social tensions. . . ."[37]

The reasons why rumor control centers did not service the black community are not difficult to fathom. In the first place, "rumor control" was automatically equated with "riot control" in the minds of many blacks—and both of these were regarded as forms of repression. Typical of this kind of thinking was the charge issued by one black newspaper that the Los Angeles Rumor Control and Information Center was guilty of "unethical activities," and had "an entire espionage network, designed exclusively for and operating exclusively against Black citizens."[38] The credibility problem was a related factor. Few centers were initiated, sponsored or based in the black community. Our own survey (see Appendix G) suggests that most rumor control centers were grafted onto existing institutions—chiefly human relations commissions, police departments and mayors' offices—better known to blacks as the white power structure. If calling most such centers

'No, ma'am, no one was stabbed last night. Someone was injured on Handy Street. Bernie Fleming, he was beat up. The police are still investigating.'

With confidence and finality, the article added: "And another rumor is quashed." But was it? Rumor Control advocates such as these would have us believe that facts have some magical power invested in them to "quash," "quell," "combat," "spike," "suppress," "abate," "counter" and "dispel" rumors—or as Williams and Erchak put it, they have the power "to break the rumor cycle."

While this approach espoused by Shibutani and others works in some situations, we have demonstrated that it is not always valid in the context of racial disorders. In this particular situation, the key element is the hostile belief set operating among members of each race, not ambiguity. As a footnote to our point, we might add that, even though much time has elapsed since the Attica tragedy and all the relevant facts have long since come in, there are many whites living in the vicinity of that correctional facility—and elsewhere—who still believe the throat-slashing stories.

The other faulty assumption upon which the rumor control center system is based is that rumors are a causal factor in the violence. For example, misinterpreting the Kerner Report, the memo issued by Detroit's Commission on Human Relations states: "Communication patterns in riots was of particular interest to the Commission. It was pointed out [in the Kerner Report] that much of the trouble occurring in the summer of 1967 was generated through distortion of facts and information."[40] The Philadelphia *Bulletin* story on rumor control (October 7, 1969), which dwelled on the role of rumor in the serious Tampa disorder of 1967, is a more graphic illustration of his thinking:

"rumor control" was insensitive, then locating th
the traditional channels of government was, a
least, shortsighted and naive.

We are not saying that whites should l
excluded from this service; for, as we have lea
our research, rumor networks, along with th
which accompany them, are found in both the
white communities. However, the inability
control centers to reach *all* segments of the
represents a signal failure of their stated objecti

This last point brings us to a key questi
centers had been able to reach the black
would it have made a difference in controllin
rumors or the violence? We think not, given o
rumor control centers were predicated on
assumptions. The first of these assumptions is
are a form of "improvised news," filling an
gap. When people are confronted with a situa
ambiguous, problematic or unclear, a solid dc
all that is needed to make troublesome rumor:
so the reasoning goes. For example, William
state:

> An alternative to rumor formation and the 'i
> news' does exist. . . . The modern society does ha
> filling information gaps, and this is the function
> centers in our cities.[39]

Similarly, the New Brunswick *Home Neu
called "A Phone Call Away . . ." on March 2
time of some school disturbances:

> The white telephone on the black desk rings
> answers. 'Sheriff Flanagan, rumor phone.'

A young black man was shot as he fled through a ghetto from a robbery. To keep from falling when he was hit, he grabbed a fence.

People poured out of neighboring buildings to see what was going on. They saw the wounded man in what they took to be a posture of surrender, his back turned, his hands up, clutching the wire fence. In minutes a rumor was rampant: 'Shot down in cold blood by a white cop as he was trying to give up!'

Tampa's toll—two dead, 16 injured, thousands of dollars of property damage.

An incident, an inflammatory rumor, and suddenly the city had a riot on its hands. The implication is clear: if there had been no rumor, there would have been no riot. Or, as a journalist writing in *Parade* magazine says: "Send a ferocious rumor into a receptive ear, and you could get a riot in return."[4][1]

The correlate to that assumption—control or prevent the rumors and you control or prevent the violence—is equally invalid. As we have tried to demonstrate with our process model, rumors do not "cause" the violence, any more than violence "causes" rumors; rather, both are part of the same process that induces collective outbursts. Therefore, rumors cannot be treated in isolation, since they are only one of several determinants which, combined with each other, lead to disorder.

Unfortunately, taking their cues from incorrect assumptions such as these, many advocates of rumor control have looked to such centers as a panacea for racial conflict and disorder. An editorial in the Elizabeth, N.J. *Journal* on August 29, 1969, declared:

The evidence indicates that many of the major urban disorders were the result of reaction by uninformed citizens to rumor. Establishment of centers where rumors can be dispelled and where the public can air its gripes is vital to continued peaceful community relations.

Another editorial, also supporting rumor control centers, in the Atlanta *Constitution* on October 17, 1971, maintained:

> Rumor is the enemy of peaceful relations, racial and otherwise. Unfounded rumors started by unbalanced persons have caused a lot of trouble in this world.
>
> The way to neutralize rumor is to check it and talk it out. The menace then generally disappears.

In a similar vein, one City Hall regular in Philadelphia was quoted as saying: "The mayor wants to have a quiet city, so we have a Rumor Central."

This line of thinking is not only simplistic, it is also counterproductive. Rumor control centers have not "hoaxed" the public. However, along with so many "solutions" smacking of gimmickry and slick public relations work, they have diverted away attention from the real issues—racism, poverty, powerlessness and all the other manifestations of inequality. Looking back now, what stands out about Tampa's disorder in 1967 is not the absence of a rumor control center at the time, but the fact that there was no black person on the city council, none on the school board, none in the fire department, and none of high rank within the police department.

If, for a moment, we could isolate rumors as a single issue, we might agree that rumors are essentially a problem of communication. But, even on this level, we would have to acknowledge that the problem is a great deal more complicated than a telephone; more subtle than a piece of news; more costly than a $126 phone bill or a $40,000 budget; it is a problem whose progress cannot be charted on a plastic overlay map, and whose solution must be more than a summertime thing.

APPENDIX A

RUMORS FROM PRESS REPORTS

What follows is a chronological list of 224 disorders in which rumors were present, taken from the various press reports cited.

Date and Location of Disorder	Source
1. May 16-17, 1967—Houston, Tex.	Facts on File (New York), Thursday, June 8-Wednesday, June 14; New York Times, 5/19.
2. June 2-5, 1967—Boston, Mass.	Boston Globe, 6/7.
3. June 14-17, 1967—Dayton, Ohio	Dayton Journal Herald, 6/20.
4. June 26-30, 1967—Buffalo, N.Y.	New York Times, 6/28-30.
5. July 9, 1967—Tampa, Fla.	Facts on File, Thursday, August 3-Wednesday, August 9.
6. July 12-17, 1967—Newark, N.J.	Newark News, 7/13-15; Facts on File, Thursday, July 20-Wednesday, July 26.
7. July 16-18, 1967—Somerville, N.J.	Somerset Messenger-Gazette, 7/20.

8. July 16-19, 1967—Cairo, Ill. *Washington Post*, 7/20; *New York Times*, 7/21.

9. July 17-19, 1967—New Brunswick, N.J. New Brunswick *Home News*, 7/18.

10. July 19-25, 1967—Minneapolis, Minn. Minneapolis *Tribune*, 7/21; *Facts on File*, Thursday, August 9.

11. July 22, 1967—Youngstown, Ohio Youngstown *Vindicator*, 7/22; *New York Times*, 7/23.

12. July 22, 1967—Wadesboro, N.C. Charlotte *Observer*, 7/23, 27.

13. July 23-25, 1967—East Harlem, N.Y. *New York Times*, 7/24; *New York Post*, 7/25; *Amsterdam News*, 7/29.

14. July 23-24, 1967—Rochester, N.Y. Rochester *Times-Union*, 8/7.

15. July 23-30, 1967—Detroit, Mich. *New York Times*, 7/24; Garden City (Mich.) *Guardian-Review*, 7/26; Detroit *News*, 8/3; *Facts on File*, Thursday, July 27-Wednesday, August 2.

16. July 24-28, 1967—Mount Vernon, N.Y. *New York Times*, 7/29.

17. July 24-30, 1967—Flint, Mich. Flint *Journal*, 7/26.

18. July 24-26, 1967—Grand Rapids, Mich. Grand Rapids *Press*, 7/27, 30.

19. July 24-25, 1967 — Pontiac, Mich.

Pontiac *Press*, 7/25.

20. July 24-27, 1967 — Toledo, Ohio

Toledo *Times*, 7/26.

21. July 24-26, 1967 — Cambridge, Md.

Hurlock (Md.) *Dorchester News*, 7/26.

22. July 24, 1967 — Portsmouth, Va.

Norfolk *Virginian-Pilot*, 7/26; *New York Times*, 7/26.

23. July 25-30, 1967 — Chicago, Ill.

Chicago *Daily Defender*, 7/27.

24. July 27-29, 1967 — Poughkeepsie, N.Y.

Poughkeepsie *Journal*, 7/30.

25. July 27, 1967 — Lorain, Ohio

Cleveland *Plain Dealer*, 7/28.

26. July 27, 1967 — Memphis, Tenn.

Nashville *Tennessean*, 7/29.

27. July 28-31, 1967 — San Bernadino, Cal.

San Bernardino *Telegram*, 8/1; Los Angeles *Times*, 8/6.

28. July 30-31, 1967 — Portland, Ore.

Ann Arbor (Mich.) *News*, 7/31.

29. July 30-August 1, 1967 — Denver, Col.

Denver *Post*, 8/2; Denver *Rocky Mountain News*, 8/12.

30. July 30-August 8, 1967 — Milwaukee, Wis.

Milwaukee *Journal*, 8/1.

31. July 30, 1967—Riviera Beach, Fla.   Miami *News*, 8/2.

32. July 31-August 2, 1967—Providence, R.I.   Providence *Journal*, 8/1-2; Providence *Bulletin*, 8/2.

33. August 1-3, 1967—Wyandanch,   *New York Times*, 8/3.
    Long Island (N.Y.)

34. August 1-2, 1967—Chicago, Ill.   *Facts on File*, Thursday, Aug. 10-Wednesday, Aug. 16.

35. August 9, 12, 1967—Chattanooga, Tenn.   Chattanooga *News-Free Press*, 8/10.

36. August 16-18, 1967—Painesville, Ohio   Cleveland *Plain Dealer*, 8/27.

37. August 16-19, 1967—Syracuse, N.Y.   *Bay State Banner* (Mass.), 9/7; *New York Times*, 8/18.

38. August 16-17, 1967—Houston, Tex.   Houston *Post*, 8/17; *Washington Post*, 8/18.

39. August 19-22, 1967—New Haven, Conn.   New Haven *Register*, 8/23; Fairfield *Sunday Herald*, 8/27.

40. August 31, 1967—Atlantic City, N.J.   *New York Times*, 8/26.

41. September 4-7, 1967—Brooklyn, N.Y.   *New York Times*, 9/6.

42. September 14-15, 1967—Chicago, Ill.   Chicago *Tribune*, 9/16; Chicago *Sun-Times*, 9/16.

43. September 19-24, 1967—Maywood, Ill.   Chicago *Tribune*, 9/25; Chicago *Defender*, 9/27.

44. September 20-21, 1967—Columbus, Ohio   Columbus *Citizen-Journal*, 10/22.

45. September 29, 1967—Philadelphia, Pa.   Philadelphia *Bulletin*, 9/30.

46. October 3, 1967—Philadelphia, Pa.   Philadelphia *Inquirer*, 10/4.

47. October 10-11, 13, 1967—Newark, N.J.   Newark *News*, 10/12.

48. October 19-29, 1967—Los Angeles, Cal.   Los Angeles *Times*, 10/27.

49. October 21, 1967—Waukegan, Ill.   Chicago *News*, 10/23.

50. October 31, 1967—St. Albans, N.Y.   Long Island *Star-Journal*, 11/1.

51. November 1-6, 1967—Pittsburgh, Pa.   *New York Times*, 11/5.

52. November 2-7, 1967—Winston-Salem, N.C.   Winston-Salem *Journal*, 11/3-7.

53. November 6, 1967—San Francisco, Cal.   San Francisco *Examiner*, 11/7.

54. November 13-15, 1967—Wilberforce, Ohio   Dayton Journal *Herald*, 11/16; Cleveland *Plain Dealer*, 11/17; *New York Times*, 11/16; Dayton *Daily News*, 1/21/68.

55. November 17, 1967—Philadelphia, Pa.   *New York Times*, 11/18.

56. November 17, 1967—Washington, D.C.   Washington *Star*, 11/18.

57. November 21-24, 1967—Chicago, Ill.   Chicago *Tribune*, 11/24.

58. December 12-13, 1967—Trenton, N.J.   Newark *Star-Ledger*, 12/15.

59. December 15, 1967—Minneapolis, Minn.   Minneapolis *Star*, 12/16.

60. January 15, 1968—Dayton, Ohio   Dayton *Journal Herald*, 1/17.

61. January 19, 1968—East St. Louis, Ill.   St. Louis *Post-Dispatch*, 1/21.

62. January 22, 1968—San Diego, Cal.   San Diego *Tribune*, 1/24.

63. February 1, 1968—Brooklyn, N.Y.   *New York Times*, 2/3.

64. February 5, 1968—Chicago, Ill.   Chicago *Tribune*, 2/6.

65. February 5-8, 1968—Orangeburg, S.C.   Charleston *News & Courier*, 3/14.

66. February 6, 1968—New Haven, Conn. — Boston *Herald Traveler*, 2/6.

67. February 21, 1968—Chicago, Ill. — Chicago *Daily Defender*, 2/21.

68. March 7, 1968—Columbia, S.C. — Columbia *State*, 3/15.

69. March 26, 1968—Linden, N.J. — Elizabeth *Journal*, 3/27.

70. April 2, 1968—Washington, D.C. — Washington *Post*, 4/4.

71. April 4, 1968—Erie, Pa. — Pittsburgh *Post-Gazette*, 4/5.

72. April 4-6, 1968—Denver, Col. — Denver *Post*, 4/5-8; *Rocky Mountain News*, 4/6.

73. April 4, 1968—Annapolis and Bowie, Md. — Baltimore *Sun*, 4/5.

74. April 4-10, 1968—Lexington, Ky. — Lexington *Herald-Leader*, 4/9.

75. April 4-8, 1968—Raleigh, N.C. — Raleigh *News & Observer*, 4/6-8; Raleigh *Times*, 4/5-9.

76. April 4-5, 1968—Tampa, Fla. — Tampa *Times*, 4/5.

77. April 4, 6, 1968—Winter Haven, Fla. — Lakeland *Ledger*, 4/7.

78. April 5-9, 1968—Cincinnati, Ohio — Cincinnati *Enquirer*, 4/10.

79. April 5-6, 1968—Oakland, Cal. Oakland *Tribune*, 4/5.

80. April 5, 1968—Pittsburg, Cal. San Francisco *Chronicle*, 4/19.

81. April 5, 8-14, 1968—Wilmington, Del. Wilmington *News*, 4/23.

82. April 5-8, 1968—Nashville, Tenn. Nashville *Banner*, 4/6.

83. April 5-6, 1968—Pine Bluff, Ark. Pine Bluff *Commercial*, 4/6.

84. April 6-7, 1968—Joliet, Ill. Joliet *Herald-News*, 4/9.

85. April 6-7, 1968—Rockville, Md. *Washington Post*, 4/8, 11; Washington *Star*, 4/8.

86. April 6-8, 1968—Gainesville, Fla. Gainesville *Sun*, 4/8.

87. April 6-7, 1968—Wilmington, N.C. Wilmington *Star*, 4/8.

88. April 7, 1968—Hamilton, N.Y. *New York Times*, 4/15.

89. April 7, 1968—Royal Oak, Mich. Royal Oak *Tribune*, 4/8.

90. April 8-9, 1968—Youngstown, Ohio Youngstown *Vindicator*, 4/10.

91. April 9-12, 1968—Trenton, N.J. Trenton *Trentonian*, 4/10; Philadelphia *Inquirer*, 4/14.

92. April 9, 1968—Reading, Pa.
Reading *Times*, 4/9; Port Allegany *Reporter-Argus*, 4/11.

93. April 9-12, 1968—Kansas City, Mo.
Kansas City *Call*, 5/3; *New York Times*, 4/12.

94. April 14, 1968—Cedar Rapids, Iowa
Cedar Rapids *Gazette*, 4/15.

95. April 27-30, 1968—Omaha, Neb.
Omaha *World-Herald*, 4/28, 30; Ann Arbor (Mich.) *News*, 4/29.

96. April 30-May 7, 1968—Cincinnatti, Ohio
Cincinnati *Post & Times-Star*, 5/3.

97. May 3-16, 1968—Newark, N.J.
New York Times, 5/10.

98. May 6-10, 1968—Dearborn, Mich.
Dearborn *Guide*, 5/16.

99. May 6-August 1968-St. Petersburg, Fla.
St. Petersburg *Independent*, 6/28.

100. May 13, 1968—Detroit, Mich.
Michigan *Chronicle*, 5/25.

101. May 18-24, 1968—Salisbury, Md.
Salisbury *Times*, 5/20; Baltimore *Sun*, 5/20, 27.

102. May 21-28, 1968—Wilkinsburg, Pa.
Pittsburgh *Post-Gazette*, 5/28.

103. May 23-24, 1968—New Haven, Conn.
New Haven *Register*, 5/28.

104. May 24-28, 1968—Ann Arbor, Mich.   Ann Arbor *News*, 5/30.

105. May 27-30, 1968—Louisville, Ky.   Louisville *Courier-Journal*, 6/16.

106. June 1-2, 1968—Natchez, Miss.   Ann Arbor (Mich.) *News*, 6/3; Detroit (Mich.) *American*, 6/4.

107. June 22-24, 1968—Denver, Col.   Denver *Post*, 6/23; *Rocky Mountain News*, 6/26.

108. July 1-6, 1968—Paterson, N.J.   New York *Post*, 7/6.

109. July 11-15, 1968—York, Pa.   York *Dispatch*, 7/16; York *Gazette & Daily*, 7/18.

110. July 12, 1968—South Bend, Ind.   South Bend *Tribune*, 7/12.

111. July 17-23, 1968—Akron, Ohio   Akron *Beacon Journal*, 7/23.

112. July 20-21, 23, 1968—Brooklyn, N.Y.   New York *Post*, 7/23.

113. July 23-26, 1968—Cleveland, Ohio   *New York Times*, 9/2; Roldo Bartimole, "The Glenville Shoot-Out: Bad Day in Cleveland," *Nation*, July 14, 1969.

114. July 27-29, 1968—Gary, Ind.   Gary *Post-Tribune*, 8/1.

115. August 6-7, 1968—Harvey and Dixmoor, Ill.

Washington Post, 8/8.

116. August 7-9, 1968—Fort Wayne, Ind.

Fort Wayne *News-Sentinel*, 8/8-10; Fort Wayne *Journal-Gazette*, 8/8.

117. August 7-12, 1968—Little Rock, Ark.

San Antonio (Tex.) *Express-News*, 8/11.

118. August 10, 1968—Fostoria, Ohio

Cleveland *Plain Dealer*, 8/13.

119. August 11-13, 1968—Los Angeles, Cal.

Baltimore (Md.) *Sun*, 8/13; Ann Arbor *News*, 8/13.

120. August 14, 1968—Bedminster, N.J.

New Brunswick *Home News*, 8/15.

121. August 14-15, 1968—Louisville, Ky.

Louisville *Courier-Journal*, 8/16.

122. August 17-20, 1968—Providence, R.I.

Providence *Journal*, 8/20.

123. August 22, 1968—Edgewater Park, N.J.

Philadelphia *Bulletin*, 8/23.

124. August 22-24, 1968—Evansville, Ind.

Evansville *Courier*, 8/25; Evansville *Press*, 8/26.

125. August 22-24, 1968—Ypsilanti, Mich.

Michigan *Chronicle*, 8/31; Detroit *News*, 8/25; Ann Arbor *News*, 8/25-26.

126. August 22-24, 1968—Wichita, Kan.
     Wichita *Beacon*, 8/27.

127. September 1, 1968—Berea, Ky.
     Louisville *Courier-Journal*, 9/3.

128. September 4, 12, 1968—Brooklyn, N.Y.
     New York *Post*, 9/5; *New York Times*, 9/5.

129. September 6, 1968—Lima, Ohio
     Lima *News*, 9/11.

130. September 12-14, 1968—Denver, Col.
     Denver *Post*, 9/14.

131. September 13, 1968—Lockport, Ill.
     Joliet *Herald-News*, 9/16.

132. September 13-14, 1968—Toledo, Ohio
     Toledo *Blade*, 9/16.

133. September 14-16, 1968—Teaneck, N.J.
     Newark *News*, 9/19.

134. September 19, 1968—Minneapolis, Minn.
     Minneapolis *Tribune*, 9/20.

135. September 19-20, 23-24, 1968—
     Bladensburg, Md.
     Washington *News*, 9/21-24; Washington *Star*, 9/23.

136. September 20-24, 1968—York, Pa.
     York *Dispatch*, 9/25.

137. September 20, 1968—Wichita, Kan.   Wichita *Eagle*, 9/21.

138. September 20, 1968—Smyrna, Del.   Smyrna *Times*, 9/26.

139. September 23-24, 1968—Louisville, Ky.   Louisville *Times*, 9/24-25 ; Louisville *Courier-Journal*, 9/26.

140. September 24-30, 1968—Trenton, N.J.   Trenton *Times-Advertiser*, 10/2.

141. September 26-October 3, 1968—   Montclair *Times*, 10/3.
     Montclair, N.J.

142. September 26, 1968—Elmira, N.Y.   Elmira *Star-Gazette*, 9/27.

143. October 8, 1968—Washington, D.C.   *Washington Post*, 10/9; Washington *Star*, 10/15.

144. October 11-18, 1968—San Francisco, Cal.   San Francisco *Chronicle*, 10/19.

145. October 13-16, 1968—Washington, D.C.   *Washington Post*, 10/16-17.

146. October 18-20, 1968—Princeton, N.J.   Princeton *Town Topics*, 10/24.

147. October 21, 27, 1968—Cleveland, Ohio   Cleveland *Press*, 10/21.

148. October 23, 1968—Blue Island, Ill. Chicago *Tribune*, 10/24.

149. October 25, 1968—St. Louis, Mo. St. Louis *Post-Dispatch*, 10/26; St. Louis *Argus*, 11/1.

150. October 28, 1968—Glendale, Md. *Washington Post*, 10/29; Washington *Star*, 10/28-29.

151. October 30-November 2, 1968—Lancaster, Pa. Lancaster *New Era*, 11/1.

152. October 30-31, 1968—South Bend, Ind. South Bend *Tribune*, 11/1.

153. October 31, 1968—Hopkinsville, Ky. Louisville *Courier-Journal*, 11/2.

154. November 3, 1968—Washington, D.C. *Washington Post*, 11/4.

155. November 11, 1968—Swanquarter, N.C. Norfolk (Va.) *Virginian-Pilot*, 11/12.

156. November 11, 1968—Hillsborough, N.C. Chapel Hill *Weekly*, 11/13.

157. December 9, 1968—Northridge, Cal. Los Angeles *Times*, 12/10.

158. December 11-13, 1968—Los Angeles, Cal. Los Angeles *Times*, 1/6.

159. February 4, 1969—St. Louis, Mo. St. Louis *Globe-Democrat,* 2/5.

160. February 13, 17-18, 1969—Pittsburgh, Pa. Pittsburgh *Post-Gazette,* 2/14; Pittsburgh *Press,* 2/18-19.

161. February 19, 1969—Baltimore, Md. Baltimore *Sun,* 2/22.

162. February 20, 26, 1969—San Francisco, Cal. San Francisco *Examiner,* 2/21; San Francisco *Chronicle,* 2/21, 27.

163. February 26, 1969—Chicago, Ill. Chicago *News,* 2/27.

164. February 27, 1969—Minneapolis, Minn. Minneapolis *Star,* 2/28.

165. March 3, 1969—Waterloo, Iowa Waterloo *Courier,* 3/4.

166. March 4, 1969—Evansville, Ill. Chicago *Sun-Times,* 3/9.

167. March 7, 10, 1969—Los Angeles, Cal. Los Angeles *Times,* 3/11, 13.

168. March 12, 1969—Santa Ana, Cal. Santa Ana *Register,* 3/13.

169. March 20, 1969—Piscataway, N.J. *New York Times,* 3/21.

170. April 5, 1969—Williamstown, Mass.   Boston *Globe*, 4/6, 9; Albany (N.Y.) *Times-Union*, 4/8.

171. April 5, 1969—Anniston, Ala.   Anniston *Star*, 4/6.

172. April 9-18, 1969—Cambridge, Mass.   Boston *Globe*, 4/24.

173. April 12-20, 1969—Ithaca, N.Y.   *New York Times*, 4/20, 27, 5/14.

174. April 25, 1969—Roosevelt (Long Island), N.Y. Long Island *Press*, 4/26.

175. April 25, 1969—Charleston, S.C.   *New York Times*, 4/29.

176. May 6-8, 1969—Camden, N.J.   Camden *Courier Post*, 6/4, 9.

177. May 6, 1969—Lorain, Ohio   Lorain *Journal*, 5/7.

178. May 9, 13, 1969—Providence, R.I.   Providence *Journal*, 5/14.

179. May 12, 1969—Tacoma, Wash.   Tacoma *Tribune and Ledger*, 5/12; Tacoma *News Tribune*, 5/12.

180. May 14-22, 1969—Chattanooga, Tenn.   Chattanooga *Times*, 5/16.

181. May 16-21, 1969—Chicago, Ill.   Chicago *Tribune*, 5/17; Chicago *New Crusader*, 5/24.

182. May 19, 1969—Newark, N.J.   Newark *News*, 5/21; *New York Times*, 5/21.

183. May 20-23, 1969—Portland, Ore.   Portland *Oregonian*, 5/22, 24; Portland *Journal*, 5/22.

184. May 21, 1969—Oxford, Pa.   Oxford *Press*, 4/30.

185. May 23, 1969—Detroit, Mich.   Detroit *News*, 6/6.

186. May 26, 1969—Champaign, Ill.   Chicago *Tribune*, 5/30.

187. June 2-7, 1969—Hartford, Conn.   Hartford *Courant*, 6/6.

188. June 3-9, 1969—Cleveland, Ohio   Cleveland *Call & Post*, 6/14.

189. June 8-15, 1969—Roxboro, N.C.   Arkansas *Gazette*, 6/15.

190. June 12-13, 1969—Trenton, N.J.   Newark *News*, 6/14; *Washington Post*, 6/14.

191. June 15-16, 1969—Sacramento, Cal.   *New York Times*, 6/18.

192. June 17-18, 1969—Madison, Ill.   St. Louis *Post-Dispatch*, 6/19.

193. June 20-July 1, 1969—Red Bank, N.J.   Red Bank *Register*, 6/23.

194. June 23, 1969—West Dallas, Tex.   Dallas *Times Herald*, 7/1.

195. June 24-25, 1969—Chicago, Ill.   Chicago *Defender*, 6/26.

196. June 25-28, 1969—Omaha, Neb.   Ann Arbor *News*, 6/26.

197. June 26-27, 1969—Kokomo, Ind.   Kokomo *Tribune*, 6/29.

198. July 5-6, 1969—Tampa, Fla.   Tampa *Tribune*, 7/7; Miami *Herald*, 7/7; *Washington Post*, 7/8.

199. July 10-13, 1969—Evansville, Ind.   Evansville *Courier & Press*, 7/13.

200. July 13-15, 1969—Jamesburg, N.J.   New Brunswick *Home News*, 7/16.

201. July 17-22, 1969—York, Pa.   Baltimore *News American*, 7/27.

202. August 22, 1969—Middlesex, N.J.   Plainfield *Courier-News*, 8/27.

203. August 31-September 4, 1969—Fort Lauderdale, Fla.   Fort Lauderdale *News*, 9/2; *New York Times*, 9/3.

204. September 1-9, 1969-Hartford, Conn.   Hartford *Times*, 9/2-5; New Britain *Herald*, 9/5; *New York Times*, 9/3.

205. September 1-2, 1969—Camden, N.J.   Camden *Courier Post*, 9/3; Newark *Star Ledger*, 9/4.

206. September 6-7, 1969—Boston, Mass.   Boston *Globe*, 9/15.

207. September 6-11, 1969—Hightstown, N.J.   Newark *News*, 9/11.

208. September 8-12, 1969—Brooklyn and Manhattan, N.Y.   *New York Times*, 9/11.

209. September 9, 1969—Birmingham, Ala.   Birmingham *News*, 9/10.

210. September 11, 1969—Vero Beach, Fla.   Cocoa (Fla.) *Today*, 9/15.

211. September 12-19, 24, 1969—Aberdeen, Md.   Baltimore *Sun*, 9/26.

212. September 17-19, 1969—Bladensburg, Md.   Washington *Star*, 9/21.

213. September 19, 22-23, 1969—Wilmington, Del.   Wilmington *Journal* 9/23.

214. September 19, 1969—Homestead, Fla.   Miami *Herald*, 9/21; Philadelphia *Inquirer*, 9/21.

215. September 22, 1969—Battle Creek, Mich.   Battle Creek *Enquirer and News*, 9/26.

216. September 23-25, 1969—Salisbury, N.C.   Winston-Salem *Journal*, 9/26; Salisbury *Post*, 9/26.

217. September 25-26, October 1, 1969—   *Newsday*, 9/27; Deer Park *Suffolk Sun*, 10/3.
      Middle Island, N.Y.

218. September 26-27, 29, 1969—Miami, Fla.   Miami *News*, 10/3; Miami *Herald*, 10/5, 12.

219. September 29-October 2, 7, 1969—   Charlotte *Observer*, 10/1, 3, 7-8.
      Asheville, N.C.

220. October 1, 1969—Denver, Col.   Denver *Post*, 10/3.

221. October 7-8, 1969—San Francisco, Cal.   San Francisco *Examiner*, 10/10.

222. October 9, 1969—South Bend, Ind.   South Bend *Tribune*, 10/10.

223. October 9-10, 13-14, 1969—Fort Pierce, Fla.   Fort Pierce *News Tribune*, 10/26.

224. October 30, 1969—Champaign, Ill.   Champaign *Courier*, 10/31.

APPENDIX B

RUMORS FROM INVESTIGATIVE ACCOUNTS

What follows is a chronological list of disorders accompanied by rumors, taken from the in-depth reports and studies cited.

1.   August 28-30, 1964—Philadelphia, Pa.

    Lenora E. Berson, *Case Study of a Riot: The Philadelphia Story* (New York: Institute of Human Relations Press, The American Jewish Committee, 1966).

2.   August 11-14, 1965—Watts (Los Angeles), Cal.

    Robert Conot, *Rivers of Blood, Years of Darkness: The Unforgettable Classic Account of the Watts Riot* (New York: William Morrow, 1968).

    Jerry Cohen and William S. Murphy, *The Los Angeles Race Riot: August 1965: Burn, Baby, Burn!* (New York: E.P. Dutton, 1966).

    Violence in the City—An End or a Beginning?, A Report by the Governor's Commission on the Los Angeles Riots, December 2, 1965.

3.   September 27-October 2, 1966—San Francisco, Cal.

    128 Hours: A Report of the Civil Disturbance in the City & County of San Francisco (1966), Compiled and Prepared by Sgt. Ford E. Long and Sgt. Richard Trueb of the San Francisco Police Department.

4.   June 11-18, 1967—Tampa, Fla.

    Tampa Police Department, *After-Action Report* (mimeo), Pt. I.

5.   June 26-30, 1967—Buffalo, N.Y.

    Frank P. Besag, *Anatomy of a Riot: Buffalo '67* (Buffalo, N.Y.: University Press, 1967).

6.   July 12-17, 1967—Newark, N.J.

Report for Action, Governor's Select Commission on Civil Disorder, State of New Jersey, February, 1968, pp. 103-144.

7.   July 14-17, 1967—Plainfield, N.J.

Report for Action, pp. 145-153.

The Road to Anarchy, Findings of Riot Study Commission of the New Jersey State Patrolmen's Benevolent Association, Inc., 1968.

8.   July 17-19, 1967—New Brunswick, N.J.

The Road to Anarchy.

9.   July 21-25, 1967—Englewood, N.J.

Report for Action, pp. 154-160.

The Road to Anarchy.

10.   December 12-13, 1967—Trenton, N.J.

Report of the School Study Panel to the Human Relations Council Serving the Greater Trenton Area. (Trenton: Human Relations Council, n.d.).

11.   February 5-8, 1968—Orangeburg, S.C.

Jack Nelson and Jack Bass, *The Orangeburg Massacre* (New York: World, 1970).

Events at Orangeburg: A report based on study and interviews in Orangeburg, South Carolina, in the aftermath of tragedy, by Pat Watters and Weldon Rougeau, Special Report, (Atlanta, Georgia: Southern Regional Council, February 25, 1968).

12.   March 15, 1968—Detroit, Mich.

Memo from Detroit Commission on Community Relations to Mayors' Offices, Human Relations Agencies, Interested Persons, regarding establishment of a Rumor Control Center. (Undated)

13.   April 4-11, 1968—Chicago, Ill.

Report of the Chicago Riot Study Committee to the Hon. Richard J. Daley, August 1, 1968.

14.   April 4-9, 1968—Washington, D.C.

Ben W. Gilbert and the staff of the *Washington Post, Ten Blocks from the White House: Anatomy of the Washington Riots of 1968* (New York: Frederick A. Praeger, 1968).

15.   April 5-9, 1968—Detroit, Mich.

Memo from Detroit Commission on Community Relations to Mayors' Offices, Human Relations Agencies, Interested Persons, regarding establishment of a Rumor Control Center. (Undated)

16.   April 6-9, 1968—Baltimore, Md.

Report on Baltimore Civil Disorders: April, 1968, by Jane Motz, Middle Atlantic Region American Friends Service Committee, September, 1968.

17.   June 25-27, 1968—Richmond, Cal.

Report Kapsis, Jim Smith, Bruce Saunders, Paul Takagi, Oscar Williams, *The Reconstruction of a Riot: A Case Study of Community Tensions and Civil Disorder,* Approaches to the Study of Violence, Lemberg Center for the Study of Violence, Brandeis University (1970).

18.   July 23-26, 1968—Cleveland, Ohio.

Shoot-out in Cleveland: Black Militants and the Police: July 23, 1968, by Louis H. Masotti and Jerome R. Corsi, A Report Submitted to the National Commission on the Causes and Prevention of Violence, May 16, 1969 (New York: Bantam Books, 1969).

19.   August 7-13, 1968—Miami, Fla.

Miami Report: The Report of the Miami Study Team on Civil Disturbances in Miami, Florida, during the week of August 5, 1968, Miami, Florida, January 15, 1969, Submitted to the National Commission on the Causes and Prevention of Violence (Washington, D.C.: GPO, 1969).

20.   September 19, 22, 1969—Detroit, Mich.

Detroit Commission on Community Relations, Education Division, Addendum to October 10, 1969 Memo on Student Unrest at Cooley High School, October 22, 1969.

21.   May 11-12, 1970—Augusta, Ga.

Augusta, Georgia and Jackson State University: Southern Episodes in a National Tragedy (August report by William Winn with D.L. Inman), Special Report, Southern Regional Council, June, 1970), pp. 1-44.

22.   May 13-15, 1970—Jackson, Miss.

Augusta, Georgia and Jackson State University: Southern Episodes in a National Tragedy (Jackson report by Ed Williams), Special Report, Southern Regional Council, June 1970, pp. 45-71.

APPENDIX C

RUMOR QUESTIONNAIRE

The following questions on rumors refer to the disturbance occurring on _____ (date indicated). Please check the appropriate line, unless otherwise indicated.

1. In general, do rumors reported to your Department or some other appropriate city agency mostly involve matters of race? (check one)

   _____ almost always
   _____ more than half the time
   _____ frequently (but not more than half the time)
   _____ occasionally (but less than half the time)
   _____ very seldom

2. Prior to the disorder, do your records show any noticeable increase in rumors reflecting racial tension? _____Yes _____ No

3. If this information was not recorded, do you *recall* that there was a noticeable increase in rumors of this kind prior to the disorder? _____Yes _____No

4. If there was an increase in rumors prior to the disorder, how far in advance of the disorder did the rumors begin? (check one)

   _____ over a year
   _____ more than 6 months
   _____ a few months
   _____ a few weeks
   _____ a few days
   _____ the day of the disorder (before the outbreak)

5. If there was an increase in rumors prior to the disorder, what was their content? (check one or more)

   _____ general predictions of trouble or violence
   _____ agitators planning violence
   _____ acts of brutality by the police

_____ reinforcements of police stationed in the area in the expectation of violence

_____ acts of brutality (such as beatings) by white citizens against Negroes

_____ acts of brutality (such as beatings) by Negro citizens against whites

_____ reprisals against the black community by whites

_____ reprisals against the white community by blacks

_____ other (please describe)

6. Prior to the disorder, were there specific issues or events in the community which seemed to give rise to the rumors?

_____ Yes _____ No

7. If answer is "yes" to No. 6, what type of issue or event? (check one or more)

_____ police issue or event

_____ school issue or event

_____ disputes over jobs, housing or welfare

_____ other (please describe)

8. Was the disorder started by an actual incident or simply by a rumor?

_____ actual incident

_____ simply by a rumor

9. If the disorder was started by an actual incident, was this incident intensified by a rumor(s)? _____ Yes _____ No

10. If answer is "yes" to No. 9, what was this rumor(s)? (please explain)

11. If the disorder was started by nothing more than a rumor (no actual incident), what was this rumor? (please explain)

12. As the disturbance continued, was there a noticeable increase in the number of rumors reported to your department or some other appropriate city agency? _____Yes _____No (please give some examples)

13. Did your city have a rumor-control agency at the time of the disorder? _____ Yes _____ No

14. Was there any attempt by a public official or agency to dispel rumors (TV broadcast, for example)? _____Yes _____No (please describe)

15. Does your city now have a rumor-control agency or center? _____Yes _____No

16. If your city does have some rumor-control agency, under whose jurisdiction is it?

17. If your answer is "no" to No. 15, are there current plans for a rumor-control center or agency? _____ Yes _____No

18. Additional comments:

APPENDIX D

RESPONDENTS TO RUMOR QUESTIONNAIRE

City	Respondent	Date of Disorder(s) (1968)
1. Albion, Mich.	C. Lindstrom Chief of Police	(1) April 7-8
2. Alexandria, Va.	Major Russell A. Hawes Chief of Police	(2) April 5-7 (3) May 17 (4) July 4
3. Annapolis, Md.	B. Kalnoske Deputy Chief of Police	(5) October 12
4. Aurora, Ill.	Robert E. Brent Sgt.-Gen. Staff Division	(6) April 7-8
5. Battle Creek, Mich.	Sgt. Gerald W. Wilbur	(7) April 4-5 (8) May 25
6. Benton Harbor, Mich.	William B. McClaran Chief of Police	(9) April 6-9 (10) April 29-May 1 (11) July 21-23

7.	Blue Island, Ill.	Lt. Harry J. Harczak	(12) October 23
8.	Bluefield, W. Va.	Andrew L. Dodson Chief of Police	(13) November 7-21
9.	Charlotte, N.C.	Marshall W. Haigler Administrative Planning Officer	(14) April 5-8
10.	Chicago Heights, Ill.	Jack Ziegler Chief of Police	(15) April 7 (16) August 11-13
11.	Coral Gables, Fla.	W.G. Kimbrough Chief of Police	(17) May 14
12.	Dayton, Ohio	R. Wasserman Administrative Assistant to Director	(18) January 15 (19) April 5 (20) September 2 (21) October 16
13.	Decatur, Ill.	S.E. Repnicke Record Supervisor	(22) April 6-7 (23) September 13
14.	Dover, Del.	William L. Spence, Jr. Chief of Police	(24) September 20

15.	Durham, N.C.	Capt. E.G. Atkins, Jr.	(25) (26) (27)	February 15 April 5-8 June 6, 26
16.	Elizabeth, N.J.	Michael D. Roy Chief of Police	(28)	May 21
17.	Fostoria, Ohio	James C. Meek Chief of Police	(29)	August 10
18.	Freeport, N.Y.	Anthony Elar Chief of Police	(30)	April 5
19.	Gainesville, Fla.	William D. Joiner Chief of Police	(31) (32) (33) (34)	March 13 April 6-8 July 30-August 1 August 20-21
20.	Homestead, Fla.	E.L. Snider Chief of Police	(35)	April 9
21.	Inkster, Mich.	James L. Fyke Chief of Police	(36)	August 4-8
22.	Jackson, Miss.	Major C.R. Wilson	(37)	April 4-6

23.	Jersey City, N.J.	Capt. Hugh Lee Record Room	(38)	September 24
24.	Kalamazoo, Mich.	Paul G. Aldo Administrative Assistant	(39) (40) (41)	April 5 July 29-30 September 25
25.	Kansas City, Mo.	Lt. Lester Harris Commander, Planning and Research Unit	(42) (43) (44) (45)	April 9-12 July 10 August 13-14 August 20
26.	Lansing, Mich.	William L. Findsen Planning Officer III	(46) (47) (48)	April 9 May 14 August 21-22
27.	Miami, Fla.	Lt. Col. Paul M. Denham Acting Chief of Police	(49) (50)	August 7-9 December 12
28.	Middletown, Conn.	Vincent S. Marino Chief of Police	(51)	August 31-September 2
29.	Mt. Clemens, Mich.	Sgt. Bernard A. Campau Youth Bureau	(52)	March 4-5
30.	Lexington, Ky.	Capt. William Riley Central Records	(53)	April 4-10

31.	Lockport, Ill.	Robert Gait Chief of Police	(54) September 13
32.	Natchez, Miss.	J.T. Robinson Chief of Police	(55) June 1-2
33.	New Britain, Conn.	Arthur P. Hayward Chief of Police	(56) May 15
34.	New Orleans, La.	Major Lucien J. Cutrera Research and Planning Division	(57) April 7-10
35.	Niagara Falls, N.Y.	James B. Gorman Deputy Supt. of Police	(58) April 5-7
36.	Northridge, Cal.	Capt. E.M. Lembke Commander, Devonshire Div.	(59) November 4-9
37.	Nyack, N.Y.	(Questionnaire unsigned)	(60) September 14
38.	Oakland, Cal.	C.R. Gain Chief of Police	(61) April 5-6 (62) September 10-18 (63) November 15
39.	Oberlin, Ohio	Robert K. Ferber Chief of Police	(64) April 9-10

No.	City	Official	Ref.	Date
40.	Ossining, N.Y.	Lt. Samuel R. Rubin, Executive Officer, Ossining Police Dept.	(65)	April 5
41.	Pacifica, Cal.	Sgt. Otto H. Satlenberger, Patrol Division	(66)	July 28-29
42.	Pasco, Wash.	Okie Miles, Capt. of Services	(67)	July 20-29
43.	Paterson, N.J.	Capt. Samuel Silvestri	(68) (69)	May 9-20 July 1-6
44.	Peekskill, N.Y.	James Nelson, Detective Sergeant	(70)	October 24-25
45.	Pittsburg, Cal.	C. F. Flynn, Chief of Police	(71) (72) (73)	April 5 April 16 July 31
46.	Port Chester, N.Y.	Eric Geldart, Chief of Police	(74)	April 5-6
47.	Portland, Ore.	Donald I. McNamara, Chief of Police	(75)	December 11-13

48.	Portsmouth, Va.	Col. C.L. Warren Chief of Police	(76)	April 8
49.	Prince George's County, Md. (Glendale)	Vincent S. Free Chief of Police	(77)	October 28
50.	Racine, Wis.	Leroy C. Jenkins Chief of Police	(78)	August 3-5
51.	Rayne, La.	Esta Lantier Chief of Police	(79)	September 15
52.	Reading, Pa.	Lt. Thomas Hess Planning Officer	(80)	April 9
53.	Richmond, Va.	Col. F.S. Duling Chief of Police	(81)	April 6-12
54.	Riverside, Cal.	John T. Cochran Intelligence	(82)	August 6-8
55.	Roanoke, Va.	Capt. E.A. Griggs	(83)	September 8-9
56.	St. Joseph, Mich.	(Questionnaire unsigned)	(84)	September 18
57.	San Antonio, Tex.	George W. Bichsel Chief of Police	(85)	April 22

58.	Seattle, Wash.	Capt. M.W. Matheson	(86) March 29, April 4 (87) July 1-4 (88) July 29-31
59.	Smithfield, N.C.	B.P. Jones Chief of Police	(89) September 22-23
60.	Spokane, Wash.	Thomas J. O'Brien Inspector of Police	(90) April 5
61.	Springfield, Ohio	I.W. Hallowell Chief of Police	(91) August 31 (92) October 11 (93) December 5-6
62.	Syracuse, N.Y.	John F. O'Conner Chief of Police	(94) April 4-7 (95) September 8-12
63.	Takoma Park, Md.	Lt. Robert E. Porter Administrative Office	(96) April 6-7
64.	Washington, D.C. (Incidents connected with Poor People's Campaign centering around Resurrection City)	John B. Layton Chief of Police	(97) April 4-9 (98) May 29-June 25 (99) October 13-16

	City	Name / Title		Dates
65.	Waterloo, Iowa	Robert S. Wright Chief of Police	(100) (101) (102)	April 9 August 17 September 13-17
66.	Weirton, W. Va.	Andrew Olenick Chief of Police	(103) (104)	July 31-August 1 September 14
67.	West Chester, Pa.	Thomas G. Frame Chief of Police	(105)	April 5-6
68.	Wilmington, Del.	(Questionnaire unsigned)	(106)	April 5, 8-14
69.	Wilmington, N.C.	H.E. Williamson Chief of Police	(107)	April 6-7
70.	Wilson, N.C.	J.E. Teel Identification Officer	(108)	April 6-7
71.	Winston-Salem, N.C.	Justus M. Tucker Chief of Police	(109) (110)	April 4-5 December 16
72.	Yonkers, N.Y.	William F. Polsen Chief of Police	(111)	May 17
73.	Ypsilanti, Mich.	Ray H. Walton	(112)	August 22-24

TOTAL: 73 Cities   TOTAL: 112 Disorders

APPENDIX E

LIST OF STATES BY REGION

1. EAST: Connecticut, Maine, Massachusetts, New Hampshire, New York, New Jersey, Pennsylvania, Rhode Island, Vermont.

2. MIDWEST: Illinois, Indiana, Iowa, Kansas, Michigan, Minnesota, Nebraska, North Dakota, Ohio, South Dakota, Wisconsin.

3. WEST: Alaska, Arizona, California, Colorado, Hawaii, Idaho, Montana, Nevada, New Mexico, Oregon, Utah, Washington, Wyoming.

4. SOUTH: Alabama, Arkansas, Florida, Georgia, Louisiana, Mississippi, North Carolina, Oklahoma, South Carolina, Tennessee, Texas, Virginia.

5. BORDER: Delaware, Kentucky, Maryland, Missouri, Washington, D.C., West Virginia.

APPENDIX F

KING AND NON-KING DISORDERS

The following is a division of our police survey sample (112 cases) into King (38) and Non-King (74) disorders.

Exhibit F.1
FREQUENCY DISTRIBUTION OF KING VS. NON-KING
DISORDERS BY MAGNITUDE

Magnitude of Disorders	Non-King %	Non-King No.	King %	King No.	Sample Total %	Sample Total No.	1968 Recorded Disorder Total %	1968 Recorded Disorder Total No.
Minor	64	47	47	18	58	65	68	389
Medium	28	21	34	13	30	34	25	144
Serious	8	6	11	4	9	10	5	29
Major	0	0	8	3	3	3	1	7
TOTAL	100	74	100	38	100	112	99	569

Exhibit F.2
FREQUENCY DISTRIBUTION OF KING VS. NON-KING
DISORDERS BY REGION

Region of the Country	Non-King %	Non-King No.	King %	King No.	Sample Total %	Sample Total No.	1968 Recorded Disorder Total %	1968 Recorded Disorder Total No.
East	14	10	18	7	15	17	28	160
Midwest	34	25	29	11	32	36	27	155
West	16	12	8	3	13	15	10	59
Border	15	11	13	5	14	16	14	77
South	22	16	32	12	25	28	21	118
TOTAL	101	74	100	38	99	112	100	569

APPENDIX G

RUMOR CONTROL CENTERS

The following is a list of cities which have had rumor control centers. Under source: PQ refers to our police questionnaire, which was mailed out in April 1969; NAPCRO, the National Association of Police Community Relations Officers, made a survey of rumor control centers which existed as of June 1970. A dash (-) indicates it is not clear which group or agency operated the center. In a few instances where a city has had more than one center, the cases are listed in the second column.

City, State	Operated By	Source
1. Akron, Ohio	—	NAPCRO.
2. Alexandra, Va.	City Manager's Office	Washington, D.C. *Afro-American*, 5/4/71.
3. Ann Arbor, Mich.	Huron High School Student Council	Ann Arbor *News*, 11/12/71.
4. Anniston, Ala.	Police Department	Anniston *Star*, 11/4/71.
5. Atlanta, Ga.	Community Relations Commission	Atlanta *Journal*, 11/17/71.
6. Baltimore, Md.	Community Relations Commission	Baltimore *News American*, 4/19/70.
7. Benton Harbor, Mich.	— Community Relations Advisory Board	PQ.

	—	Benton Harbor Area Schools Advisory Council	St. Joseph *Herald-Press*, 2/26/71.
8.	Birmingham, Ala.		
9.	Bloomfield, N.J.	Commission on Civil Rights	NAPCRO.
			Bloomfield *Independent Press*, 5/28/70.
10.	Boston, Mass.	Mayor's Office Office of Human Rights	NAPCRO.
11.	Buffalo, N.Y.	Mayor's Office	NAPCRO.
12.	Champaign, Ill.	Citizens Education Council	Champaign-Urbana *Courier*, 11/8/70.
13.	Charlotte, N.C.	Mayor's Office Human Relations Committee	PQ; Charlotte *Observer*, 2/27/71.
14.	Chicago, Ill.	Commission on Human Relations	NAPCRO.
15.	Chicago Heights, Ill.	Cook County Sheriff's Department	PQ.
16.	Cleveland, Ohio	—	*Wall Street Journal*, 4/12/68.
17.	Columbus, Ohio	Human Relations Commission	NAPCRO.

18. Dallas, Tex.	Police Department	Dallas *Times Herald*, 7/1/69; NAPCRO.
19. Dayton, Ohio	— Human Relations Council (West Dayton)	PQ.
	— Human Relations Council (East Dayton)	Dayton *Journal Herald*, 8/28/70.
20. Decatur, Ill.	Community Relations	PQ.
21. Denver, Col.	Mayor's Office	Denver *Post*, 4/6/68; NAPCRO.
22. Detroit, Mich.	Commission on Human Relations	Wyandotte *News-Herald*, 4/10/68; NAPCRO.
23. Durham, N.C.	Police Department Community Relations Unit	PQ.
24. East St. Louis, Ill.	Police Department (Five police community relations storefronts)	East St. Louis *Journal*, 12/4/69.
25. Easton, Pa.	Mayor's Office	Easton *Express*, 8/25/71.
26. Elizabeth, N.J.	— Police Department	PQ; Elizabeth *Journal*, 12/9/70.
	— Community Service Center	

27.	Eugene, Ore.	Oregon University	Eugene *Emerald*, 4/13/71.
28.	Evansville, Ind.	—	Evansville *Press*, 7/17/69.
29.	Flint, Mich.	Prosecutor's Office	Flint *Journal*, 6/4/68.
30.	Grand Rapids, Mich.	Office of Community Relations	Grand Rapids *Times*, 9/24/70.
31.	Greensboro, N.C.	Concerned Citizens for Schools	Greensboro *News*, 9/3/71.
32.	Hartford, Conn.	—	Hartford *Courant*, 6/7/69.
33.	Huntsville, Ala.	Police Department	Birmingham *News*, 10/15/70.
34.	Inkster, Mich.	Wayne County Board of Supervisors	PQ.
35.	Jackson, Mich.	Communications Sub-committee on the Schools' Advisory Committee	Jackson *Blazer*, 12/4/71.
36.	Jackson, Miss.	Parent-Teachers' Association	*Washington Post*, 2/15/70.
37.	Joliet, Ill.	—	Joliet *Herald-News*, 4/9/68.
38.	Kalamazoo, Mich.	City Administration	PQ.
39.	Kansas City, Mo.	— Police Department Public Information Unit	PQ.

	City	Organization	Source
		— Mayor's Office	NAPCRO.
40.	Kokomo, Ind.	Human Relations Commission	Kokomo *Tribune*, 8/28/70.
41.	Lancaster, Pa.	Mayor's Office	*Report on Rumor Control Center.*
42.	Lansing, Mich.	Lansing Area Council of Churches and Community Services Council	PQ.
43.	Lawrence, Kans.	Student Mobilization for Peace	Lawrence University *Kansan*, 5/8/70.
44.	Lawrence, Long Island, N.Y.	Five Towns Economic Opportunity Council	*Newsday*, 6/4/69.
45.	Lexington, Ky.	Police Department	PQ.
46.	Linden, N.J.	—	Elizabeth *Journal*, 8/29/69.
47.	Lockport, Ill.	Police Department	PQ.
48.	Los Angeles, Calif.	Independent agency funded by government funds and private donations	NAPCRO.
49.	Louisville, Ky.	— Louisville Area Council of Churches	Louisville *Courier-Journal*, 6/16/68.

50.	Lubbock, Tex.	— Police Department Community Relations Division	NAPCRO.
		Human Relations Commission	Lubbock University *Daily*, 10/9/72.
51.	Memphis, Tenn.	— Police Department — Chamber of Commerce	NAPCRO; Memphis *Tri-State Defender*, 4/29/72.
52.	Menlo Park, Calif.	Stanford University	Menlo Park *Recorder*, 5/20/70.
53.	Miami, Fla.	— Police Department Public Information Unit — Dade School Board	PQ; NAPCRO. Miami *News*, 5/9/70.
54.	Michigan City, Ind.	YMCA	Michigan City *News-Dispatch*, 7/17/70.
55.	Middletown, Conn.	Police Department	PQ.
56.	Milwaukee, Wis.	Commission on Community Relations	NAPCRO.
57.	Nashville, Tenn.	Urban League	Nashville *Tennessean*, 8/7/71.
58.	New Brunswick, N.J.	Sheriff's Department	New Brunswick *Home News*, 3/23/69.

59.	New Castle, Pa.	Mayor's Office	Pittsburgh *Courier*, 11/7/70.
60.	New York City, N.Y.	Mayor's Office Urban Task Force	NAPCRO.
61.	New Orleans, La.	Community Organization, partly funded by O.E.O.	NAPCRO.
62.	Newark, N.J.	Police Department	Newark *Star-Ledger*, 4/9/68; NAPCRO.
63.	Newport News, Va.	Newport News School Board	Newport News *Times-Herald*, 8/20/71.
64.	Niagara Falls, N.Y.	Police Department	PQ.
65.	Normal, Ill.	Illinois State University	Muncie *Ball State News*, 11/11/70.
66.	Northridge, Calif.	— Los Angeles Police Department Intelligence Division — NAACP	PQ.
67.	Oakland, Calif.	Police Department Communications Section	PQ; NAPCRO.
68.	Oklahoma City, Okla.	Commission on Human Relations	NAPCRO.

69. Philadelphia, Pa.	– Commission on Human Relations	Philadelphia *Bulletin*, 10/7/69.
	– Olney High School Advisory Committee	Olney *Times*, 3/11/71.
70. Phoenix, Ariz.	Human Relations and Fire Department	NAPCRO.
71. Piscataway, N.J.	Mayor's Office (Manned by Civil Rights Advisory Commission)	New Brunswick *Home News*, 3/22/69.
72. Plainfield, N.J.	—	Plainfield *Courier-News*, 7/3/70.
73. Portland, Oreg.	Citizens for School Support	Portland *Press*, 5/27/70; NAPCRO.
74. Prince George's County, Md. (Glendale)	– Police Department – Board of County Commissioners	PQ.
75. Raleigh, N.C.	Women in Action for the Prevention of Violence and its Causes	Raleigh *News and Observer*, 6/28/71.
76. Richmond, Va.	Human Relations Commission	Richmond *Times-Dispatch*, 8/31/70.
77. Riverside, Calif.	Mayor's Office	Riverside *Enterprise*, 4/6/71.
78. Rochester, N.Y.	—	NAPCRO.

79.	Rockville, Md.	Commission on Human Relations (Montgomery County)	Gerald M. Erchak, *Rumor Control in Civil Disorders* (Batelle Memorial Institute, September 6, 1968), p. 15.
80.	St. Paul, Minn.	Mayor's Office Department of Human Rights	NAPCRO.
81.	Salisbury, Md.	—	Baltimore *News American*, 5/21/68.
82.	San Bernardino, Calif.	Human Relations Commission	Pomona *Progress-Bulletin*, 12/10/70.
83.	San Diego, Calif.	Volunteer	San Diego *Union*, 3/29/70.
84.	San Francisco, Calif.	Human Rights Commission	NAPCRO.
85.	San Mateo, Calif.	Human Relations Commission	Burlingame (Cal.) *Advance-Star*, 1/26/72.
86.	Seattle, Wash.	—	PQ; NAPCRO; Seattle *Times*, 1/20/73.
87.	South Bend, Ind.	Human Relations Commission	South Bend *Tribune*, 10/10/69.
88.	Springfield, Ohio	Police Department Chief of Detectives	PQ.

89.	Stillwater, Okla.	Oklahoma State University	Stillwater *O'Collegian*, 11/18/70.
90.	Syracuse, N.Y.	Police Department Intelligence Division	PQ.
91.	Tampa, Fla.	County School System	Tampa *Times*, 7/22/71.
92.	Utica, N.Y.	Council of Churches	Utica *Observer-Dispatch*, 9/6/70.
93.	Washington, D.C.	— Urban League — U.S. Senate—special lines. Each Senator connected with Capitol Police — D.C. Health and Welfare Council — Citizens Information Service	*The Washington Post*, 5/24/68. *The Washington Post*, 5/22/68. Philadelphia *Bulletin*, 3/9/69. Philadelphia *Bulletin*, 3/9/69.
94.	Wayne County, Mich.	Community and Human Relations	Mt. Clemens Macomb *Daily*, 4/11/68.
95.	Wichita, Kans.	Police Department	Wichita *Eagle*, 8/24/68.
96.	Wilmington, Del.	—	Wilmington *Journal*, 9/23/69; Philadelphia *Bulletin*, 9/23/69.
97.	Wilmington, N.C.	Human Relations Agent	PQ.

Notes, Chapter 1

1. Scholars have been in substantial agreement with one another in defining the word "rumor." For example, see Robert H. Knapp, "A Psychology of Rumor," *Public Opinion Quarterly,* vol. 8, no. 1 (Spring 1944): 22; Gordon W. Allport and Leo Postman, *The Psychology of Rumor* (New York: Henry Holt, 1947), pp. ix-xi; and Warren A. Peterson and Noel P. Gist, "Rumor and Public Opinion," *American Journal of Sociology,* vol. 57, no. 2 (September 1951): 159. However, for a different and more functional definition, see Tamotsu Shibutani, *Improvised News: A Sociological Study of Rumor* (New York: Bobbs-Merrill, 1966), p. 17. Shibutani regards rumor as "a recurrent form of communication through which men caught in an ambiguous situation attempt to construct a meaningful interpretation of it by pooling their intellectual resources."

2. Shibutani, *Improvised News,* p. 22.

3. While stories about concentration camps have never been confirmed, it is easy to see how such reports arose. Title II of the Internal Security Act of 1950 authorized the attorney general, upon declaration of an "internal security emergency" by the president, to hold in detention centers persons he believed "probably will engage in . . . acts of espionage or sabotage." As Attorney General Ramsay Clark stated flatly, there "have been and will be no concentration camps." However, the situation was clouded by an article in the *Atlantic Monthly* (May 1969) which quoted Deputy Attorney General Richard Kleindienst as saying that disruptive student demonstrators "should be rounded up and put in a detention camp." The Deputy Attorney later denied having made the statement. The Act was subsequently repealed by Congress in September 1971.

4. See George Rudé, *The Crowd in the French Revolution* (New York: Oxford University Press, 1967), p. 223; and Leo Gershoy, *The French Revolution and Napoleon* (New York: Appleton-Century-Crofts, 1964), pp. 119-21.

5. Sidney B. Fay, *The Origins of the World War,* vol. 1 (Toronto: The Free Press, 1968), p. 27; also 1966 edition, vol. 2, p. 141.

6. Oliver Perry Chitwood, *A History of Colonial America* (New York: Harper, 2nd ed., 1948), p. 634.

7. Patriotic historians have the dubious distinction of having further compounded these distortions, elevating them to the realm of popular mythology, by improperly terming the tragedy the "Boston Massacre."

8. Knapp, "Psychology of Rumor," p. 22.

9. Theodore Caplow, "Rumors in War," *Social Forces,* vol. 25, no. 3 (March 1947): 298-302.

10. See, for example, Frederick C. Bartlett, *Remembering* (London: Cambridge University Press, 1932).

11. Allport and Postman, *The Psychology of Rumor,* pp. 75-115.

12. T.M. Higham, "The Experimental Study of the Transmission of Rumour," *British Journal of Psychology,* vol. 42 (March and May 1951): 42-55.

13. See Herbert M. Schall, Bernard Levy and M.E. Tresselt, "The Sociometric Approach to Rumor," *Journal of Social Psychology,* vol. 31, First Half (February 1950): 121-29; Melvin L. DeFleur, "Mass Communication and the Study of Rumor," *Sociological Inquiry,* vol. 32, no. 1 (Winter 1962): 51-70; H. Taylor Buckner, "A Theory of Rumor Transmission," *Public Opinion Quarterly,* no. 29, vol. 1 (Spring 1965): 54-70; and Peterson and Gist, "Rumor and Public Opinion," pp. 159-67.

14. Shibutani, *Improvised News,* p. 27.

15. Ibid., p. 26.

Notes, Chapter 2

1. John Hope Franklin, *From Slavery to Freedom: A History of Negro Americans,* 3rd ed. (New York: Knopf, 1969), p. 73.

2. See Hon. J.T. Headley, *Pen and Pencil Sketches of the Great Riots* (New York: E.B. Treat, 1882), in Robert M. Fogelson and Richard E. Rubenstein, advisory eds., *Mass Violence in America* (New York; Arno Press and *The New York Times,* 1969), p. 28.

3. Headley, *Pen and Pencil Sketches,* pp. 29-30.

4. This action recalls a similar response by an American president more than 200 years later, when, following the enormous outbreak of rioting in Detroit in the summer of 1967, Lyndon Johnson proclaimed a day of prayer.

5. Headley, *Pen and Pencil Sketches,* pp. 41-42.

6. Ibid., p. 43.

7. Quoted in David J. Jacobson, *The Affairs of Dame Rumor* (New York: Rinehart, 1948), p. 64.

8. The Charleston *Mercury,* October 11, 1860; quoted in Kenneth M. Stampp, ed., *The Causes of the Civil War* (Englewood Cliffs, N.J.: Spectrum, 1961), p. 125.

9. The Trenton *Gazette,* January 3, 1861; in Stampp, *Causes of Civil War,* pp. 15-16.

10. Stampp, *Causes of Civil War,* p. 5.

11. Franklin, *From Slavery to Freedom,* p. 439.

12. The reader has undoubtedly realized that all the rumors treated thus far concern whites. Regrettably, there are relatively few first-hand historical accounts by blacks in our early history. This, coupled with the fact that even sympathetic white observers in the past (such as Frederick Law Olmsted) had little direct contact with blacks, helps explain the paucity of historical data concerning rumors among blacks. Nevertheless, we shall have much to say

24. St. Louis *Post-Dispatch* (Evening Edition), July 7, 1917, and *Post-Dispatch* (Sunday Morning Edition), July 8, 1917.

25. Rudwick, *Race Riot at East St. Louis,* pp. 38-39. This incident recalls the so-called "Cleveland shoot-out" between the police and a group of black militants in July 1968. Immediately, the press portrayed this clash as a deliberate ambush of the police. Only later was it discovered that the situation was far more complicated and that, in all probability, a series of provocative actions made by the police actually precipitated the disorder.

26. Franklin, *From Slavery to Freedom,* p. 480.

27. The Chicago Commission on Race Relations, *The Negro in Chicago: A Study of Race Relations and a Race Riot* (Chicago: University of Chicago Press, 1922), reprinted by Arno Press and *The New York Times* (1968), p. 585. (Hereafter cited as *Chicago Commission on Race Relations.)*

28. Arthur I. Waskow, *From Race Riot to Sit-In, 1919 and the 1960's: A Study in the Connections between Conflict and Violence* (Garden City, N.Y.: Anchor Books, 1967), p. 22.

29. New York *Tribune,* September 1, 1919.

30. Franklin, *From Slavery to Freedom,* p. 483.

31. New York *Tribune,* September 1, 1919, and New York *Evening Telegram,* August 31, 1919.

32. Omaha *World-Herald,* October 1, 1919.

33. Telegram from John E. Morris, Commanding, Omaha, to Major General Leonard Wood, 6:09 P.M., September 29, 1919, War Dept. MSS in Waskow, *From Race Riot to Sit-In,* p. 113.

34. Omaha *World-Herald,* October 2, 1919.

35. *Arkansas Gazette,* October 2, 1919.

36. Waskow, *From Race Riot to Sit-In,* p. 134.

37. Franklin, *From Slavery to Freedom,* pp. 482-3.

38. Chicago Commission on Race Relations, p. 572.

39. Ibid., p. 5.

40. Ibid., p. 25.

41. Ibid., p. 571.

42. Ibid., p. 571.

43. Ibid., pp. 569-70.

44. Ibid., p. 569.

45. Ibid., p. 29.

46. Ibid., pp. 21-22.

47. Ibid., p. 575.

48. Ibid., p. 577.

49. Knapp, "Psychology of Rumor," pp. 24-25; Allport and Postman, *Psychology of Rumor,* pp. 10-13.

Notes

about such rumors when we begin our formal inquiry.

13. Leon Litwack, *North of Slavery: The Negro in the Fr* *1790-1860* (Chicago: University of Chicago Press, 1961), pp. 100-? also Franklin, *From Slavery to Freedom,* pp. 234-5.

14. Allen D. Grimshaw, "A Study in Social Violence: Urban Rac the United States," (Ph. D. diss., University of Pennsylvania, 178-80.

15. Large-scale, direct, violent clashes between the races have tr been labelled "race riots." However, the use of the term is unfort least several respects. First, the term has been used extremely loosel a broad spectrum of collective behavior, ranging from slave revolts t Second, the term is still used to describe outbreaks which, while ra necessarily involve direct confrontations between the races (fo where the dominant mode of violence involves the destruction of Adding to the confusion is the tendency, particularly on the part media, to describe as "race riots" extremely small disorders, such between blacks and whites.

The author uses the term "race riot" to describe a type of civil involving aggressive behavior by whites against blacks or by bl whites, and characterized by: a precipitating incident (usually minor event regarded as insulting or unjust); quickly followed by ous outburst of violence on the part of the aggrieved group; whi panied by a corresponding loss of social control.

16. Elliot M. Rudwick, *Race Riot at East St. Louis, July 2, 1?* dale, Ill.: Southern Illinois University Press, 1964), p. 28. To dat been few case histories of riots. Rudwick's thorough and illumina is therefore an extremely valuable contribution to our knowledg ject.

17. "Select Committee to Investigate Conditions in Illinois Interfering with Interstate Commerce between the States" (Unp script of the Congressional hearings concerning the East St. 1917), pp. 2391-93. In effect, the rumors concerning "big emp legitimized by the so-called Walker Committee, following the support of labor organizers, the Committee blamed the violenc ate conspiracy of employers to import "an excessive and abno of blacks into East St. Louis. Blacks and "big employers" wer together under the same conspiratorial umbrella—very democrati

18. St. Louis *Star,* May 29, 1917; and Belleville *News-Dem* 1917; quoted in Rudwick, *Race Riot at East St. Louis,* p. 30.

19. Rudwick, *Race Riot at East St. Louis,* p. 87.

20. Ibid., p. 37.

21. May 29 and June 3, 1917 in Ibid., p. 34.

22. Ibid., p. 44.

23. Ibid., p. 71.

50. Chicago Commission on Race Relations, p. 6.

51. Ibid., p. 637.

52. Ibid., p. 19.

53. Ibid., p. 595.

54. Ibid., p. 26.

55. The *New York Times*, July 28, 1919.

56. The *New York Times*, July 28, 1919.

57. The *New York Times*, July 28, 1919; August 4, 1919.

58. Chicago Commission on Race Relations, p. 636.

59. The *New York Times*, August 26, 1919.

60. The *New York Times*, August 27, 1919.

61. *The Complete Report of Mayor LaGuardia's Commission on the Harlem Riot of March 19, 1935*, in Robert M. Fogelson and Richard E. Rubenstein, advisory eds., *Mass Violence in America* (New York: Arno Press and *The New York Times*, 1969), p. 7. (Hereafter cited as LaGuardia Commission.)

62. LaGuardia Commission, pp. 8-9.

63. The Harlem riot differed from those previously discussed, in that there were no major clashes between the races. Virtually all the violence was directed against property and took the form of extensive window-breaking and looting.

64. LaGuardia Commission, p. 10.

65. LaGuardia Commission, p. 12.

66. LaGuardia Commission, p. 11. Mayor LaGuardia never formally issued the Commission's report to the public. In obtaining and later publishing the report in 1936, the *New York Amsterdam News* charged that the Mayor had found it "too hot, too caustic, too critical, too unfavorable." The Mayor's response recalls the rather lukewarm reaction to the Report of the National Advisory Commission on Civil Disorders by President Lyndon B. Johnson. Apparently riot commissions, like little children, are meant to be seen and not heard.

67. The zoot-suit seems to have originated in the East and was identified with blacks in Harlem. In southern California, Mexican-American youths became associated with this garb, which featured long suit coats, trousers pegged sharply at the cuff, and yard-long watch chains. "Zooters," or "zoot-suiters," wore their hair long, full and well-lubricated.

68. Ralph H. Turner and Samuel J. Surace, "Zoot-Suiters and Mexicans: Symbols in Crowd Behavior," *American Journal of Sociology*, vol. 62, no. 1 (July 1956): 16-17.

69. Carey McWilliams, "The Zoot-Suit Riots," *The New Republic*, vol. 108, no. 25 (June 21, 1943): 818-20.

70. This stereotyped portrayal in the press of Mexican-Americans as criminals recalls the findings of the Chicago Commission concerning the press treat-

ment of blacks which have been already cited. For a general assessment of the press along these lines, but in a non-riot context, see Noel P. Gist, "The Negro in the Daily Press," *Social Forces*, vol. 10, no. 3 (March 1932): 405-11; also see Noel P. Gist, "Racial Attitudes in the Press," *Sociology and Social Research*, vol. 17, no. 1 (September-October 1932): 30.

71. Turner and Surace, "Zoot-Suiters and Mexicans," p. 20.

72. Both quotes cited in "Zoot-Suit War," *Time*, June 21, 1943, p. 18.

73. Ibid.

74. The Los Angeles *Times*, June 9, 1943.

75. Los Angeles *Daily News*, June 8, 1943.

76. In the absence of clashes between whites and blacks, the violence cannot be termed a "race riot" in the strictest sense of the word. For a popular account of the riot, see Walter White, "Behind the Harlem Riot," *The New Republic*, vol. 109, no. 7 (August 16, 1943): 220-22. For a comparison of the disturbances in Harlem in 1935 and 1943 with other riots, see Grimshaw, "A Study in Social Violence," Appendix E, "The Harlem Disturbances of 1935 and 1943: Deviant Cases?", pp. 374-77.

77. "The Taut String," *Time*, vol. 42, no. 6 (August 9, 1943): 19.

78. *Committee to Investigate the Riot Occurring in Detroit on June 21, 1943: Factual Report*, Submitted by H. J. Rushton, W.E. Dowling, Oscar Olander and J.H. Witherspoon (mimeo), p. 10. Usually referred to as the "Dowling Report," because of the important role played in the committee's proceedings by William E. Dowling, Prosecuting Attorney. In view of the many assertions of plots regarding other riots, it may be worth citing the report's finding that the riot in Detroit "was not planned" and "was not inspired by subversive enemy influence" (p. 15). Adding further significance to this finding is the fact that all four individuals comprising the committee were connected with law enforcement agencies.

79. Dowling Report, p. 10.

80. Alfred McClung Lee and Norman Daymond Humphrey, *Race Riot* (New York: Dryden Press, 1943), p. 27.

81. Robert Shogan and Tom Craig, *The Detroit Race Riot: A Study in Violence* (New York: Chilton Books, 1964), p. 54.

82. Lee and Humphrey, *Race Riot*, p. 44.

83. Ibid., p. 38.

84. LaGuardia Commission, p. 12.

85. The reader may recall the rumors circulating among another minority group, the Chicanos, in Los Angeles, to the effect that servicemen had molested Mexican women.

86. The findings concerning the press refer almost exclusively to newspapers. Only one instance was recorded in which another segment of the news media was involved in spreading a rumor—i.e., a local radio station in Detroit, which broadcast a faulty report about armed blacks headed for the city from

Chicago. The inability to uncover other instances of misreporting by radio stations, in all likelihood, was due to the general unavailability of this kind of data, rather than any qualitative differences in reporting between the various branches of the media.

87. The *Arkansas Gazette*, October 2, 1919.

Notes, Chapter 3

1. Robert H. Knapp, "A Psychology of Rumor," *Public Opinion Quarterly*, vol. 8, no. 1 (Spring 1944): 31-33.

2. Ibid., p. 32.

3. Gordon W. Allport and Leo Postman, *The Psychology of Rumor* (New York: Henry Holt, 1947), p. 43.

4. Bernard Hart, *Psychopathology: Its Development and its Place in Medicine* (Cambridge, England: Cambridge University Press, 1939), p. 121.

5. Herbert M. Schall, Bernard Levy, and M.E. Tresselt, "A Sociometric Approach to Rumor," *Journal of Social Psychology*, vol. 31, First Half (February 1950): 122.

6. Warren A. Peterson and Noel P. Gist, "Rumor and Public Opinion," *American Journal of Sociology*, vol. 57, no. 2 (September 1951): 166.

7. C.G. Jung, *Analytical Psychology*, Constance E. Long, trans. (New York: Moffat Yard and Company, 1916), pp. 176-90.

8. Hart, *Psychopathology*, p. 120.

9. Allport and Postman, *Psychology of Rumor*, p. 196.

10. Ibid., p. vii.

11. Ibid., p. 193 (emphasis added).

12. Ibid., p. 198.

13. Ibid., pp. 198-99.

14. Hart, *Psychopathology*, p. 94.

15. Ibid., p. 112.

16. Ibid., p. 114.

17. Allport and Postman, *The Psychology of Rumor*, p. 200.

18. Tamotsu Shibutani, *Improvised News: A Sociological Study of Rumor* (New York: Bobbs-Merill, 1966).

19. Shibutani, *Improvised News*, p. 40.

20. Ibid., p. 17.

21. For a journalist's account of the Chappaquiddick incident, see Jack Olsen, *The Bridge at Chappaquiddick* (Boston: Little, Brown, 1970).

22. "The Taut String," *Time*, (vol. 42, no. 6 (August 9, 1943): 19.

23. Walter White, "Behind the Harlem Riot," *The New Republic,* vol. 109, no. 7 (August 16, 1943): 220-21.

24. Elliott M. Rudwick, *Race Riot at East St. Louis, July 2, 1917* (Carbondale, Ill.: Southern Illinois University Press, 1964). See especially pp. 27-29.

25. Shibutani, *Improvised News,* p. 131.

26. Ibid., p. 40.

27. Ibid., both quotes from p. 148.

28. Ibid., p. 46.

29. Ibid., pp. 98-99.

30. For an expanded account of this episode, see Edgar Morin, *Rumour in Orléans* trans. Peter Green (New York: Pantheon Books, 1971).

31. See Knapp, "Psychology of Rumor," pp. 28-29; Allport and Postman, *Psychology of Rumor,* pp. 14, 29-31; and Shibutani, *Improvised News,* pp. 185-200.

32. Raymond M. Momboisse, *Rumors* (Sacramento, Cal.: MSM Enterprises, 1968), pp. 7-8.

33. Alfred McClung Lee and Norman Daymond Humphrey, *Race Riot* (New York: Dryden Press, 1943).

34. Ibid., pp. 109-10 (italics added).

35. Ibid., p. 112.

36. Jerry Cohen and William S. Murphy, *The Los Angeles Race Riot: August, 1965: Burn, Baby Burn!* (New York: E.P. Dutton, 1966), p. 227.

37. Letter to this writer from Jerry Cohen, dated June 4, 1969.

Notes, Chapter 4

1. See especially Neil J. Smelser, *Theory of Collective Behavior* (New York: The Free Press, 1962); Allen D. Grimshaw, *A Study in Social Violence: Urban Race Riots in the United States* (Ph. D. dissertation, University of Pennsylvania, 1959); Allen D. Grimshaw, ed., *Racial Violence in the United States* (Chicago: Aldine Publishing Company, 1969); Allen D. Grimshaw, "Interpreting Collective Violence: An Argument for the Importance of Social Structure," in eds., James F. Short, Jr. and Marvin E. Wolfgang, "Collective Violence" in *The Annals of the American Academy of Political and Social Science* vol. 391 (September 1970): 9-20; and John P. Spiegel, "Toward a Theory of Collective Violence," paper delivered to the American Psychiatric Association, Divisional Meeting on "Violence and Aggression," Chicago, November 15-16, 1968.

2. Richard E. Rubenstein, *Rebels in Eden: Mass Political Violence in the United States* (Boston: Little, Brown, 1970), p. x.

3. John P. Spiegel, "Toward a Theory of Collective Violence," pp. 14-15.

4. For an excellent discussion of the exclusion of blacks seen from an historical perspective, see John Hope Franklin, "The Two Worlds of Race: A Historical View," in "The American Negro," *Daedalus,* Proceedings of the American Academy of Arts and Sciences, vol. 94, no. 4 (Fall 1965): 899-920.

5. Quoted in Franklin, "The Two Worlds of Race, p. 900.

6. Franklin, "The Two Worlds of Race," p. 919.

7. "How Whites Feel About Negroes: A Painful American Dilemma," *Newsweek,* vol. 62, no. 17 (October 21, 1963): 44-57.

8. "Black and White: A Major Survey of U.S. Racial Attitudes Today," *Newsweek* vol. 68, no. 8 (August 22, 1966): 25-26.

9. Jeffery Mayland Paige, *Collective Violence and the Culture of Subordination: A Study of Participants in the July 1967 Riots in Newark, New Jersey, and Detroit, Michigan* (Ph. D. diss., University of Michigan, 1969), especially pp. 55-87; also *Report of the National Advisory Commission on Civil Disorders* (Washington, D.C.: GPO, 1968), pp. 73, 76-77. (Hereafter cited as Kerner Commission)

10. *The Politics of Protest: Violent Aspects of Protest and Confrontation,* A Staff Report to the National Commission on the Causes and Prevention of Violence, prepared by Jerome Skolnick (Washington, D.C.: GPO, 1969), p. 6.

11. Shortly after the Pirates had defeated the Baltimore Orioles, hundreds of happy fans (some of whom got carried away) spilled into the streets. Almost 100 persons were arrested (mostly for intoxication), another 128 injured, while some minimal looting was reported.

12. For a discussion of hostile beliefs as they relate to intergroup conflict in general, see Smelser, *Theory of Collective Behavior,* especially pp. 101-30.

13. Studies conducted by the Kerner Commission provide some evidence to support this assumption—at least for black rioters. See Kerner Commission, pp. 73-77; and Paige, *Collective Violence,* pp. 67-77.

14. Thomas F. Pettigrew, *A Profile of the Negro American* (Princeton, N.J.: D. Van Nostrand, 1964), p. 193.

15. The Chicago Commission on Race Relations, *The Negro in Chicago: A Study of Race Relations and a Race Riot* (Chicago: University of Chicago Press, 1922), reprinted by Arno Press and *The New York Times* (1968), p. 452. (Hereafter cited as Chicago Commission on Race Relations.)

16. Chicago Commission on Race Relations, p. 438.

17. Figures taken from *Task Force Report: Crime and Its Impact—An Assessment,* The President's Commission on Law Enforcement and Administration of Justice (Washington, D.C.: GPO, 1967), p. 78.

18. For a more extensive analysis of the correlates of crime involving blacks, see *Crimes of Violence,* A Staff Report to the National Commission on the Causes and Prevention of Violence, prepared by Donald J. Mulvihill and Melvin M. Tumin, with Lynn A. Curtis (Washington, D.C.: GPO, December

1969), vol. 12, pp. 417-32; Marvin E. Wolfgang and Bernard Cohen, *Crime and Race: Conceptions and Misconceptions* (New York: Institute of Human Relations Press—The American Jewish Committee, 1970); Pettigrew, *Profile of the Negro American,* 136-56; and *Task Force Report: Crime and Its Impact—An Assessment,* pp. 60-76.

19. For an interesting examination of the race problem along these lines, see Calvin G. Hernton, *Sex and Racism in America* (New York: First Evergreen Black Cat Edition, 1966).

20. W.J. Cash, *The Mind of the South* (New York: Alfred A. Knopf, 1957), pp. 114-17.

21. Eldridge Cleaver, *Soul on Ice* (New York: Dell Publishing Co., Inc., 1970), p. 26.

22. Richard Hofstadter, *The Paranoid Style in American Politics and Other Essays* (New York: Alfred A. Knopf, 1966).

23. Hofstadter, *Paranoid Style,* p. 32.

24. *The Autobiography of Malcolm X,* with the assistance of Alex Haley (New York: Grove Press, 1966), pp. 268-69. (Hereafter cited as *Autobiography of Malcolm X.*)

25. See Raymond A. and Alice H. Bauer, "Day to Day Resistance to Slavery," *The Journal of Negro History,* vol. 27, no. 4 (October 1942): 388-419; also Kenneth M. Stampp, *The Peculiar Institution: Slavery in the Ante-Bellum South* (New York: Alfred A. Knopf, 1969), ch. 3, pp. 86-140.

26. The inclination of whites to dismiss or disregard the various forms of black protest is nothing new. To cite but one example from the past: according to Dr. Samuel Cartwright, runaway slaves were suffering from a "disease of the mind," which he called "Drapetomania." The first symptom was a "sulky and dissatisfied attitude." However, with "proper medical advice," the good doctor argued, this disease could be cured. (See Stampp, *The Peculiar Institution,* p. 109).

27. Robert M. Fogelson and Robert B. Hill, "Who Riots? A Study of Participation in the 1967 Riots," *Supplemental Studies for the National Advisory Commission on Civil Disorders* (Washington, D.C.: GPO, July, 1968), p. 243.

28. Edward Vaughn quoted by Roger Beardwood, "The Fortune Study of the New Negro Mood," *Fortune,* vol. 77, no. 1 (January 1968): 146.

29. *Autobiography of Malcolm X,* p. 371.

30. See Paige, *Collective Violence,* pp. 75, 88-90.

31. While considerable dispute remains on all these issues, the interested reader may find the following sources useful: David N. Daniels, Marshall F. Gilula and Frank M. Ochberg, eds., *Violence and the Struggle for Existence* (Boston: Little, Brown, 1970; Anthony Storr, *Human Aggression* (New York: Atheneum, 1968); Konrad Lorenz, trans. by Marjorie Kerr Wilson, *On Aggression* (New York: Harcourt, Brace & World, 1966); John P. Spiegel, "Violence

and the Social Order," *ZYGON/Journal of Religion and Science,* University of Chicago, vol. 4, no. 3 (September 1969): 222-37; and "Aggression and Violence," Special Section in *The American Journal of Psychiatry,* vol. 128, no. 4 (October 1971): 431-74.

32. For example, see *Task Force Report: The Police,* the President's Commission on Law Enforcement and Administration of Justice (Washington, D.C.: GPO, 1967), especially ch. 6, pp. 144-215; also Kerner Commission, ch. 11, pp. 157-69.

33. Cleaver, *Soul On Ice,* pp. 121-22.

34. Ibid., p. 125.

35. Smelser, *Theory of Collective Behavior,* p. 243.

36. Franklin, *From Slavery to Freedom,* p. 485.

37. Grimshaw, *A Study in Social Violence,* p. 21.

38. Kerner Commission, p. 68.

39. Stanley Lieberson and Arnold R. Silverman, "The Precipitants and Underlying Conditions of Race Riots," *American Sociological Review,* vol. 30, no. 6 (December 1965): 888.

40. The one major exception to this last point is the enormous wave of disorders which followed the assassination of the Rev. Dr. Martin Luther King, Jr., in 1968. At least 200 disorders occurring in every section of the country were recorded. For an analysis of the King assassination as a precipitating event, see The Lemberg Center for the Study of Violence, "April Aftermath of the King Assassination," *Riot Data Review,* no. 2 (August 1968): 67-72.

41. In order to avoid confusion, future references to the triggering incident will be referred to as the precipitating—not crystallizing—event.

42. When it comes to blacks, the police are not without their own sensitivities. Under the provisions of a new city ordinance issued in 1970 in Toledo, Ohio, it is now illegal to call a policeman "pig." In a special message to all members of the police division, the city Safety Director ordered arrests made for such violations, adding that persons making noises such as "oink oink" were also subject to arrest. In 1971, a young man in Fairfax, Virginia, was charged with disorderly conduct for singing "Old MacDonald Had a Farm"— twice, emphasizing the word "pig"—in the presence of a policeman. A judge sentenced the defendant to sitting on a pigpen fence for an hour so that he could observe the difference between the police and swine.

43. "Select Committee to Investigate Conditions in Illinois and Missouri Interfering with Interstate Commerce between the States" (Unpublished transcript of the Congressional hearings concerning the East St. Louis riots in 1917), p. 2391 (italics added).

44. "Return to 12th Street: A follow-up survey of attitudes of Detroit Negroes," Detroit *Free Press,* October, 1968.

45. Tamotsu Shibutani, *Improvised News: A Sociological Study of Rumor* (New York: Bobbs-Merrill, 1966), p. 40.

Notes, Chapter 5

    1. See Jane A. Baskin, Joyce K. Hartweg, Ralph G. Lewis and Lester W. McCullough, Jr., "Race Related Civil Disorders: 1967-1969" (Lemberg Center for the Study of Violence, Brandeis University, 1972).

    In this chapter we will use the Center's working definition of civil orders: Events involving crowd behavior, characterized by either damage to persons or property, or defiance of civil authority, or aggressive disruptions which violate the civil law (such as building seizures). Crowd behavior refers to the activities of four or more persons acting in concert. Defiance of civil authority is characterized by one or more of the following types of behavior: (1) disobedience of the orders of civil authorities such as local, state and federal officials and (2) physical attacks upon such authorities and/or their symbolic equivalents such as police cars, police stations, etc.

    Race-related civil disorders are identified as norm-violating events characterized by aggressive or violent behavior by members of one racial or ethnic group against members of another or their symbolic equivalents. Such behavior is characterized by one or more of the following factors: (1) *group membership:* identification of the participants with their racial group is salient; (2) *motivation:* individuals become involved in an aggressive incident because of a sense of injustice or because of feelings of hostility toward the other group; (3) *choice of targets of aggression:* the objects of aggressive behavior—whether persons or property—symbolize the hostility of one group toward another.

    2. Baskin, et al, "Race Related Civil Disorders," p. 12.

    3. Thomas F. Pettigrew, *A Profile of the Negro American* (New York: D. Van Nostrand, 1964), p. 192.

    4. Stokely Carmichael and Charles V. Hamilton, *Black Power: The Politics of Liberation in America* (New York: Vintage Books, 1967), p. ix. For a discussion of the transition from the civil rights to the black power movement, see William L. O'Neill, *Coming Apart: An Informal History of America in the 1960's* (Chicago: Quadrangle Books, 1971), pp. 158-94.

    5. Lemberg Center for the Study of Violence, *Six-City Study: A Survey of Racial Attitudes in Six Northern Cities—Preliminary Findings* (mimeo, Brandeis University, 1967), p. 9. (Hereafter cited as *Six-City Study*). The six cities were Akron, Dayton, Boston, San Francisco, Pittsburgh and Cleveland.

    6. *Six-City Study*, p. 22.

    7. Baskin, et al, "Race Related Civil Disorders," p. 20.

    8. See Appendix A of this volume for a complete list of disorders obtained from news clips by date, city and news source.

    9. See Appendix B for a complete list of investigative accounts covering the 22 disorders.

    10. As one example of this problem: informal talks with the police by this writer and her associates, on a number of occasions, would elicit a response that their city "didn't really have a race problem"—despite glaring evidence to

the contrary. We might also note, however, that the denial response was not uncommon among other public officials as well.

11. A copy of the rumor questionnaire appears in Appendix C.

12. These figures are somewhat lower than the totals found in the Lemberg Center report, "Race Related Civil Disorders: 1967-1969," published in 1971. These differences are due to revised data collection procedures and to the fact that the figures used here only refer to clear-cut cases of racial disturbances. The Center's report included "equivocals"—cases in which it was unclear whether they met the CDC's criteria for disorders. However, in no way do the differences affect our study.

13. The list of cities which responded to the questionnaire appears as Appendix D.

14. For a list of the states included in each region, see Appendix E.

15. More specifically, for every disorder, a number ranging from 1 (low) to 4 (high) was assigned to each variable, as follows:

Disorder in Hours		*Number of Participants*		*Amount of Property Damage*	
3 hrs. or less	= 1	100 persons or less	= 1	$1,000 or less	= 1
4-9 hrs.	= 2	101-200 persons	= 2	$1,001-$99,000	= 2
10-14 hrs.	= 3	201-500 persons	= 3	$100,000-$499,000	= 3
15 or more hrs.	= 4	More than 500 persons	= 4	$500,000 or more	= 4

Then, for each disorder, the three variables were given an aggregate weight. An overall number signifying the magnitude could then be assigned to each disorder: 1 was considered minor; 2 was medium; 3 was serious; and 4 was major.

16. Alfred McClung Lee and Norman Daymond Humphrey, *Race Riot* (New York: Dryden Press, 1943), pp. 109-10.

17. Gordon W. Allport and Leo Postman, *The Psychology of Rumor* (New York: Henry Holt, 1947), p. 193 (emphasis added).

18. Lee and Humphrey, *Race Riot,* p. 109.

19. Allport and Postman, *Psychology of Rumor,* pp. 193-96.

20. Federal Bureau of Investigation, U.S. Department of Justice, *Prevention and Control of Mobs and Riots* (Washington, D.C.: GPO, 1967), pp. 25-26.

21. John Molleson, "The Explosive Power of Rumors," *Parade,* May 19, 1968 (emphasis added).

22. *Report of the National Advisory Commission on Civil Disorders* (Washington, D.C.: GPO, 1968), p. 173.

23. See Questions 2, 3, 8, 9, 10, 11 and 12 of the rumor questionnaire in Appendix C.

24. See Exhibits F.1 and F.2 in Appendix F.

25. See Questions 2 and 3 of the rumor questionnaire in Appendix C.

26. See Question 4 of the rumor questionnaire in Appendix C.

27. See Question 6 of the rumor questionnaire in Appendix C.

28. Despite our respondents denial of precipitating events, our records showed they occurred in Durham, N.C., 2/15; Gainesville, Fla., 3/13; Pittsburg, Cal., 4/16; Benton Harbor, Mich., 4/29-5/1; Riverside, Cal., 8/6-8 and Blue Island, Ill., 10/23. These newsclips were the basis of summaries found in two Lemberg Center publications. For summaries of Durham and Gainesville, consult *Riot Data Review*, No. 1 (May, 1968), pp. 14 and 24; for Pittsburg and Benton Harbor, see *Riot Data Review*, No. 2 (August, 1968), pp. 48 and 53; for Riverside, see *U.S. Race-Related Civil Disorders*, May 1, 1968-August 31, 1968, p. 45; for Blue Island, see *U.S. Race-Related Civil Disorders*, September 1, 1968-December 31, 1968, p. 40.

29. See Question 7 of the rumor questionnaire in Appendix C.

30. These figures do not include the six cases taken from news clips. The six divide into the following categories: one "police"; three "schools"; one "living conditions"; and one "alleged discrimination."

31. Also, in the months prior to a disturbance in Miami August 7-8, 1968, there was a buildup of tension in the black community over a highly publicized get-tough policy announced by the chief of police. This policy included the frequent display of shotguns and dogs by Miami Police in black neighborhoods, and aggressive use of the Miami stop-and-frisk law. See *Miami Report: The Report of the Miami Study Team on Civil Disturbances in Miami, Florida, during the week of August 5, 1968*, Miami, Florida, January 15, 1969, submitted to the National Commission on the Causes and Prevention of Violence (Washington, D.C.: GPO, 1969), p. 3. Nevertheless, while noting an increase in rumors before the disorder, the acting chief of police responding to our questionnaire did not check "police" as an issue.

32. There can be little doubt that the murder of the Rev. Dr. Martin Luther King, Jr., was perceived not only as an act of injustice but also as a severe blow to blacks everywhere. The sense of loss and injury among blacks was much greater than among whites, and this contrast has been documented for Dr. King's native city. A study conducted by the Center for Research in Social Change at Emory University revealed that, of the 300 blacks and 300 whites interviewed in Atlanta, 78 percent of the blacks, as compared to 30 percent of the whites, reported their immediate reaction as "very shocked, sad,"—whereas one percent of the blacks, as compared to 14 percent of the whites, reported their immediate reaction as "indifferent." See Fred R. Crawford, Roy Norman and Leah Dabbs, *A Report of Certain Reactions by The Atlanta Public to the Death of the Reverend Doctor Martin Luther King, Jr.*, Center for Research in Social Change, April 4, 1969, Series A, Report No. 1, Appendix B, Table 7.

33. *Report of the National Advisory Commission on Civil Disorders* (Washington, D.C.: GPO, 1968), p. 68.

34. See Questions 8 and 9 of the rumor questionnaire in Appendix C. Question 8 also asked if the disorder might have been started "simply by a rumor?" Not one of the respondents (out of 112 cases) answered "yes," confirming a point made in the last chapter—i.e., that rumors do not occur "out of the blue" and are invariably linked to some kind of event.

35. As there was apparently some confusion as to whether or not the assassination of the Rev. Dr. Martin Luther King, Jr., constituted a precipitating event, our discussion here will be limited to non-King disorders.

36. The Chicago Commission on Race Relations, *The Negro in Chicago: A Study of Race Relations and a Race Riot* (Chicago: University of Chicago Press, 1922), reprinted by Arno Press and the *New York Times* (1968), p. 5.

37. *Committee to Investigate the Riot Occurring in Detroit on June 21, 1943: Factual Report,* Submitted by H.J. Rushton, W.E. Dowling, Oscar Olander and J.H. Witherspoon (mimeo), pp. 9-10.

38. See Question 12 of the rumor questionnaire in Appendix C.

39. Lenora E. Berson, *Case Study of a Riot: The Philadelphia Story* (New York: Institute of Human Relations Press, The American Jewish Committee, 1966), p. 21.

40. Out of 181 cases, one lone rumor exaggerating the amount of violence was found among blacks.

41. Carmichael and Hamilton, *Black Power*, p. 155.

42. Robert Conot, *Rivers of Blood, Years of Darkness: The Unforgettable Classic Account of the Watts Riot* (New York: William Morrow 1968), p. 200.

43. The findings from our police survey indicated that rumors did not seem to occur very often at this point. Therefore, the relevant issue here is, when they did, whether or not the various kinds of rumors would approximate the percentage of those occurring at other stages.

44. Two of the 22 cases—Augusta, Ga. and Jackson, Miss.—actually occurred during the first six months of 1970.

45. The reader should be alerted to the fact that the total number of rumors from the historical sample was originally 70. Three cases were eliminated subsequently because the race of the group circulating the rumor was not clear.

46. This kind of rumor count for the 1960s disorders was done previously (Exhibits 5.9 and 5.10). In undertaking the same task for our World Wars I and II sample, we should note that statements by public officials and the press falling into the realm of rumor were not counted as a general rule. However, in a couple of instances, there is evidence that a given news story gained currency in the community—such as the *Washington Post* "rape" story which helped trigger a disorder in that city in 1919. These cases were included in the sample.

47. Trenton *Times-Advertiser,* October 2, 1968; Providence *Journal,* May 14, 1969. In compiling the figures for our news clip samples, both of these cases were place; in the "other" category.

48. At the same time, we should recognize that a sizable number of racial disorders occurred in our nation's schools. While members of both races were frequently, although not always, involved, these clashes tended to be limited to small-scale fights which could in no way be compared to the race riots of the past.

49. Rumored predictions of violence among blacks soared from 8 to 21 percent, and may be attributable to the newer style of disorder. The reader may remember from our previous discussion that the more recent predictions tended to have an aggressive, threatening quality, with *whites* as the principal targets. The character of these rumors was very much in line with the aggressive role of blacks. However, it is also noteworthy that this type of rumor among blacks scored only 7 percent on our news clip sample, leaving the meaning of the above findings in doubt.

50. As noted earlier, rape rumors fell from 20 to 0 percent. We have already indicated that it is not clear whether that type of rumor was no longer really present or whether our data had simply failed to pick it up. However, assuming for the moment the existence of such rumors, it is likely they would have been far less common than in the past, given the changed nature of disorders.

51. Referring back to Table 11, police and civilian brutality rumors among blacks accounted for 66 percent of the total. But, as we noted later, 20 out of the 33 conspiracy rumors were in the nature of "official brutality," upping the grand total for the brutality theme to 77 percent.

52. Marilynn Rosenthal, "Where Rumor Raged," *Transaction* (now Society), vol. 8, no. 4 (February 1971): 36.

53. Twenty-eight percent said "frequently (but not more than half the time"; 18 percent replied "more than half the time"; and 23 percent indicated "almost always." On the other side, 17 percent answered "occasionally" and another 14 percent said "very seldom." See Question 1 of the rumor questionnaire in Appendix C.

Notes, Chapter 6

1. International Association of Chiefs of Police, Professional Standards Division, *Civil Disorders: After-Action Reports: A Report to the Attorney General of the United States* (Spring 1968), p. 41.

2. Marilynn Rosenthal, "Where Rumor Raged," *Trans*action (now **Society**), vol. 8, no. 4 (February 1971): 41-42. Rosenthal was careful to point out that, while this type of police reaction was widespread, it was by no means universal: "While the police in Redford, Dearborn and Livonia were escalating their rhetoric and mobilizing their communities, police officials in other communities responded to the rumors in a somewhat more restrained fashion." p. 42

3. *The Report of the President's Commission on Campus Unrest* (Washington, D.C.: GPO, 1970), p. 440.

4. Rosenthal, "Where Rumor Raged," p. 42.

5. Robert Kapsis, Jim Smith, Bruce Saunders, Paul Takagi, Oscar Williams, *The Reconstruction of a Riot: A Case Study of Community Tensions and Civil Disorder*, Approaches to the Study of Violence (Lemberg Center for the Study of Violence, Brandeis University, 1970), p. 60.

6. *128 Hours: A Report of the Civil Disturbance in the City & County of San Francisco* (mimeo, 1966), Compiled and Prepared by Sgt. Ford E. Long and Sgt. Richard Trueb, p. 18.

7. Albert J. Reiss, Jr., "Police Brutality . . . Answers to Key Questions," in Michael Lipsky, ed. *Law and Order: Police Encounters* 2nd ed. (New Brunswick, N.J.: Transaction Books, 1973).

8. Terry Ann Knopf, "Sniping—A New Pattern of Violence?" *Transaction* (now **Society**), vol. no. 9 (July/August 1969): 26.

9. Terry Ann Knopf, *Youth Patrols: An Experiment in Community Participation,* Approaches to the Study of Violence (Lemberg Center for the Study of Violence, Brandeis University, 1969).

10. David P. Riley, "Should Communities Control Their Police," *Civil Rights Digest,* U.S. Commission on Civil Rights, vol. 2, no. 4 (Fall 1969): 28.

11. Three other inmates were also killed by other inmates during the occupation.

12. Russell G. Oswald, *Attica—My Story,* edited by Rodney Campbell (Garden City, N.Y.: Doubleday, 1972).

13. Oswald, *Attica,* p. 42.

14. Quinn was a prison guard who was seriously injured during the initial takeover. Several hours later, he was removed from the prison and taken to Rochester General Hospital where he died two days later.

15. Besides the set of hostile beliefs held by the white officials, other factors contributed to the spread of these atrocity stories. Information on the condition of the hostages was not available until Thursday night. Many inmates had been committed for crimes of violence and thus were capable of flashes of rage. Homosexual practices in the prison, including acts of rape, aroused fears of sexual abuse. Inmates hurled defiant threats at the state police: "Come on in here, pigs, and we'll kill all the hostages." Finally, although no hostages were killed by the inmates on the day of the assault, two hostages who survived suffered slash wounds on their necks and several others were struck with blunt instruments wielded by inmates.

16. Oswald, *Attica,* p. 42.

17. *Attica: The Official Report of the New York State Special Commission* (New York: Bantam Books, 1972), p. 328. Hereafter cited as McKay Report.

18. McKay Report, p. 339.

19. Oswald, *Attica*, p. 69.

20. McKay Report, p. 105.

21. Oswald, *Attica*, p. 12.

22. Ibid., p. 234.

23. For a general assessment of the media along these lines, see Terry Ann Knopf, "Media Myths on Violence," *Columbia Journalism Review*, vol. 9, no. 1 (Spring 1970): 17-23.

24. Robert J. Glessing, *The Underground Press in America* (Bloomington, Ind.: Indiana University Press, 1970), p. 153.

25. In the last two years, a number of underground papers have folded. In some instances, however, their place has been taken by a different kind of alternative urban weekly. In Boston, for example, the demise of the radical *The Ole Mole* coincided with the emergence of two commercial weeklys known as the Boston *Phoenix* and *The Real Paper*. Less strident and less bound by ideology than most radical papers (although clearly sympathetic to the political Left), these publications have done some excellent investigative and analytical reporting and have continued to broaden their readership base.

26. Contrary to widespread belief, the press council idea is not new. Great Britain and other European countries have had operative councils for years. New Zealand and three Canadian provinces have recently started councils; Minnesota now has a statewide council initiated by the Minnesota Newspaper Association; while Honolulu and several smaller U.S. communities have local councils. To date, however, there has been no stimulus for the proliferation of local, state or regional councils here. A national council, some adherents believe, might serve as a spearhead to this process.

27. The decision was by no means unanimous within the ranks of the *Times*. John B. Oakes, the *Times'* editorial page editor, was a member of the task force which recommended the formation of the council.

28. Reginald Stuart, "Survey of Southern Black Journalists," *South Today: A Digest of Southern Affairs*, vol. 3, no. 11 (July/August 1972): 6.

29. Certainly none of the approaches used in this country has been quite so drastic as the one adopted by the government of South Korea. Early in 1972, 19 persons were arrested on charges of spreading rumors—in effect, making speaking a crime.

30. See Appendix G for a list of cities known to have had rumor control centers.

31. *A Study of "Rumor Control" or Information Centers in Major Cities of the United States*, National Association of Police Community Relations Officers (mimeo, June 30, 1970), p. 5.

32. Walter L. Webb, "Rumor Control During Civil Disorder," Management Information Service, International City Managers' Association, vol. 1, no. L-1 (January 1969): 1.

33. *Mass Media and Violence*, A Staff Report to the National Commission

on the Causes and Prevention of Violence, prepared by David L. Lange, Robert K. Baker and Sandra J. Ball (Washington, D.C.: GPO, November 1969), vol. 11, p. 161.

34. *Report of the Chicago Riot Study Committee to the Hon. Richard J. Daley,* August 1, 1968, p. 57.

35. *The Washington Post,* May 24, 1968.

36. Memo from Detroit Commission on Community Relations to Mayors' Offices, Human Relations Agencies, Interested Persons, regarding establishment of a Rumor Control Center. (Undated, p. 6.)

37. Memo from Detroit Commission on Community Relations, p. 6.

38. Los Angeles *Herald-Dispatch,* February 4, 1971.

39. Larry Williams and Gerald Erchak, "Rumor Control Centers in Civil Disorders," *The Police Chief* vol. 36, no. 5 (May 1969): p. 28.

40. Memo from Detroit Commission on Human Relations, p. 1.

41. John Molleson, "The Explosive Power of Rumors," *Parade* (May 19, 1968): 16.